Personality Development for Business

4th edition

ALLIEN R. RUSSON
Professor of Management
College of Business
University of Utah

Western Iowa Tech-IMC
3475

Published by

K41   **SOUTH-WESTERN PUBLISHING CO.**

CINCINNATI   WEST CHICAGO, ILL.   DALLAS   PELHAM MANOR, N.Y.
PALO ALTO, CALIF.   BRIGHTON, ENGLAND

Library of Congress Catalog Card Number: 72-89731

ISBN: 0-538-11410-X

2 3 4 5 6 7 8 K 8 7 6 5 4

Printed in the United States of America

PREFACE

What is the empty space in the typical young person's makeup? Most of you have sufficient skill, knowledge, and ability to go into the business world and tackle the job you are given. However, if you are going into business for the first time — or are returning after an extended absence — you may be aware of something missing. This "something" is usually a lack of confidence, a fear of rejection, an uncertainty of your worth as a human being. You may be afraid you will be unable to fit into your work group, that you will be rejected, that you cannot get along well with others.

This book is written to help you fill in your missing space, to help you develop your true personality. In your anxiety, you may have built up a mask to cover the real you. That mask is seldom as attractive, however, as the real you it is covering up. Yet, in the modern business world, no one has the time to bring out your best self. It is as if we were living in an *instant* society. Travel between cities is now completed in minutes instead of days. Complex business problems are solved by computers in seconds instead of days or weeks. Is it any wonder that this *instant* factor should spill over into the way employers react to new workers?

Your new employer expects instant efficiency, but he also hopes that you will fit instantly into the business team. Such a situation puts a heavy burden on you as a new employee. Because everyone expects you to be at ease in the new situation, you become even more nervous and worried. Because you try too hard to please, you are unable to keep cool when your employer reprimands you. Because you react with anger or hurt feelings, you are judged as lacking poise.

There is, of course, no easy road to the kind of personality the business world needs and wants. The rewards that come to you if you have efficiency plus personality, however, make the journey worthwhile, no matter how difficult. The first step is the most important one: You must want to improve. You must be willing to face yourself, "warts and all," as Abraham Lincoln said to his photographer. When you can accept yourself, just as you are, you will have taken that first step.

Moreover, when you accept yourself, you begin to lose your defensive reaction to the "sandpaper" parts of your personality. You may find that you need to be more careful about grooming, about your appearance. You must not be defensive and overreact when someone points this fact out to you. Instead, you start working on the part that needs improvement. How does your voice sound to others? Do you know? Have you ever heard a recording of your own voice? If not, here would be a good place to start. How would you describe your attitude? Is it negative? Do you look on the darker side most of the time? If you do, you can change your negative attitude by following the ideas in the chapters that follow. Is conversation with others easy for you? Can you give and take praise without embarrassment? Can you forget yourself and think about the other fellow, putting yourself in his shoes?

You will be the kind of person who fits in with the business team if you can get rid of negative feelings and attitudes. Being negative, after all, is nothing more than a habit; and habits can be changed. You will discover that happiness or unhappiness is not the result of what happens to you. It is the result of how you take what happens to you. Much of the unhappiness you complain about comes from your negative habits of thinking and speaking.

Start working now on just one part of the *you* the other person sees, hears, or perceives. As your appearance, your way of speaking, and your attitudes begin to improve, you will find that your feelings about yourself improve as well. Instead of a self-image that seems hopeless, you will begin to develop a positive self-image, one that can walk fearlessly up that road to success.

ALLIEN R. RUSSON

contents

v

part
one

the ninety percent factor

chapter 1

success — ninety percent personality

If you had three wishes, what would they be? Happiness? Riches? Popularity? Peace of mind? Fame? Service to others? You can think of many other wishes that you would like to have if someone could wave a magic wand and give them to you. But the magic wand isn't working these days. Most of us must develop a do-it-yourself kit and build our own three wishes. One packet in your do-it-yourself kit contains a most important ingredient. That ingredient is personality. If you are to make your three wishes come true, your personality may be the deciding factor. In fact, in any kind of success — in your work, your friendships, your marriage — your personality is the key.

SUCCESS IN BUSINESS

Success in business is based not only on your abilities and how you work, but also on your *attitude* toward your work. Success is based on your knowledge and skill, but it is also based on how you look, how you talk, and how you act. In other school courses, you will build skills and acquire a background in literature, art, science, business, economics. But this is not enough. If you want to be a success in business, you must have the kind of personality that fits into the office team. You must get along well with other workers in business. Developing your business personality will be the purpose of this course.

There are two sides to business success: efficiency and satisfaction of needs. The first, efficiency, is foremost in people's minds. If you are efficient in your work, you are doing well; you are a success. The other side is satisfaction of needs, and it is less well known.

3

Everyone has basic physical needs: to have shelter from the cold; to have food when hungry; to be safe from harm. The need to share with others, to be part of a group, is a strong human need. The need to achieve and to acquire possessions is present in most of us, as is the need to have others recognize our achievements. These needs must be met if we are to be happy in our work.

You may be a success in your work, then, if you work efficiently and if your basic needs are met. It is quite likely that these two sides will work together. When your efficiency improves, this improvement may cause you to feel more secure. And when you feel more secure, you may find yourself working still more efficiently.

HOW SUCCESS IS ACHIEVED

If you are convinced that you should develop your personality, how do you go about it? If you should analyze the personal traits that make up a good personality, you might include a smile, a pleasant voice, a friendly attitude, the use of tact. These would certainly be some of the signs of a good personality, but what is underneath these surface signs? A personality can grow only when such growth is based on deeper habits of mind and heart.

A genuine liking for other people is an important habit of heart. If you like someone, you will want to put him at ease; and, presto, you will forget your own ill-at-ease feelings. Self-confidence is an important inner trait. To develop self-confidence, it is wise to do your best to excel. You will then have a reason to be assured, to forget your inadequacies. Naturalness is another habit, a habit of mind. To be natural, you must keep out anxiety, for anxiety causes you to think of yourself, how you look, how you walk, how you talk. This makes you self-conscious — the very opposite of being natural.

Building the inner and outer habits of personality is not an easy matter, but it is a task that will bring rich dividends. Personality is not achieved by picking up a few tricks, nor can it be gained by memorizing facts. To build desired traits, you must *want* to improve; you must *believe* that you *can* improve. With knowledge and belief as the foundation, you can do the right things with a positive aliveness, and your personality will grow. The following steps will help you reach this goal:

1. Determine the type of personality you wish to possess and decide to develop within yourself those habits, attitudes, and traits that will best express that personality.
2. Keep constantly before you the image of the kind of person you wish to become. This mental picture must be so clear and so constantly present that your mental processes and your ways of conduct will bring satisfaction only if they stand approved by this mental personality.

3. Analyze yourself. Discover and acknowledge the weaknesses in your make-up. Face these facts squarely and decide to remove the objectionable factors and substitute new strength for any weakness that stands in the way of your reaching your objective.
4. Exercise the traits of the personality you wish to possess. Only the constant practice of the acceptable conduct will encourage the development of desirable traits and a pleasing personality.

Positive Work Attitude

One of the important factors in success is your attitude toward your job. A positive work attitude can be the difference between success and mediocrity. If you like your work, you will have a positive attitude; if you dislike it, your attitude will be negative. No one likes to be around a negative person. This is just as true in business as it is in personal relations. If you complain, if you say it can't be done, you will be defeating yourself.

Every beginner has a lot to learn; but if your attitude is favorable, you will learn faster and your learning time will be excused by others. How does a positive work attitude manifest itself?

Enthusiasm. A good work attitude includes enthusiasm, both for the work and for the firm that employs you. Enthusiasm is actually nothing more than positive energy. When you are enthusiastic, you accomplish seeming miracles. And the best part of enthusiasm is that it is "catching." If you are enthusiastic, a co-worker may find his "down-in-the-dumps" feeling has disappeared. Enthusiasm is a trait that contributes a major share to what goes into success.

Willingness to learn. A beginner does have a lot to learn. People expect it. They do not expect the learning process to go on forever, though. The beginner who needs to be told something only once is considered a paragon, and the one who learns the new routines and facts without being told is rare, indeed. Everyone makes mistakes, but the beginner with a good work attitude seldom makes the same mistake twice.

Getting along with people. Perhaps the most important factor in a positive work attitude is getting along with people; this involves understanding yourself, the other person, and the way you choose to influence the other person. Where do you begin? Begin with the most difficult part — understanding yourself. You may wonder why understanding yourself is more difficult than learning how to influence others. The answer lies in the years that have been devoted to self-deception. We look at ourselves through rose-colored glasses. We can see the faults of others, but we cannot see our own. Or, if we do see them, we "rationalize" — find excuses for the unattractive sides of our personalities and our characters. So the first step is to take a good look at yourself. Some of the tools for doing this will be discussed in Chapter 2.

The next step is to look for something to like in that person with whom you wish to get along. Liking *something* in others must precede having the other person like you. It may seem an oversimplification, but much of getting along with people consists of just such "turnabouts." If you want to be liked, you must like others. If you want to be *interesting*, you must be *interested* — in the other person's ideas, problems, and suggestions. If you want others to adjust to your wishes, you must first learn to adjust to theirs. Others will overlook your failings more readily if you develop tolerance toward their failings.

Flexible goals. Another factor that helps you achieve a positive work attitude — and success — is having an objective or goal. In today's world, however, you can be certain of one fact of life: Our world is changing so rapidly that no one can predict the work you will be doing three years from now. The job you are preparing for today may have disappeared by the time you finish school. How can you set definite goals in such a changing world? Your grandparents probably believed you should "hitch your wagon to a star." Even they, perhaps, may have had doubts about their abilities to reach their stars, stars that seemed to go farther and farther away from them as they struggled to reach them.

Today, such fixed goals are completely useless. Our stars refuse to stay put. All you can do is use your star as the navigators did before the days of the compass — to set your direction. You can say, "I'm going *toward* that star." That's all. You can decide on some general kind of work, something you like, something in which you have some ability. But be ready for change. You may need to retrain, even after you get your job. Some experts say the job of the future will last only two or three years before the worker will need to learn new skills, become expert on a new machine, take courses to fit him or her for some new development in the work.

Then, too, there is our shrinking workweek. With machines doing so much of the work our hands did in the past, you must plan for more hours away from your work. What will you do with those extra hours? Recreation is only part of the answer. Decide now, before the need arises, on some way in which you can be of service. How can you help your neighborhood, your town, your country? Volunteer work in hospitals, reading for the blind, tutoring disadvantaged children — these and other opportunities are waiting for someone with an hour or two a week. Clean-up drives are waiting for you, as well as involvement in the ecology movement. Worthwhile service means you can use your leisure time to benefit yourself as well as benefit others.

Your goals, then, must be flexible; they must include worthwhile leisure-time activities. Moreover, they must be realistic. You must look at your abilities, your interests, your training, your work habits, and your personal qualities with an objective eye. For instance, if you can't make yourself write a letter, you should think twice before deciding to be a professional writer. If you have never passed a mathematics course with a B or better grade, you should probably not decide to become an engineer just because engineering seems a thrilling profession. If you don't like to take responsibility, you should not aspire to be the manager of the company.

Remember, too, the chance factor. A person who decides to become a personnel manager cannot entirely control his destiny. He can do much to achieve this objective, but he cannot be certain that he will become a personnel manager. Certainly many other people aspire toward the same goal, and not all who compete can succeed. Therefore, even though he obtains the necessary education and works in personnel offices, even though he studies and develops attractive personal traits, elements of chance may not enable him to become a personnel manager. His goals must be flexible enough that he will not be frustrated. He must consider that he still has his training and the knowledge that he has acquired; that he is utilizing this preparation, if not in the capacity in which he wants to use it, in a worthwhile form of service; that he has contributed his best ability in the position in which his business placed him. Anyone who can say these things of his career has reason to hold his head high. However, in obtaining the preparation for personnel director, he acted as wisely as he could. By obtaining such training, he increased his chances of reaching his goal. Because training and work cannot assure success, do not withdraw from the competition. To withdraw is certain defeat. To run well in the race is a noble feat.

Plan your goals carefully in terms of the investment of time and work which you want to make. The goals which you set will have great influence on your life. Happiness and success may not be synonymous terms for you. Weigh them in the balance. Try to reconcile the conflict if one exists.

In setting goals and planning their attainment, you cannot always be definite or specific. You can decide only the direction in which you wish to move. You can be prepared. Many opportunities you must seek for yourself. The opportunities which you will find cannot be anticipated with exactness. Some element of chance necessarily exists although you can do much to control that element of chance by training, a good record, habits of industry, and desirable personal traits. New avenues of opportunity may open to you, opportunities that you cannot now even imagine. If you have the necessary training and personal qualities, you may find employers will compete to obtain your services.

Read the life stories of persons who succeeded. You find few accounts of sudden fame, power, or wealth. You read of their long, hard struggles and of overpowering desire to win their fights.   Although success is not assured through hard work, you cannot name any person who has reached a lifetime goal who has not left a trail of hard work behind.

Basic Factors of Success

Just as there is no royal road to learning, so there is no smooth path to success. That road has not yet been paved. Every person who has traveled on it has learned how to take the bumps, how to make the grade. In 1970 a survey was made to determine the factors making for success in clerical work. It was found that a similar survey, made in 1949, had come up with almost the same factors. It is interesting to note that the first two in the 1970 study were (1) dependability and (2) accuracy in performing operations. The first two in the 1949 study were (1) accuracy in performing operations and (2) dependability. These two factors cannot be over-emphasized.

The 20 factors of greatest importance revealed in the 1970 study were the following:

1. Dependability
2. Accuracy in performing operations
3. Ability to follow instructions accurately and without repetition
4. Attendance, tardiness, and strict observance of break and lunch periods
5. Speed in performing operations — amount of acceptable work produced
6. Capacity for remembering necessary details, figures, and instructions
7. Initiative and/or resourcefulness
8. Personal appearance — appropriate dress and grooming
9. Ability to maintain harmonious working relations with others
10. Physical fitness for the work
11. Ability to work under pressure or abnormal conditions, such as meeting deadlines, multiple assignments, and extra work
12. Industry
13. Personality — cheerfulness and/or charm
14. Neatness and orderliness and maintenance or arrangement of physical surroundings, such as desks, files, and floor
15. Does not lose excessive time in personal telephone calls, talking with fellow workers, going to the rest room, and other personal activities
16. Ability to make judgments or decisions quickly and accurately
17. Natural ability and aptitude and attitude for the job
18. Acceptability of work — is within acceptable work standards for the job
19. Ability to organize work
20. Ability to suggest improvements in work techniques and operations[1]

---

[1]Fred S. Cook and Frank W. Lanham, "R & D," *Business Education World* (March-April, 1971), p. 13.

If we were to build a pyramid to success, using all 20 of these factors, we would have six as the foundation stones. Let's begin with the first three of these factors.

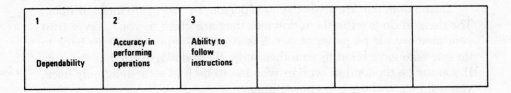

1	2	3			
Dependability	Accuracy in performing operations	Ability to follow instructions			

Figure 1-1. Base of Success Pyramid

Dependability. If someone says you are dependable, what does he mean? In most cases, he means you do what you say you will do. It sounds quite simple, doesn't it? Yet workers with the best of intentions are often labeled as undependable. They hate to hurt another's feelings by saying "No." They say they will get the report out by five o'clock, but they really know they won't be able to do it. A dependable person, however, does not say "Yes" unless he is certain he can carry out his promise. In fact, when you say you will do something, you have — in effect — signed a contract. A written contract, of course, would seem more important to you; but a spoken promise is just as important. If you, as a worker, are dependable, you will do your work well. You will not be an alibi artist. If you make a mistake, you will admit it and suggest a way of correcting it; you will suggest a solution.

Accuracy in performing operations. Accuracy is a result of having pride in your work. More and more these days employers are saying that they can't find workers who want to do a good job, who have pride in their work, who are actually artisans in what they do. If you are accurate in paper work, you learn to check everything. You proofread carefully. If you are uncertain of the spelling of a name or of an address, you look it up in the files or in the telephone directory. If you deal with numbers, you check them carefully. Just as you have learned to be a defensive driver, you must learn to check the same way. Anyone can make an error; you are there to see that no error goes past you.

Ability to follow instructions. Any office job or selling job involves instructions. These instructions may be in written form, in which case they must be followed to the letter. Sometimes, however, the writer of the instructions may not be too clear. In that case, all you need to do is rephrase the instructions in numbered form. Itemizing the instructions is simply listing them in detail, item by item.

Itemized instructions are easy to follow. You can check each one off as you do it, and you can make sure you are following them in their proper sequence.

Instructions that are given to you in person, by voice, are more difficult. The thing to do is write them down as they are given to you. Never trust your memory. If no paper or pencil is available, repeat the items back to the one who gave them to you; then write them down as soon as you can. If you can be the kind of worker who has to be told something only once, you will be a real asset to your company.

Build Your Own Self-Confidence

In reading the life stories of successful persons, you may decide there is little you hold in common with such famous people. These men and women seemingly had special abilities that they developed. They made use, however, of what they had.

You, too, have individual talents. Discover them; employ them; develop them. Of what use are your own special gifts and talents if you ignore them? Of what use is a course of training if you do not employ the lessons it would teach? Do not blame fate if you do not make use of the power and the ability that have been given you.

Your mental attitude is of greater value than your mental capacity. Just at the time when you think you have exhausted all your resources, there comes a deciding moment demanding more of you than you think you possess. If you fail to meet the test, if you stop trying, you lose the prize. A belief in yourself is essential to success; there must be such a sense of self-confidence and self-assurance that failure, no matter how often repeated, cannot get you down. The strength of will of the individual determined to succeed is the deciding factor in measuring his success.

Do not expect that success will come quickly and easily; rather, be prepared to build it carefully and slowly. Profit by your unpleasant experiences, interpret them as opportunities for broadening your outlook, for displaying your own inner powers of resistance, and "keep on keeping on." Believe in yourself, in your ability, in the sureness of the final outcome.

FOLLOW-UP ACTIVITIES

1. If you wish to succeed in getting the job you want, follow these steps:

   a. Make an inventory of your skills, your abilities, your knowledge, and your personal qualities.

b. Make an inventory of the skills, abilities, knowledge, and personal qualities you will need on the job.

c. Acquire any knowledge, skill, and business information you now lack.

d. Develop the personality traits and behavior patterns needed in the job.

Select a job for which you are preparing. Discuss with the class steps c and d.

2. What opportunities does your community afford for furthering your progress in business through additional educational advantages? If no such opportunities are afforded, what are your plans, once you are employed, for additional schooling?

3. Assume that you have obtained the job you want but would like to be promoted. What are some of the steps you should take to become promotable?

4. By what outward signs do you judge people when you first meet them?

5. The following test is designed to help you discover if you have the qualities that cause others to like you. Answer each question by underlining "Yes" or "No" at the end of each question.

1. If you make a promise, do you always keep it? (Yes No)
2. If someone, a friend or a co-worker, or a member of your family, is in need of help, do you give that help cheerfully? (Yes No)
3. Are you frequently witty in a sarcastic way? (Yes No)
4. Do you have a tendency to gain attention by "topping" the remark made by the previous speaker in a conversation? (Yes No)
5. Are you usually ill at ease with strangers? (Yes No)
6. Are you critical of others when you feel they are at fault? (Yes No)
7. Can you usually avoid being bossy? (Yes No)
8. Are you able to avoid ridiculing other people when they are not present? (Yes No)
9. Do you frequently laugh at the mistakes of others? (Yes No)
10. When others make mistakes (in fact, in grammar, in pronunciation) do you correct them? (Yes No)
11. Do you smile easily? (Yes No)
12. Are you able to praise and compliment other people easily? (Yes No)
13. Do you frequently try to reform other people? (Yes No)
14. Are you able to keep your personal troubles to yourself? (Yes No)
15. Are you suspicious of other people's motives? (Yes No)
16. Do you frequently borrow the belongings of others? (Yes No)
17. Do you enjoy gossip? (Yes No)
18. Are you able to keep out of other people's business most of the time? (Yes No)
19. Do you avoid talking about yourself, your belongings, your successes most of the time? (Yes No)
20. Do you ever use belittling words when referring to those who differ from you in religion, race, politics, or beliefs? (Yes No)

If you are well liked by most of your acquaintances, you will probably answer "Yes" to Questions 1, 2, 7, 8, 11, 12, 14, 18, and 19. Your "No" answers should be to Questions 3, 4, 5, 6, 9, 10, 13, 15, 16, 17, and 20. Give yourself five points for each answer you underlined that corresponds to the instructions given. If your total score is below 70, perhaps you are turning people off.

CASE PROBLEMS

1. The Working Mother

Mary Chamberlain's husband has left her with three small children to support. Mary is working nights at present, cleaning offices in a large office building. The pay is not high; she must ride the bus to and from the building; and she does not enjoy the work. Mary learns that she can qualify for a work-study grant at a nearby community college where she can learn computer programming. The only drawback is the hours. Mary's present job is from 10 p.m. to 3 a.m. Since she must leave at 9 in order to get to the downtown office and does not return until 4 a.m., she is away from her children most of the night. Mary leaves her children (ages 12, 10, and 7) alone while she works, but the woman in the next-door apartment looks in on them just before she retires at 11. Mary's school hours would be from 10 a.m. to 4 p.m. All of the children are in school and would thus be alone for about an hour each day.

1. Is there a primary objective that Mary should keep in mind?
2. What long-term objective do you feel Mary should consider?
3. What would you do if you were in Mary's situation?
4. Assuming you believe Mary should take the work-study grant, suggest ways in which she could solve the problem of her children's welfare when she is not at home.

2. Dead End?

Joan Ellsworth majored in secretarial science at a two-year business college. After she graduated, she tried for several weeks to find a job as a private secretary, but with no success. Finally, she found a job as a clerk-typist in a large life insurance company. She has been working now for nearly a year. Her supervisor is pleased with her work. While Joan's salary is not large, she has had two raises in the last six months. The physical conditions in the office are extremely good; there are also many fringe benefits that are attractive. The routine work Joan is doing, however, is below her abilities. While attending school, Joan did extremely well in shorthand and in simulated office procedures. Now, she fears she will lose her shorthand speed because of lack of practice.

1. Put yourself in Joan's place. What are some of the possible solutions to the problem?
2. After evaluating the possible solutions, which one would you take?

3. To Speak or Not to Speak

Marilyn Clark's employer has had a bad day. He has given reprimands to several of the employees and discharged one salesman. When Marilyn answers his ring to take dictation, he reproves her for being late. He had sent Marilyn on an errand a few minutes before, and she could not have returned earlier. When he says, "Why don't you ever get here promptly? I always have to wait for you," it is too much for Marilyn. She answers, "Because I had gone to the filing room to find those papers you wanted!" Her employer then says coldly, "You may go back to your more important work. I'll dictate to one of the others."

1. Evaluate Marilyn's handling of this situation.
2. What would you do in a similar case?
3. Is it helpful to fix the blame? Why or why not?

4. Short- or Long-Term Goals?

Patrick Hyde had always wanted to be a lawyer. Both his father and grandfather had been attorneys, and Patrick had always been certain of his career. After three years of college, however, he was told that his grades were not high enough for him to be accepted by the School of Law. Patrick's schoolwork slipped badly after this news, and his counselor, Mr. Cannon, called him in for an interview. During the interview, Patrick told Mr. Cannon that he had no other interests. He added, "If I can't be a lawyer, I won't be anything." At this point Mr. Cannon asked about the other courses Patrick had taken in high school and college. Among other things, Patrick mentioned that he had taken typing and shorthand in high school and had reached a high level of skill in both subjects. Mr. Cannon then suggested that Patrick find a part-time job as a stenographer in a law office while taking a reduced load in college.

1. What advantages to Patrick do you see in this suggestion?
2. Will firsthand knowledge of legal work give Patrick a more realistic idea of his goal?
3. What effect do you think working part-time will have on Patrick's grades in college? Why?
4. Do you think working as a legal stenographer may help if he is later accepted in a school of law?

5. Start at the Top?

Mr. Harwood, the vocational counsellor at Lincoln High School, asked Ben Garcia to apply for a job as general clerk with the A-One Trucking Company. Ben had just graduated and he was well qualified for the work. He got the job. The salary was good, and the boss was fair, but after a month Ben quit his job. He told Mr. Harwood that he could have stayed on the job forever and never had a chance to do anything but what he had done every day for a month — routing, checking, and keeping routine records.

Mr. Harwood called to check with Mr. Wellington, the self-made owner of the A-One Trucking Company, to see what was wrong. Mr. Wellington said, "Too anxious to be vice-president. Ben told me he didn't see how he could get anywhere in this business. He wanted to get ahead too fast. He couldn't see the chance that was right here waiting for him."

1. Do you agree with Ben's attitude about getting ahead? Why or why not?
2. How long does it take in a new position before an employee is worth his salary?
3. Do you think any vocation or profession is free from drudgery?
4. If you were a beginning worker, what would be your attitude toward routine work?

chapter 2

what makes you tick?

How many faces has success? One face, of course, is efficient and effective work: doing your job well. Another face is work satisfaction: enjoying your work. A third face is the ability to work as a part of a team. Working as a team is more than being well liked. Most of us do want to be liked. No one who watches television or reads a popular magazine can doubt this statement. To many young people being popular is the most important goal in their lives. Frequently, however, this desire is coupled with an utter lack of knowledge of how to achieve popularity. That is why each new mouthwash, perfume, hair style, or fashion is adopted so rapidly by so many people. They are seeking some way to escape from their sense of loneliness, of being shut away from love, recognition, and acceptance.

Teamwork, however, is more than personal popularity. Before you can become a good teamworker, you must learn all you can about yourself. You must discover what makes you tick. Most of you have had at least one difficult relationship in your life. There has been at least one person whom you could not understand, who seemed to bring out your resentment, your anger, your dislike. What we want to find out in this chapter is what *we* do to contribute to the difficulty. Personal problems do not arise because one person is entirely at fault. If we cannot get along with someone, there must be something *we* do that triggers the problem.

THE STAIRWAY OF NEEDS

Part of that something is being able to look away from oneself. You have heard the word *outgoing*, and this means just the opposite of *self-centered*. If you can learn to be outgoing, this one ability will solve many

15

of your problems.   Everyone knows the devastating effects of self-consciousness. You may be happy and relaxed until someone asks you to stand up and speak before a group. Immediately, you wonder what to do with your hands; you worry about the way you stand; your voice sounds strange to your ears. Why can't you think about the audience and forget yourself? The reason is that certain needs must be filled first.

A famous psychologist has written that everyone climbs a stairway of needs. As soon as our first-step needs are filled, or partly filled, we want to move on to the second step. The higher up the stairway we can go, the more effective we can become. First, everyone must satisfy his physical needs. He must have food when he is hungry, water when he is thirsty, shelter from the cold. Until these physical needs are met, no one can think of anything else.

When we do have enough to eat, shelter from the elements, and enough clothing to keep us warm, we experience a discontent. We want something more. We are ready for the second step: the need to be safe from harm. If you fear that an earthquake may engulf you at any minute, the need to be safe from this danger would take precedence over a need to be popular. It is useless to sell a man a "hyacinth for his soul" when he is starving for bread, and a man trapped in a burning building wants nothing but to be rescued. There is more to the second step than physical safety, however. We also need security. We must feel that our job is safe, that nothing will suddenly throw us back to that first step again. But let us assume that our safety and security needs have been partly met. Again, we feel dissatisfied; again, we want something else. We are now ready to move on to the third step.

The third need is to belong, to establish social relationships, often called interpersonal relations. You have seen this in certain grades in school. In junior high school, for example, teenagers may join a gang to become a member of a group. With this need to belong comes a desire to dress as others do, to become such a conformist that the slightest deviation from what "everyone does" cannot be tolerated.

At the third step you also have a great need to be loved — for yourself alone — not for your car, or your skills, or your big brown eyes. This is the stage where people fall in love, where nothing seems so important as being the greatest person in the world to one other human being. One aspect of the needs stairway is that most of us stop at the third stage. We daydream about achieving some kind of recognition, but we may not work at it. Daydreaming is so much easier; when we daydream we do not run the risk of failure. So, if you are bothered and unhappy about your own inadequacies, take heart. You are a member of the minority that is beginning to rise to the top.

When you suddenly find that love and belonging are not enough, that you want to be recognized, to be admired for what you have *done*, then you will know that you are trying to reach the fourth step on that stairway of needs. In this stage you may go too far: you may antagonize others in your determination to gain recognition. The fourth stage, however, is the one demanding an *outgoing* personality. When you have reached it, your self-improvement campaign can begin.

In Chapter 1 the "turnabout" method of getting along with people was mentioned. This same "turnabout" can be a part of finding esteem — both the esteem of others and self-esteem. No one is proud of his own actions and accomplishments all the time. In fact, the more renowned an individual may be, the more likely he will be striving to achieve still more. Also, the more you know about the goal you are trying to reach, the farther you will seem to be from reaching it. Remember this: Every person of high position was once in your shoes. Everyone has had to work his way through a jungle of self-doubt.

WHO YOU ARE

Besides understanding the need level for which you are striving, it is important for you to know who you are. You may be thinking, "I know who I am." But do you? The way you feel inside, the way you behave toward others, your self-control, your self-respect — these indicate who you really are. Sometimes your life can go badly because your self-image, the way you think you are, is not the truth of who you are.

Your Three Selves

Your self-image is affected by three ego states, according to Dr. Eric Berne.[1] An ego state is the way you feel about something and the way that feeling causes you to behave. These three ego states are all present and operating in each of us. They are the Parent ego state, the Adult ego state, and the Child ego state.

When you act as your parents did, or as some other person who took the place of your parent, you are in your Parent ego state. Listen closely to what is going on in your head. Do you hear statements like these: "You look sloppy in that outfit," "You'll never learn to play the piano," "You are so stupid," "Don't drive so fast," or "This room is a mess"? If you do, your Parent self is operating. You are still saying to yourself the things your parents once said to you. In a sense, you have become your own parent. Unfortunately, most of these parental statements you are making to yourself (and to others) are critical.

---

[1]Eric Berne, *Games People Play* (New York: Grove Press, 1967). See also Muriel James and Dorothy Jongeward, *Born to Win* (Reading, Massachusetts: Addison-Wesley Publishing Company, 1971).

On the other hand, your Parent self may want to take care of other people, give them advice, see that they do the right thing. Even though your intentions are good, the person you advise may resent it. The Parent in you may give others the impression that you are bossy, critical, or overbearing.

You can also think for yourself. You can look at a situation, decide what the sensible alternative is, and act. When you behave in this fashion, you are being your Adult self; you are in your Adult ego state. The Adult ego state operates much as a computer does:

Computer	*Your Adult*
Data fed into the machine	You see, hear, and feel what is going on right now
Machine processes the data	You think the matter over
Answers come out of the machine	You act according to what you think is best

When you are behaving from your Adult self, you are able to deal objectively with facts, free from personal feelings and opinions. Your Adult self helps you to act from how you think, not from how you feel.

The third ego state, your Child self, is different for each one of you. The child you once were is still in you. When you are in your Child ego state, you behave in a child-like way. Some child-like behavior is undesirable after you have grown up, but some of it is good. The Child in you is

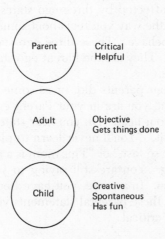

Figure 2-1. Your Three Selves

the self that feels free, that likes to discover new things, that is able to be spontaneous. It is your Child self who can laugh and have fun. But just as no one likes a selfish, spoiled child, so no one likes you to whine or to sulk. Such child-like behavior *is* undesirable.

Your Transactions with Others

All three of your ego states must operate if you are to develop your personality, but your Adult self must be in charge. Your Adult self learns to listen to what goes on inside you. Your Adult self thinks things over and decides whether to use the behavior of the Parent or of the Child. The Adult asks, "Is this behavior appropriate right now?" The Adult self drives the car, although the Child self and the Parent self are available when needed. If the Parent self or the Child self drives the car, there may be a smashup.

Much of the trouble we have in dealing with others comes from what Berne calls "crossed transactions." An example of a crossed transaction is the following: An Adult question is asked by the supervisor: "Millie, have you seen the file on the new Bakersfield contract?" This question, however, is answered by Millie's Child ego state: "You are always picking on me. I can't keep track of every file in the office!" Millie is letting her Child self drive her car.

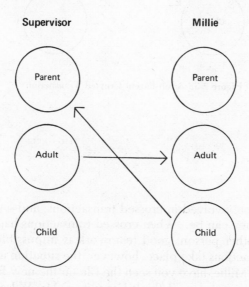

Figure 2-2. Adult-Child Crossed Transaction

Let's look at another type of crossed transaction. The supervisor asks, "Millie, have you seen the file on the new Bakersfield contract?" and Millie's Parent self answers: "If you took care of this department the way you should, there wouldn't be any necessity to look for lost files!" Millie is letting her Parent self drive her car; there is going to be another smashup. This particular smashup may leave lasting scars. No one likes to have a bossy subordinate tell him or her what to do. It is wise, therefore, to be careful to avoid reacting as a Parent self to an Adult transaction.

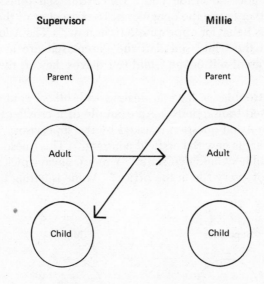

Figure 2-3. Adult-Parent Crossed Transaction

We've all been involved in crossed transactions, and we all know how uncomfortable they can be. When crossed transactions happen, we move away from the other person; good teamwork is impossible. When complementary transactions take place, however, the situation is pleasant. The supervisor says, "Millie, have you seen the file on the new Bakersfield contract?" Millie now answers, "I think I saw it on Mr. Wilson's desk. Shall I get it for you?" Millie's Adult self answered an adult question. Her Adult self is driving her car.

Supervisor   Millie

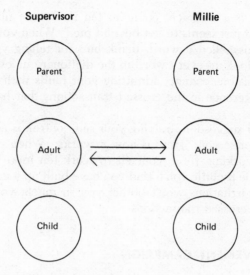

Figure 2-4. Complementary Transaction

See if you can tell *who is speaking* when you talk with someone. If you are careful to respond to the speaker from the same ego state as the stimulus statement or question, you can avoid getting into many difficulties with the people around you. When someone speaks to you in a child-like way, answer in the same fashion. For example, a "kidding" statement is best answered with more kidding. If you take the kidding seriously, you are guilty of a crossed transaction. Also, if someone speaks seriously to you, you will offend that person if you answer in a flippant manner. Just keep in mind *who* is speaking; learn to answer in a way that causes complementary transactions and not crossed ones.

Putting Starch in Your Adult

What can you do if many of your transactions with others result in quarrels, hurt feelings, broken friendships? One important action you can take is to strengthen your Adult self. Two suggestions for putting starch in your Adult are made here: admitting your faults and training your self-control.

Admitting your faults is hard; we all have a reflex action that responds with anger when we are criticized. But it really is helpful to learn to accept criticism without trying to defend yourself. When someone tells you your room or office is a disgrace, count to ten in Roman numerals and say, "Yes, I know. It just seems to get beyond me." When your boss blows up because you misspelled a word, thank him for telling you. Then, from that day forth, look up every word in the dictionary unless you are sure of its spelling. This one change, admitting your faults with good grace, will make a big difference in the crossed transactions that have been ruining your life.

The second suggestion, training your self-control, is also hard; but the results will surprise you. Here is how it works: When you are tired and want to stop working, force yourself to work ten more minutes. That's all it is. But little by little you'll find you have built up a great deal of inner strength; small irritations won't bother you so much; you'll find it much easier to avoid crossed transactions.

YOUR IMPROVEMENT CAMPAIGN

You have now learned something about your need level and your ego states. The next step is to do something about what you have learned.

You, Too, Can

You have seen the ads, "YOU, TOO," can play the piano, paint a landscape, write a novel. For your self-improvement campaign, let's borrow this phrase. You, too, can improve. It's guaranteed. What you must do first, though, is look at *this year's* model very carefully. Imagine yourself as a product — this year's model. Put yourself on the drawing board; analyze the product in every detail. What are the good points? (Remember to start with the positive, always.) List them. You will find that this activity is self-propelling, too, because as you write down one good point, it will remind you of another. After you have exhausted your plus qualities, see if you can group them into three or four categories. For example, you might use a breakdown for appearance, mental abilities, and emotional qualities.

Now, take up the emotional category list and check the "Room for Improvement" traits that you have. It is best to start here because, believe it or not, you can talk about your emotional difficulties more objectively than you can about your looks or your brains. Somehow they seem more flexible, more capable of being changed. Because of this, you feel less resentment about these faults. If you have a tendency to put off until tomorrow what should have been done today, you may look upon this trait somewhat indulgently. You cannot be complacent, however, about being covered with freckles or having a long, pointed nose. These "born-with" traits must be left until we build up our objectivity.

Beginning with the emotional category, let's label it *Attitudes* — a more neutral word. Now, from your list, select the trait that has the most references that are considered negative. If you have listed procrastination, you may find you have also listed failing to take care of your clothes properly, forgetting to return library books, losing things, and so on. All of these faults might be lumped under the heading *Procrastination*. You put off giving attention to doing things as you should. This trait, then, is the one with which you begin your improvement campaign.

Take up another sheet of paper. There is a reason for this suggestion. We impress upon our minds the importance of an action or thought much more completely when we write it down than when we merely think about it. Thoughts are the most elusive phenomena we have. You may have a brilliant idea and think: "That's good. I must remember that." But what happens? You *don't* remember it! It fades away almost immediately unless it is captured on paper. In a similar way, writing down a list of things to be done is one step toward doing them.

On a piece of paper, then, write the title, "To Be Done Thursday," or whatever the next day happens to be. The best time to write this list is just before retiring. Below the title, list numbers 1 through 5. It is better to start with not more than five things to be done. Remember, we are encouraged by success, so make it easy for you to succeed the first time.

After you have written your column of numbers, write opposite No. 1 the most difficult, most disagreeable job you have to do tomorrow. Beneath that, write the next most important job, and so on down to number 5. Think hard about your list; visualize yourself doing these things, perhaps in more than one way. Then place the list where you will be sure to see it the first thing the next morning.

When you wake the next morning and are ready for the day, start on that first job. *Do not* do all of the short, easy jobs first. You may think that you will finish the easy jobs first so that you will have nothing else on your mind and can concentrate on the big job. This is a fallacy. When you finish the short, easy jobs, you will have *nothing* on your mind. You will be tired and will probably decide to wait until tomorrow to get at that hard job.

After item No. 1 is finished, begin No. 2, and upon completion of that task, begin the next one. You may not finish all the items on the list, but that is all right. The most difficult job has been finished, and you should give yourself the heartiest of congratulations. Forget the items at the bottom of the list that you did not reach, and just add them to the next day's list. Concentrate on what you *did* do, not what you *did not* do.

Accentuate the Positive

You have probably already learned that negative statements should be avoided when you write or speak to others. The main thing that is wrong with a negative attitude or statement is that negatives are contagious. You know, yourself, that you can get up in the morning with a feeling of well-being. Yet, if you meet four or five friends during the day who tell you of depressing happenings, who complain about their lot, or — worst of all — who criticize you and call attention to your mistakes, your mood of happiness will soon disappear. The other side of the coin is just as contagious, however. Although you may be tired and discouraged, your mood changes when you meet someone who gives you a sincere compliment or who greets you with a smile.

The step to take, then, is to accentuate the positive and eliminate the negative. Being negative is actually nothing but another of those habits discussed in Chapter 1. Just to prove this, you might try an experiment. On the left side of a folded sheet of paper, write "Negative Statements"; on the right side, write "Positive Statements." Choose an hour of the day that is about average for you. Avoid five o'clock in the afternoon, for this is a low period for most of us. Now keep track of the negative and positive statements you make during that hour. Don't try to be different from the way you normally talk, but make a record of each positive and each negative statement. Did you have more negative or more positive statements at the end of the hour? You will be quite unusual if your positive statements outnumber the negative ones. This is because our culture encourages negativism. Most of us tend to say nothing about the good things in our lives. We may go so far as to say, "What a beautiful day," but we are more likely to complain about life's irritations than to give praise.

The next step, after you have found your score, is to start a "Let's be more positive" campaign. Watch yourself. When you start to complain about a teacher, an assignment, the weather, or your financial state, stop. See if you can twist your statement around so that it will be positive. For example, if you get a test paper back with a C- on it, you may start to say, "How awful! I'm below average." Instead, just for this experiment, say, "How about that! I passed!" This may seem ridiculous to you, but it is guaranteed to have a remarkable effect on your moods and emotions. With concentrated effort, you can all but eliminate negative thoughts — with their destructive effects — from your life.

No More Self-Pity

Besides being more positive in what we say, we must get rid of another bad habit — self-pity. Let's wipe out once and for all the "poor little me" feeling. You have heard the old proverb about the man who had no shoes and complained until he met a man with no feet. This is the way to erase those self-pitying thoughts that will — unless we are on guard — creep into our minds. There is too much self-pity in the world, and in its train comes an even more destructive emotion — resentment.

One way to cure resentment is through action. Don't just sit there and brood. Do something! Any kind of positive action will help eliminate resentment, but the best cure is action that you enjoy. Perhaps you have done poorly on a test and you deeply resent the fellow who got the top grade. Thinking about your resentment — nursing it to keep it warm — will not help; neither will additional study while you are in a resentful mood. Instead, do something you enjoy that is active. Play tennis, join a square dance group, paint scenery for the drama club — anything that is fun.

YOUR SUCCESS PYRAMID

In Chapter 1, we described the first three blocks of your pyramid to success. In this chapter, three more of the blocks will be described. These blocks will complete the base of your success pyramid.

Attendance and Punctuality

In today's permissive age, few people outside the work force can appreciate the necessity for always being on the job and always being there on time. You would very likely consider taking money from the cash register as dishonesty, something you would never do. Yet failure to come to work, tardiness in coming to work, tardiness in returning from lunch periods and coffee breaks are just as serious, just as dishonest as taking money from the cash drawer. Attendance and punctuality are within your power, too. You may be doubtful of your skill, your manners, your appearance; but you need not be doubtful of your ability to get to work every day a few minutes before your work day begins. Attendance and punctuality form an important block at the base of your pyramid to success. Don't let this particular block crumble. Be there — and be on time.

Amount of Acceptable Work Produced

The next block in the foundation of your success pyramid is your ability to produce. Speed, alone, is not the answer; rather, efficiency is the

1	2	3	4	5	6
Dependability	Accuracy in performing operations	Ability to follow instructions	Attendance and punctuality	Amount of acceptable work produced	Remembering necessary details

Figure 2-5. Base of Success Pyramid

key. The way to build up your work production has three parts: (1) an efficient work station, with your tools within easy reach, (2) repeated practice on the parts of the task that slow you down, and (3) an objective that increases as you improve. For example, if your work output on letters transcribed in an hour is now four, you would first see that your dictionary, your letterheads, carbon sheets, second sheets, and envelopes are within easy access to your typewriter. Your eraser or correction tool is always in the same place on your desk. Second, you would practice assembling the carbon pack, rolling it into the typewriter, setting your margins, and typing the first part of the letter until you could perform the entire operation smoothly and efficiently. Third, you would set an objective of five mailable letters an hour. When you reach your objective, you move it to six mailable letters an hour. The same procedure can be used with any kind of work. Remember, though, that your objective must be to increase the amount of work while maintaining high quality of work.

Remembering Necessary Details

Clerical workers of all types *must* develop their ability to work with details. The sixth block at the foundation of your success pyramid is the capacity for remembering necessary details, figures, instructions, and the like. The memory part of the rule, however, is to remember to write everything down. *Never* trust your memory alone. Strangely enough, the mere fact that you have written down the telephone message, the file number, the date of the important meeting seems automatically to improve your memory of these details, facts, and figures. If you forget to write down these notes, your memory will not come to your aid.

FOLLOW-UP ACTIVITIES

1. *Meeting New People.* One of the most difficult ways of becoming more outgoing is taking the initiative in meeting new people. To help you overcome this universal tendency toward "inwardness," you are to meet, entirely through your own efforts, 5 men and 5 women (of any age). Exactly four weeks from today you are to report the results of the project in the following form:

1. Name	Short Biography	Situation (How we met)	Opener (What I said)

Remember, you must have ten names and *you* must make the first move. No one else may introduce you. The short biography should contain at least four items of information about each person.

Follow your report with a paragraph of evaluation of the experience. How did it affect you? Will it change your future behavior? What have you learned about people in general?

2. *Learning to Be Positive.* As a follow-up of the project described on pages 23 and 24, keep a list of all the positive statements you make during one hour. Time the project so that it is on the same day of the week and the same time of day. If your new number of positive statements is the same (or fewer) than before, try the experiment again the next day. Do this until you form the habit of the positive approach.

3. *Helping Others to Be Positive.* Now that you are aware of the benefits of being positive, see if you can change the behavior of others by giving them positive reinforcement. Do you have a parent, sister, brother, girlfriend, boyfriend, or co-worker who does something that bothers you?

   a. Describe in detail the situation you wish to improve.
   b. Formulate in detail your plan to increase praise and decrease criticism.
   c. Keep an accurate record of your actions and the results.

4. Keep a list of the times you refrain from answering defensively when you are criticized. See if you can strengthen your Adult self by agreeing with your detractor. Evaluate the experience. Did you see any helpful results?

5. For one day, try to keep as many of your transactions with others on a complementary basis as you can. Try particularly to refrain from answering in a flippant manner when someone says something seriously to you. For example, if you are paid a compliment, try to say something helpful to the other person. If someone says, "What good looking slacks," don't say, "They're two years old"; but answer more like this: "How nice of you to notice." Report on the results.

6. *Making and Strengthening Friendships.* Few of us could live happily without friends. Try the following steps in winning new friends:

   a. Step One: All day Monday smile at those you meet at school or at work. Praise at least one person you greet.
   b. Step Two: On Tuesday relay a kind or encouraging word to every close associate you talk to during the day.
   c. Step Three: On Wednesday seek out someone in need of a friend and invite him or her to do something with you.
   d. Step Four: On Thursday choose a stranger to talk with and discuss only his or her affairs.
   e. Step Five: On Friday write a friendly letter to someone.

Evaluate the experience of the week. Do you feel more friendly with someone? Has anyone made friendly overtures to you?

7. As has already been said, you should possess the ability to estimate the other person so that you may determine what line of conduct you are to follow in order to please the other person. Remember, however, that the other person is sizing you up and evaluating your personality through your appearance, words, and conduct.

How do you think an employer would estimate you on the following list of traits, and on what outward evidence would an employer base an opinion?

muscular coordination	clumsy muscular reaction
persistent	a quitter
sociable	unsociable
careful	careless
accurate	inaccurate
industrious	lazy
enthusiastic	indifferent
self-confident	inferiority complex
ambitious	satisfied to "get by"
punctual	dilatory
adjustable	obstinate
optimistic	pessimistic
patient	impatient
thrifty	spendthrift
modest	vain

CASE PROBLEMS

1. Child, Adult, or Parent

Betty Varner is a private secretary in the firm of Strong Electronics, Inc. She has been working four years, after graduating from an excellent junior college. Betty's parents were very strict, and she has always been a perfectionist. Her superior, Mr. Bartlett, was a kind, fatherly man, and Betty has worked happily and well. Two weeks ago, however, Mr. Bartlett was transferred to San Francisco and Betty was assigned to his replacement, Mr. Kearny. The new man is brilliant and efficient, but he is somewhat short on patience. He speaks crisply and concisely to everyone. In Betty's anxiety to please, she finds herself making many errors. This fact in itself distresses Betty, but when Mr. Kearny criticizes her work rather sharply, Betty bursts into tears. Mr. Kearny takes her tears in stride, but he becomes extremely irritated with Betty's continued apologies for her previous errors. Finally, he asks the personnel manager to transfer Betty to another office

1. Put yourself in Betty's place. Is there anything you can do to eliminate this overly sensitive attitude? Can you detect any causes for perfectionism that are not particularly praiseworthy?
2. What should a beginning worker's attitude be toward criticism? How about the experienced worker? Do you think being able to "take it" will increase or decrease further criticism?
3. If you were the personnel manager, would you tell Betty the reason for her transfer?
4. What suggestions, as personnel manager, could you give Betty to help her overcome her desire for perfection in everything?
5. Would you say that Betty is operating from her Adult ego state? Explain your answer.

2. Getting the Lowdown

Joe Garcia has just started in his first job as a salesman in the men's furnishings section of a large department store. One of the older employees, Mr. Parker, asks Joe to lunch at the end of his first week in his new job. During lunch the older man talks freely and critically about the head of the department, the management policies of the store, and how hard it is to inject any new ideas. Joe agrees with Mr. Parker, adding that he has found it rather hard to work with Mr. Green, the head of the department. "He seems to know all the answers," Joe says, "and doesn't respect the ideas of others. I guess he's afraid they might be better than his own."

The next day Joe is called to the general manager's office and berated for criticizing the department manager. Joe immediately realizes that his luncheon companion has reported Joe's comments. He is very angry and decides he will be less friendly with the older employees in the future.

1. What do you think of Joe's solution to the problem? Can you suggest another solution that might be more effective?
2. What should a new employee's attitude be toward early friendship with other employees?
3. If you had been Joe, how would you have answered Mr. Parker when he criticized the policies and management of the store? Why?
4. Was Mr. Parker speaking from his Parent self, Adult self, or Child self? Explain.

3. Does Defensiveness Pay?

Max Nelson has been very happy and successful as a junior accountant with Patterson and Lee, Tax Accountants. One afternoon in April his superior, Mr. Mitchell, could not find an important document connected with a case on which Max had been working. He called Max to his office and accused him of losing the document. Ordinarily a quiet man, Mr. Mitchell began a tirade of accusations and threats against Max. Max tried to remain calm but continued to insist that the document was clipped with the others when he had placed them on Mr. Mitchell's desk that morning. In utter dejection, Max returned to his office. Just before closing time Mr. Mitchell came into Max's office and told him that the document has been found. Apparently Mr. Mitchell had enclosed it with some other papers that he sent to another company. It had just been discovered by one of the mailroom employees. Mr. Mitchell apologizes sheepishly and promises to avoid such a display in the future. Max goes home and thinks the matter over. He has been unusually conscientious in his work and his pride has been hurt deeply. He decides to leave the firm and calls the senior partner, Mr. Patterson, the next morning and resigns.

1. What do you think of Max's actions? Discuss particularly his calm when accused by Mr. Mitchell, his decision to resign, and his call to Mr. Patterson.
2. What was Max's motivation for resigning from his position? On what stage of need fulfillment was he operating?
3. What other alternatives can you suggest in this case? Which of the alternatives, including Max's decision, would you choose?

chapter 3

changing ourselves and others

You have read in the first two chapters of this book that success is 90 percent personality. Just what does that statement mean? Does it mean that skill, knowledge, and ability are valueless? No. The statement means that you need all three to *get* the job in the first place. Keeping that job, however, calls for another ingredient. You must be able to get along with other people. The 90 percent factor, by the way, comes from a study that surveyed the reasons why clerical workers *lost* their jobs. In this survey it was found that 90 percent of the reasons given for job dismissal were personal ones. In other words, personality problems may cause you to lose your job, even though you have skill, knowledge, and ability.

"I LOVE HUMANITY. IT'S PEOPLE I CAN'T STAND."

This statement, by Charlie Brown, expresses what many of us feel. In the abstract, humanity is fine. You love humanity. But there are those awful people cluttering up your life: your co-workers, your supervisor, the supervisor's boss. In addition to these problems, however, you will very likely have the same kinds of difficulties with the people in your personal life. Your roommate may be hard to get along with; your fiance(e) or mate may be demanding; later on, your children will present problems. There will never be an end to problems with people, but you can arm yourself with a helpful way of handling the ones that come up in your life.

You Can't Change Others with Criticism

The most frustrating aspect of human relations is discovered when you try to change someone else. Your best friend mispronounces words.

So, with the best intentions, you correct him. Is your friend grateful? Does he thank you for your interest in his self-improvement campaign? No, he is not grateful and he does not thank you. He resents your meddling, and he resents it deeply. Furthermore, just to show you who is boss, he does not improve. Or say you are a newly married husband. You see that your wife is not an economical shopper, so you give her a lecture on how to buy. What happens? Your wife flies into a tantrum, bursts into tears, and presents you with the job of buying groceries from now on. Or perhaps you fancy yourself as a crusader; you imagine the thrills of redeeming lost souls and with true reforming zeal marry a man who is charming but shiftless. You know that love will conquer all and that you can turn your playboy into a captain of industry. Alas, before many months have passed you must admit your mistake. Your playboy will never change because *you* want him to. If he changes, it will be because *he* has decided to reform himself.

Don't Fight the Problem

Another fallacy in this wilderness of problems with people is the belief held by many that you can talk the problem away. You can say, "This should not be," and all may agree with you; but it still *is*. So, when you are up for promotion and possess all the needed abilities and skills only to have the boss's nephew get the promotion, don't try to fight the problem. Bosses' nephews will continue, no doubt, to be promoted. Fighting the problem should be avoided; it will not alter the situation.

What you should do when the other fellow is obviously wrong and you are obviously helpless is to let it go. Chalk this one up to experience. Do something else for awhile, something that is enjoyable for you. Let your resentment out of your system through some kind of positive activity. In almost every language there is a proverb to the effect that we should change what we can change but accept what we cannot change.

Try to Change Yourself

So far, problems with people as a topic has taken on a rather negative hue. If we can't change others and can't fight the problem, what can we do? There is one thing left. There is one person you can make fun of without having an organized group send you scathing telegrams. There is one person you can "get tough with" without fear of reprisal. There is, in fact, one person whom you *can change* — yourself.

The mere changing of your own attitudes is a remarkably enlightening experience. If you have been having trouble with your supervisor and he has been criticizing you at great length and in graphic detail, you — being human — have probably retaliated in some way. Perhaps you have been sullen; you may have answered abruptly; or you may have threatened to quit if he didn't like the way you were doing things. What would happen if, instead, you said sincerely, "I know I made a terrible error, Mr. Burns. You are absolutely right to tell me about it. Is there anything I can do to repair the damage I have done?" No matter how formidable Mr. Burns may be, he could hardly fail to respond in a reasonably positive manner. And, if he were really human beneath that cold exterior, he may say, "That's all right. We'll forget it this time."

Changing yourself is the best kind of reforming you can possibly do. But how should you start? What faults do we all have in common? Everyone is an individual. How can we draw up rules for self-improvement that will be applicable to everyone? Well, there is one trait that most of us can improve. We can all learn to have a positive attitude. Or do you think you already have a positive attitude? Perhaps you do; but you will be unique, indeed, if you do not occasionally say something disparaging about a coworker or grumble and complain about (1) the weather; (2) your work; (3) your teacher or boss; (4) your grades or your pay, among other things. Everyone is negative some of the time.

Eliminate the negative. At a lecture on human relations, the speaker was giving the audience some rules for living. One of the rules was to stop expecting perfection in this world. One member of the audience immediately raised her hand. "What's wrong with being a perfectionist?" she snapped. The speaker smiled, "Your tone of voice when you asked that question, for one thing," she answered. Negative feelings, negative attitudes, negative words — all are depressors of the spirit. They all take us — and our hearers — down instead of up. We are climbing toward happiness or, at least, we would like to think we could do so. If happiness could be envisioned as lying at the top of a long stairway with unhappiness at the bottom, each negative thought or word would take us one step down. Each positive thought or word would take us one step up.

How can you tell if you need to work on this negative habit? Let's try an experiment. Take an ordinary three-hour period when you are free to say what you think. From six to nine in the evening is usually a time of relative freedom, or from three to six on a Sunday afternoon. Arm yourself with a scratch pad and a pencil. Every time you think or say something negative, write it down. This means *everything*, including, "Is it hot enough for you?" and "I wish Miss J. would wear something besides that blue dress." Just plain, ordinary negative things that all of us say and think. At the end of the three-hour period, read them over. You will be surprised at the number of items you have written. You will wonder when you had time to say or do *anything* positive, which may explain why some of us don't do more things of a positive nature.

Accentuate the positive. A negative attitude usually creeps up on us because it is so easy to be negative. It takes no effort to let a feeling of self-pity steal over you. There are disappointments in every day. The easy way is to let them engulf us. It does take effort to replace negative thoughts with positive ones, but it is time and effort well spent. The way to start is to take the first steps:

1. *Smile*. If you make yourself turn the corners of your mouth up instead of down, it will be easier to think of something positive to say. A gloomy expression is another habit that is easy to acquire. Make a real effort to look pleasant and interested in what is going on around you. You know, under the stimulation of your interest, those around you may become interesting!

2. *Say something pleasant once every hour*. This step is not intended to be funny. There are many people in the world who never say anything pleasant. So, for your second step, think of something positive, good-natured, or complimentary to say to someone once each hour. This will do wonders to those around you, but it will also keep you so busy thinking of positive things to say that you won't have time to be negative.

3. *Change your negative statements to positive ones*. The third step is to change your negative statements in midstream. Say your roommate reaches into the closet and knocks your best coat on the floor. Without thinking, you start to say, "Why can't you watch what you're doing?" But you catch yourself before you get that far. You say, "Why can't — I help you find what you want?" At first, this kind of thing may strike you with a hollow, insincere ring. Your roommate may think you have lost your mind. But keep it up for at least a week. You may be surprised at the way your relationships with people improve.

4. *Change a negative problem into a positive situation*. After you have practiced on positive statements for a week, you are ready to attack a negative problem. Look around you for some negative situation. Is there a co-worker you dislike? Is there a friend who rubs you the wrong way? Whatever it is, try the positive approach. Remember, you are not to be the culprit; you are to be the victim. But you will still try to change the situation by being positive. Let's say there is a friend who gets on your nerves. He talks about himself all the time. He boasts about everything — his car, his job, his school. You think that, without a doubt, he is the most conceited person you ever met. You may think, "What can I say that is positive that he hasn't already said over and over?" That doesn't matter. Say it anyway. You meet him at lunch and you don't even have time for a greeting before he starts right in to tell you about a test on which he knew all the answers. Why not say, "Jerry, I wish I had your confidence." If you keep out the sarcasm and say it sincerely, this may cause Jerry to stop and think a minute. He probably doesn't have too much confidence, and his

bragging is in the way of whistling in the dark. He may say, "To tell you the truth, I have always thought you were the confident one." If something like this should happen, the hostility on both sides will begin to evaporate. You say, "But how do you know this is the way it would go?" No one knows exactly how a conversation will go. We know, however, that this kind of approach results in a positive reply nearly all the time.

Your campaign to become more positive will get you over a big hurdle. When you learn to look at problems with a positive attitude, you can begin to solve them more easily.

LET'S USE BEHAVIOR MODIFICATION

A more positive attitude will surely make a difference in your campaign to change yourself. It will do even more. You can use a combination of positive attitudes and what psychologists call behavior modification to change others. These psychologists are convinced that personality is *caused*. You were not born with a chip on your shoulder. That chip grew on your shoulder because of the way someone else treated you. In a psychology class this theory was tested in the following experiment.

One of the students in the class was an unpopular "plain Jane." She was a loner; she did not mix with the other students; she had no dates; she dressed in a "ho-hum" way. Two of the male students in the class decided to see if they could change her personality by "rushing" her for a few weeks. They asked her for dates; they talked to her at every opportunity; they told her how much fun she was to be around; they treated her as if she were a beautiful, popular girl. After a few weeks of this "rush" treatment, the plain Jane disappeared. Now the girl talked freely, laughed with the others, was at ease with the other students. She dressed much more attractively. In short, she became the kind of girl the two fellows had been pretending she was. Soon, in fact, the original experimenters had a hard time finding the girl with any free time for them.

The reason for the change in Plain Jane was reinforcement, a word meaning reward. The girl was rewarded for being attractive even before she was attractive. Nevertheless, the reward worked just as well as it would have if she had been given a prize for being the most popular girl in the class. This theory, called behavior modification, means that if we want someone to change, we must make changing worth his while. If you feel unhappy and someone asks you why you are looking so sad, you may feel comforted, but you are not likely to change. But if someone says, "You look so nice in that blue dress. It exactly matches your eyes," you may find yourself feeling happier.

The rule of reinforcement says that people act in ways that bring some kind of reward. If you want to change your behavior, you must have some payoff, some reward. You will not change if no one notices what you have done. Being ignored is painful. If what you do results in indifference, you stop doing it. You know, yourself, that you need to have someone pay attention to you. If you can't get attention for being good, you'll try getting attention by being bad. You can stand anything but indifference.

One of the reasons why punishing has never helped much in changing what you do lies right here. Punishment is a kind of attention. If you want attention and the only kind you can get is punishment, you will behave in such a way that you will be punished. Punishment is better than nothing.

Someone has said that there are three kinds of people in this world: those who make things happen, those who watch others making things happen, and those who don't realize anything is happening. You will have a happier and more effective life if you can turn yourself into the kind of person who makes things happen. How can you do that?

Changing Yourself With Behavior Modification

If you are going to use behavior modification to change yourself, you will first need to have your own personal system of rewards. One of you may like to take your car apart and put it back together again; another may prefer to listen to music or sit in a quiet corner and read a favorite book. The thing to do is to think about *you*. What do you like to do best? Take a piece of paper and write down 10 to 20 activities that you enjoy. Of course, these activities must be possible in your present circumstances. You can't say you would like to spend a million dollars because you don't have a million dollars. Just write down the activities you enjoy most, the ones that are possible right now.

When you have your list of rewards drawn up, draw up a contract. You promise yourself that you are going to change in some way. You may decide to study more effectively. You may decide to control your bad temper. Whatever your behavior change is going to be, write it down. Suggestions for writing up your contract are found at the end of Chapter 4. Then you set up a system of rewards. If you follow your program of change for one hour, you get a certain reward. If you continue for an entire day, you get a better reward, and so on. But remember: the reward is important — just as important as the change in your behavior. If you fail to give yourself the reward, you will stop trying to improve.

Using Behavior Modification to Change Others

Using behavior modification to change the actions of others is simple. If the desired behavior shows up in the other person, you praise him. If the kind of behavior you dislike is shown, you walk away; you say nothing; you ignore it. The rule of reinforcement sounds so simple, really, that you may not believe that it works. Before you decide, though, try this simple plan with someone who bothers you. For example, you have a friend who constantly complains. While you like the friend, his habit of complaining is annoying to you. You decide to try behavior modification. Every time the friend complains, criticizes, finds fault, you make some excuse and leave. If this action seems too drastic, you merely look away and seem to be paying no attention. On the other hand, when the friend says something positive, or expresses an interest in you or in other people in a positive way, you listen; you make positive comments; you praise your friend for his helpful attitude.

When you are alone, write down how many negative comments the friend made before you started your plan. Then keep track of the negative comments made each time you use reinforcement to bring about more positive comments. You may be surprised to find that before too many sessions have passed, your friend will have become less negative, less critical.

In a recent national magazine, Duke Ellington stated that his doctor once told him that the bug disease kills more people than any other disease in the world. He states that it is very important, therefore, not to let anything bug you. If children bug you, behavior modification can be used with a token system. You simply find or make some small colored disks. You decide with the child what the payoff on the disks is going to be (10 disks to be exchanged for an extra half hour of television or a trip to the ice cream stand). Then you give the child a token when you catch him being good. This means you don't have a regular schedule. You just happen to notice the child at varying times. If he is studying, or picking up his clothes, or playing quietly alone or with others (or if you find that he has completed some assigned task), you hand him a token, give him a word of praise, and tell him why he is receiving the token.

You may need help, at first, in giving praise. (A great many people find it hard to give praise to others.) Practice using the following words and phrases:

Good	I'm pleased with that
That's right	Great
Exactly	I like that
Good job	That's interesting
Thank you	Good thinking

Another thing: It is better to praise the work or the action rather than praise the person. Avoid telling the child he is a good boy or a wonderful child. For some reason, praise of this kind gives the child a guilty feeling, perhaps because he knows he is *not* so wonderful as all that.

You are now armed with two weapons for making things happen. You are developing a positive attitude and you are using behavior modification to change yourself and others. Now you are ready to tackle the third weapon: learning how to make decisions. What a lot of time we could save if we could just make decisions quickly. We have a decision to make; we debate endlessly; we ask advice from friends and relatives, all of whom give us conflicting replies; we decide to wait until the next day to make up our minds — only to have the whole process repeated. A way out of this dilemma is available. The first step is to decide whether the decision is a major or a minor one. If the decision is which movie to see or which dress to wear, we flip a coin — and abide by the decision. If the decision is a major one, however, one that involves important stakes, we need another method.

DECISIONS INVOLVING PEOPLE

A logical way of solving problems with people is one that has been used for many years in science and in business. It is sometimes called the scientific method. We are going to change the method slightly, however, because we are going to use five steps to solve problems with people — in other words, people difficulties. The five steps are answers to the following questions: (1) What is the problem? (2) What are the facts? (3) What is my overall objective? (4) What are some possible solutions? and (5) Which is the best solution?

What Is the Problem?

The first step in solving a problem is to state it clearly and concisely. This may sound easy, but there is nothing more difficult. You may know something is wrong — but you don't know exactly what. Someone has said that a problem well stated is a problem half solved. How should you state the problem? One way is to ask a question. Care must be taken, however, not to give judgments in the statement of the problem. Be objective; do not favor anyone. Just state the problem in specific terms.

For example, assume that you have been working in an accounting department for two years. The supervisor, Mr. Phillips, suddenly retires because of ill health and you are promoted to his position over the head of John Tyler, a veteran of the company and the person who expected to be made supervisor. John is polite to you but noncooperative. He does his job and that's all. Worse still, the other workers in the division — consisting of 22 workers — are beginning to take sides. How would you state this problem? It is *not*: Why should John Tyler act like this? It is *not*: Should a junior accountant be promoted over the heads of those who have been in the firm longer than he? The problem is concerned with what you should do about the situation as it is. It could, of course, be stated in more than one way, but one possibility is the following: What steps can I take to improve the morale and production of this accounting division in light of the resentment felt over a newcomer's being made supervisor? You will notice that there is no question of right or wrong in this statement of the problem. Neither is there any attempt at a solution, which should be the last of the steps and not the first. This statement is also objective, another necessary feature.

What Are the Facts?

When you answer the second question, "What are the facts?" You must be careful to write down only facts, not opinions or moral judgments. You must keep out all prejudice, all "oughts" and "shoulds." For instance, it is not a fact if you say John Tyler is acting like a spoiled child. A statement of this kind implies a judgment of the facts rather than a statement of them. An objective statement of the same implication would be that John Tyler does not cooperate to the extent he did before the promotion. The facts, then, should be stated without emotional coloring.

After you have stated as many real facts as you can that apply to the situation, to the problem you wish to solve, it is helpful if you will arrange them so that the most important facts — the ones that make a difference in the solution — are at the head of your list.

What Is My Overall Objective?

The third step is the hardest one. Perhaps you have never really thought about your main goal in a particular situation. It really helps, though, if you can force yourself to write exactly where you want to go, exactly where you are headed. In the John Tyler problem, for example, your overall objective may be to keep your job. You don't want to be fired; you don't want to resign in favor of John Tyler in order to have peace restored to the department. If you are having problems with your wife or your husband (and you love him or her in spite of everything), your overall objective would be to stay married. If you are failing in school and you can't keep up the payments on your new car, your overall objective would probably be to act in a way that would be most beneficial to your future. Which would be of the greatest long-range benefit to you: To stay in school and fit yourself for your future work or to drop out of school, get a mediocre job, and keep up the payments on your car? You can see that if you think the question through logically, you can decide what your real objective is.

What Are Some Possible Solutions?

The fourth step is to write down as many solutions to your problem as you can think of. One way of clearing the way for a good solution is to write down the extreme solutions first. Extreme solutions are seldom the best ones. In our problem, such solutions would be: (1) fire John Tyler; (2) resign from your job as supervisor; (3) resign from the company. Now the way is clear to devote your attention to constructive solutions, those which would take into consideration the complex human relation factors involved, yet would be forward looking in terms of getting the work of the division done well.

What Is the Best Solution?

The last step is to choose the best solution. The best solution will meet the two parts of the following standard: (1) The most important facts in step two must have been taken care of. That is, the best solution must solve the situation as it stands as far as the important elements of the problem are concerned. (2) It must help and not hinder us in reaching our overall objective.

In the problem under discussion, the best solution might have a number of parts. There would be first, the solution in terms of John Tyler, the resentful employee. It might be well to ignore his negative attitude and begin to build a better feeling between the two of you. This could begin by asking him, without making too much of it, to take charge of some project. This could be followed by commendation for any good work that he does. The best solution for you, as a new, inexperienced supervisor, would be to give yourself time to grow into the job. One fact of life in any kind of work is that authority cannot be maintained on an equality basis. In other words, there must be some distance between the one in authority and the ones over whom such authority exists. You must not expect to be liked by all of the workers under you. Because you have been chosen by your superiors to do a job, however, you should do all you can to make that job a success. An impersonal attitude toward negative feelings of others, plus a sincere determination to merit your workers' respect, will go a long way toward bringing about the needed change in their attitudes. If you keep your attention on getting the work done, while you are fair and positive toward those who work under you, you should expect the morale of the division to improve in time.

You are now armed with your third weapon for becoming a person who makes things happen. With the five-step decision-making method, you are equipped to solve the problems that come up in every possible line of work — as well as the problems that come up in your personal life. One reason for the success of the five-step method is the mental attitude you must adopt if you are to follow the first three steps. You cannot answer the first three questions (What is the problem? What are the facts? and What is my overall objective?) until you become detached emotionally from the problem. When you can shelve your emotions temporarily and put your Adult self in charge, you may find that the correct decision appears to you before you get to step four. The secret of good decision making is to use mental judgment rather than the emotional pitfalls of "getting even" or "showing who is boss." Practice in making decisions by the five-step method is also one of the best-known ways of putting starch in your Adult self.

YOUR SUCCESS PYRAMID

In the first two chapters you have seen how the base of your success pyramid is built. The next level of the pyramid is built with five blocks. Three of these blocks are described here.

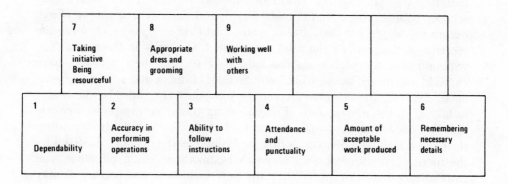

7 Taking initiative Being resourceful	8 Appropriate dress and grooming	9 Working well with others		

1 Dependability	2 Accuracy in performing operations	3 Ability to follow instructions	4 Attendance and punctuality	5 Amount of acceptable work produced	6 Remembering necessary details

Figure 3-1. Second Phase of Success Pyramid

Taking Initiative and Being Resourceful

A newcomer in the business world may find it troublesome to know just how far he should go in the matter of doing things on his own. Sometimes the rules of the organization make it necessary to follow a set pattern in everything that is done. In most cases, however, the follow-the-rules phase lasts only a short time. Before long you will be faced with an emergency. The boss who is to sign all orders is in the hospital or the boss who insists that he sign all letters is out of town. When something of this nature happens, the only thing you can do is weigh the matter carefully. What would be the results if you followed the rules? Would you lose an order? Would you cause a visiting executive to take the wrong plane? If the consequences of following the rules are worse, in your judgment, than acting on your own, you must have enough initiative to act on your own. The only requirement is that you think the situation through carefully, making your decision on the basis of facts and objectives and not on panic.

Resourcefulness is a help at any level of business. If you can make do with whatever is at hand, you are being resourceful. You are resourceful if you can look ahead to possible consequences of two actions and choose the one more likely to meet with success. In fact, the motto THINK will help you be more resourceful.

Appropriate Dress and Grooming

Dress and grooming are discussed in detail in Chapters 5 and 6. Remember, though, that the world of business is more conservative than schools, colleges, the entertainment world, and the world of sports. First, before you apply for the job you want, visit that company. Observe the secretaries, the head of the sales department, the teller in the bank. You will find that the higher up the ladder of success these workers have climbed, the more "businesslike" will be their clothing and general appearance. Second, after you have taken the job you want, don't be the leader in taking up the newest fad. For one thing, fads are expensive because they don't last long. The main reason for letting others be the first to adopt the newest fashion, however, is that the fashion leader will be criticized by the more conservative bosses in your organization. As a beginner, you can't afford that criticism. When the new fashion is accepted, you may safely join in. Until you are secure in your job, however, you shouldn't take chances.

Working Well with Others

Since all 15 chapters in this book are concerned with working well with others, only one factor is mentioned here — the quality of cheerfulness. No single trait will so endear you to your co-workers, your supervisors, and your bosses as the ability to look on the bright side, to deal with others with a light touch. Cheerfulness is a virtue, even though we seldom hear anyone preach about it, and it is one that makes working well with others remarkably simple. Don't take things too hard, keep a light touch, and your work with others will be smooth and successful.

FOLLOW-UP ACTIVITIES

1. Each Monday afternoon, make a list of the negative statements you make during a three-hour period. Try to keep the time of day the same each week. Also, after you have become more proficient, make a list of the negative statements you change to positive ones, and finally a list of the positive statements you make. Try to eliminate the negative habit in six weeks.

2. Deliberately choose the most difficult person you know, and begin a campaign to improve your relationship with him or her. Once a week, write the extent of progress you have made. Date each report.

3. Quick judgments are sometimes made without knowing all of the facts of the case. Make a list of negative statements made to you by others. Opposite the statements, write what you believe may have caused the person to be negative. Is there a reason other than dislike for you?

4. Describe a human relations problem that exists among those of your acquaintance. Go through the five steps given in this chapter, from stating the problem to choosing the best solution. Try to be completely objective. Submit your problem for evaluation.

5. Practice being cheerful until cheerfulness becomes a fixed part of your personality. Act and look cheerful, no matter how you feel. Stand up straight; smile at everybody; look like the world is yours. Try this exercise for one week and report the results.

6. Time yourself on making decisions. Begin first with little things: what to wear, what to order, what route to take when you go on an errand. Keep a record of how many seconds it takes you to make up your mind. Your eventual goal is to make instant decisions on little things and quick decisions on more important matters.

7. Choose a time-consuming job you must do. Estimate the time it usually takes you to complete the task. Now try to cut the time down one half. Continue to time yourself when similar jobs come up until you have reached the goal of completing time-consuming jobs in half the time now spent on them.

8. Does somebody bug you — your roommate, boyfriend, girlfriend, wife, husband, parent, brother, sister, co-worker? Be positive and don't nag them or complain about it. See if you can change their behavior. Use the positive reinforcement approach and compliment them for appropriate behavior. Ignore the behavior that annoys you. Use the following plan:

   a. Describe in detail the situation you wish to improve.
   b. Formulate in detail your plan to increase praise and decrease criticism. Using "X" as a symbol each time you praise and "O" each time you criticize, record your campaign on a calendar for a week.
   c. Report the results.

CASE PROBLEMS

1. Discrimination

George, a black boy, has been brought up in a white neighborhood. Sensitivity about his differences has prevented him from adjusting to the mockery, persecution, and abuse of his playground associates. When George reached high school he was shy, withdrawn, and refused to answer questions in class or speak to the other students.

1. Why was George treated as he was?
2. Have you ever been discriminated against? How did you feel? What did you do?
3. Do you ever ridicule people around you who are different from you? Why or why not?

2. Getting Even

Jean Miller had worked a year in a large company that employed 20 regular typists in a typing pool. During this time some of her friends had received promotions as stenographers to various supervisors and executives. Jean felt that she was as efficient as those who were advanced. Every time a girl was promoted from the typing pool, Jean showed her resentment by sulking for a week. She knew, of course, that she should not show these negative emotions; but she wanted Miss Share, the supervisor, to know how she felt. She had disliked Miss Share's crisp manner from the moment she had seen her. She was sure that Miss Share returned the feeling and was doing everything she could to prevent Jean from being promoted. You are a friend of Jean's. You have not wanted to interfere before this, but you now believe that something must be done. What would you say to Jean? Give the conversation, with the replies you believe Jean would probably make.

part
two

personality is what you see

chapter 4

your health is showing!

Someone has said that all a young person needs is good parents and good health. Let us assume that all of you have good parents. At least, parents usually do the best they can. But the health of a young adult depends, unfortunately, upon him — unfortunately, because good health is seldom appreciated until it is in danger of slipping away.

How *do* you feel? Do you have colds and flu every winter? Do you get headaches frequently? Do you feel week and dizzy at 10 in the morning and 4 in the afternoon? How about your endurance? Can you stand up under long hikes? Do you play tennis? Do you swim? It may be that *you* do these things, but far too many of our young adults have, seemingly, never been out of a car in their lives! They ride to school; they ride to meetings; their fathers drive them around their paper routes. It is to be expected that their muscle tone may leave something to be desired.

Whatever your present state of health, you should resolve at once to maintain it or, if need be, to improve it. Improving your health will be like opening a door to greater vitality and enjoyment of life, so do it gladly. It pays off in the long run.

GOOD HEALTH HABITS

First of all, good health is the result of good health habits. If you smoke too much, skip meals, take sleeping pills to go to sleep and pep pills to wake up, there can be only one ultimate conclusion: Your health will break down. Of course, the opposite is true. To build up your health, you must develop and maintain the kind of health habits that increase your general well-being.

Think Thin!

The recent growth of reducing salons, weight-watching organizations, and books on dieting points up a serious health problem in our present affluent society. Most of us eat too much of the wrong foods. Obesity, or overweight, is perhaps our number one health problem. It is a hard one to solve, moreover, because many overweight individuals do not realize they eat too much. They are hardly conscious that they *are* eating, as a matter of fact. Certain experiments have shown that, instead of responding to hunger as a normal person does, the overweight individual responds to other cues: hot-dog stands, smells of cooking, commercials on television, a bowl of potato chips, a candy store. He has actually made a habit of eating when he sees, smells, hears, or reads about food.

If you are a few pounds over your normal weight, you are lucky. It is fairly easy to lose three pounds: by drinking lots of water, eating high-protein foods only, by cutting each meal in half, by refraining from between-meal snacks. Any of these methods will do the trick. If you are 20 or more pounds above what you should be, however, you should see a doctor. Get the doctor's O. K. on a regimen of diet and exercise. And stick with it. You will be better looking, happier, and more popular. Most important of all, you will add years to your life. It is the fatties — not the good — who die young!

Stand Up Straight!

The first habit to develop is good posture. You can work at this habit anytime, anywhere. It is not necessary to invest in expensive equipment for practicing good posture. Neither is it essential to set aside 15 minutes a day for such practice. All you have to do is say to yourself, several times an *hour*, "Stand tall," "Sit tall," — and then do it!

Good posture does not mean throwing your shoulders back; it means stretching your ears upward. Imagine you are trying to reach the ceiling with your ears. This is the way to start. Just reach up with those ears and the rest of your body will automatically follow suit. You will find yourself slumping now and then, of course. But back you will go into good posture if you remember to stand tall, to reach upward.

The second part of good posture is *abdomen in*. This can be practiced while walking, standing, or sitting; and it takes a good bit of practice to develop a strong muscle tone that keeps a flat abdomen all the time. Just keep practicing. After you have learned to stand tall, it will be much easier to keep your abdomen pulled in.

Another part of good posture is good walking position. Feet should be pointed straight ahead — not pointed out and not pointed in. If you walk in this manner, stretching tall, your arms will fall naturally at your sides; and you will probably realize another dividend, better relaxation. Many of us are tense partly because we stand or sit in a tense "shoulders-up" position. Remember, the shoulders should not stretch up — just the ears.

Fun and Games

Another part of good health is recreation. Every young adult — and older ones, too — should have some plain fun now and then. The choice, however, must be left to each individual. Do you like organized sports? If you do, your problem will be solved quickly. Bowling, golf, tennis, basketball, football, baseball, hiking, swimming, skiing — the list goes on and on. If you like sports, see that you play your favorite game at least once a week, and more often if you can spare the time.

What if you don't like sports? The important point is that participation is the key to recreation. You do not get the same benefit from merely watching a basketball game on television. You must be active in the game or sport if you are to get the greatest benefit from it.

The healthiest people are involved in something they *enjoy*. So — get involved. Are you stagestruck but lacking in acting experience? Then volunteer to help paint scenery, sell tickets, sweep out the stage. Would you like to write on the school paper but have no background in this sort of work? Then offer to sell advertising, act as a reporter, or type other people's stories. Participation is the great advantage that comes from working in extracurricular activities. There is always room for someone who is willing to work and who will start at the bottom. If your recreation is relatively sedentary, however, you must get your exercise in some other way. Walking, especially if done at a good clip, is excellent exercise. Another method of exercise available to all is calisthenics. Even five minutes a day, done regularly and with vigor, will do wonders for you. If you exercise in no other way, this type is a must.

You Are What You Eat

If you ever pick up a home magazine, you know what you should eat; but do you? Are you one of the skip-breakfast, grab-a-donut-at-ten, skip-lunch, have-a-candy-bar-at-four kind of people? There is a very good chance that you are. If so, now is the time to reform. No one can function at anywhere near his best without good food.

At the risk of repeating what you have heard many times before, an adequate diet includes protein (meat, fish, eggs, milk), whole grain cereals, and fresh fruits and vegetables every day. You don't need as many starches as many of us eat. Most of us eat too many sweets. The quickest way to get into a vicious circle, by the way, is to overeat sweets. This creates insulin, which demands more sweets, which creates more insulin — and away we go. The carbohydrate habit can be broken, however, mainly by making sure that your diet is adequate in the whole grains that provide the B vitamins.

If you will try a balanced diet for one month, you will be convinced. Clear eyes, clear complexion, abundant energy — all of these will be natural by-products. Why not try it?

Do You Get Your Eight Hours?

Perhaps you don't get enough sleep. In these days of frantic overdoing, it is quite likely that the adage "Early to bed and early to rise" is seldom followed. But good sleep habits can be developed, just as can good eating habits. If you have formed the habit of staying up late — to watch the late-late show, let us say — you may find it impossible to get to sleep if you go to bed at 10:30.

The thing to do, then, is to taper off gradually. If midnight has been your retiring hour for quite some time, make it 11:45 for a week or two. Then, when you get into bed, imagine that your hands are made of heavy pieces of lead. Think "Heavy, heavy, heavy. My hands are heavy, heavy." Repeating these words to oneself seems to help many people drop off to sleep. After you have learned to go to sleep at 11:45, cut it back to 11:30, and so on until you can go to sleep in time to get seven to eight hours of sleep a night.

While you are working on this project, you may find that taking "cat-naps" of ten minutes now and then through the day helps you to get the rest that you need. Even if you do not go to sleep, relaxing completely in an easy chair for ten minutes or so will soon become a most refreshing pause.

YOUR MENTAL HEALTH IS SHOWING, TOO

The word "psychosomatic" has become a part of the general vocabulary of most readers in the last few years. It means the interrelationship of mind and body. In its customary usage, it designates those bodily ills which are psychologically caused. Ailments that were once regarded as imaginary, or dismissed as nerves, are now considered by many to be bodily symptoms caused, at least in part, by mental conflicts.

Some of these conflicts come from our wishes vs. our tendency to conform to the "shoulds" of life. We want to be a "good girl" or "good boy," and this wish comes in conflict with some of the things we want to do or be.

One of the "shoulds" that may cause trouble is the one relating to our feelings toward our parents, our brothers and sisters, our friends, our mates. We should love them; everyone knows this. But some of the time we just don't. This gives rise to a real conflict; and the greater the desire to be "good," the greater the conflict.

EMOTIONS AND MENTAL HEALTH

To be able to feel deeply the good things of life is a real blessing. Positive emotions make our lives worth living. But what about the negative emotions? What do they do to us? When you are seized with anger, hatred, jealousy, fear, worry, can you handle your usual tasks with efficiency and skill? In most cases, you cannot. The destructive emotions are just that. They destroy peace of mind, well-being, and often physical health. Is there anything we can do to control the destructive emotions?

How to Control Emotions

In order to control any emotion that may be a problem to you — jealousy, worry, fear — you must first identify it, describe it, state what it is. In Chapter 3 you learned to state the problem as the first step in the problem-solving process. You should do the same thing with a destructive emotion: define the emotion. What is worry, for example? You might say that it is a nameless dread for which you can find no real cause.

Step two in our campaign to control destructive emotions is to write down what the emotion does, what its manifestations are. In the case of worry, you might say it causes sleeplessness or, in some cases, sleeping too much; lack of appetite or overeating; headaches; mental blocks; lack of physical coordination, so that you drop objects that you attempt to grasp or drive a car in an erratic manner; poor memory for facts that you know. Excessive and prolonged worrying may cause you to become depressed.

Step three is to give an example, in your own life or in the life of someone you know, of what the emotion has brought about. This serves as a dramatic object lesson, showing vividly why it is wise to learn to control this emotion. In the case of worry, there is hardly a student anywhere who has not had the experience of worrying over an examination to such an extent that he is unable to think at all. If he could have relaxed, the knowledge he actually possessed would have been at his disposal, but he could not relax. This kind of experience shows the destructiveness of worry better than any number of abstract statements.

Step four consists of writing down all of the possible *actions* that might help to control the destructive emotion. In the case of worry, the list might include the following:

1. Set aside a certain time of day, or day of the week, for worrying. Then, when a worrisome thought enters your mind, just file it away to be worried about on Thursday!

2. Do something about the cause of the worry. If you worry about finances, start a budget; if about failing a course in school, study an extra half hour a day; if about being an old maid, have a party and invite several eligible men. This way of controlling emotions is an excellent one because it gets behind the emotion itself to one of its possible causes.

3. Invent some mental process that will automatically take place whenever the tendency to give in to the emotion arises. In the case of anger, you might think of something beautiful — a lovely lake you have seen, a strain from your favorite musical selection, a line from a favorite poem. In the case of worry, one of the best devices is a slogan. Some of these are old, old saws, but they are still around because they have proved their effectiveness through the centuries. Such slogans as "Take one step at a time," "Rome was not built in a day," "What will it matter in a thousand years?" and the slang slogans, "So what!" and "To heck with it!" might help in the case of worry.

4. Forget the past. This is an important rule in the case of most of the destructive emotions. We get angry at a best friend and rake up old resentments from the past, and we find we no longer have a best friend. This is a particularly vicious habit in the case of married or engaged couples. It is almost impossible to hear someone rebuke us for a past action without retaliating in kind. Too frequently words are spoken that cause wounds that can never be healed. Whatever the emotion you are working on, forget your past failures. The past is gone; nothing can be done about it; so let it go.

5. Do or say something positive in line with the emotion. If you hate someone or dislike someone intensely, the best way to get rid of this emotion is to do something positive, something considerate, for that person. It is almost impossible to dislike someone for whom you have just done a kindness. The magic does not work, however, if you expect *any* kind of reward for your good deed. Don't expect to be thanked. The kindness should be done merely because it is good for *you* to do it. There will be intangible benefits, but don't look for a reward. In fact, the best way to accomplish this is to do something considerate anonymously; this is guaranteed to take the sting of hatred away from that person.

What Emotions Say

Whatever our emotional difficulty — fear, anger, jealousy, hate, worry — there is a reason for its being there. Sometimes the reason is the exact opposite of what the emotion appears to be. It may be the other side of the coin. If you are jealous of someone's affection, for example, this does not say that you love the person deeply. It says instead that you are insecure about your own worth. You cannot believe that you are worthy of love; therefore, you cling possessively to the person who is closest to you. If you hate someone, this emotion says that you feel unappreciated. You are filled with resentment because your talents, beauty, ability, or knowledge have not received recognition, while someone else's have. Then this person has had the effrontery to belittle you in some way! It is the belittling that triggers the dislike, but the lack of appreciation is the real cause.

Envy is another resentful emotion, but here we are not sure of our abilities; we would like to be brilliant or talented or beautiful, but we feel we are not. The envious emotions say that we are insecure and that we resent this insecurity.

Worry, the kind that has no known cause, comes from hostility that we refuse to admit. That is why it is important that we take a good look at worry and at ourselves. We must admit that we are not paragons of virtue, that we may have negative feelings toward those we should love.

What We Should Say to Emotions

No matter what the emotion may be that is making your life miserable, you must not let it have its say. Learn to control it. Listen to what it tells you; then do something to change the situation that brings the emotion about. This means that you should become more lovable instead of being jealous and possessive. It means that you should become more appreciative of the accomplishments of others. Sooner or later someone will, in return, become appreciative of your accomplishments. Don't waste your life waiting for people to come to you. Take the first step. Then, while you are appreciating the achievements of others, work hard to become an expert at one thing. Many of us try to be musicians, writers, actors, debaters, athletes, and school political leaders all at once. No one can succeed in so many different fields. Choose the one activity that gives you the most satisfaction and that you do reasonably well. Then concentrate on that activity. Be willing to start at the bottom. Be willing to work on the team. It will not be long before your worth is recognized.

MASKS AND MENTAL HEALTH

Do you wear a mask a good deal of the time? If you don't, you are most unusual. Nearly all of us hide behind a mask. We dislike someone, yet we are exceptionally kind to that person to cover up the way we really feel. We like another person more than we want him to know; again, we hide behind a mask of indifference. Of course, if we did not mask our true feelings occasionally, the civilized world could not go around. Politeness and manners are really masks in a way; they are necessary with many of the people we know. If we always wear a mask, however, we are not in the best of mental health.

Each of you should have at least one person with whom you can take off your mask. Each of you should have one person with whom you can be real — just plain you. That one person should be someone you trust, someone who trusts you. With that person you should be able to say anything: your fears, your hopes, your dreams — even your nightmares. With that person you should be able to be honest, completely honest both in answering questions and in volunteering information about yourself.

This friend with whom you can be real, be honest, be yourself, may be older or younger than you, the same sex or the opposite; it makes no difference. One writer, a psychiatrist, has called this feeling of openness with another person "the transparent self." If you can be transparent with another person, there is an added dividend: *You* discover who you are. In fact, this doctor believes that you do not really understand yourself until you have made some other person understand you. When you can talk freely and openly with another person, you will not feel so alone. You will have a friend with whom you can share the way you are, a friend who will never repeat what you have said to anyone else; and you will be a friend who will never repeat anything he or she has said to you.

Masks are bad for any kind of close relationship. If you are married, you should *tell* your husband or wife the way you feel. Don't expect him or her to read your mind. If you are upset because your boyfriend forgot your birthday, say so. If you are embarrassed because you used the wrong fork at the formal dinner he invited you to, tell him so. Secrets between people who are in a close relationship can do great damage.

An open and honest relationship will be better able to withstand the upsets that always come along. If your children should break rules, they will be helped more by your honest expression of disapproval than they will be by a lecture on how hurt and disappointed you are. If you say what you honestly feel, you will help them. If you hide your real feelings because you are afraid you will lose their love, you will turn them into young tyrants.

Taking off your mask takes courage; it also takes practice. Start now. Find some friend with whom you can be your real self. Then you will gradually develop the strength to go without your mask more and more. A life free of masks is a happier, more effective life.

YOUR SUCCESS PYRAMID

The next three blocks on your success pyramid are made up of a physical fitness for the work, ability to work under pressure, and industry.

Physical fitness for the work

Chapter 4 is a good review for the tenth block of your success pyramid. You have probably had the experience of taking an examination after you sat up all night trying to cram the information into your head. You know how difficult it is to make decisions, to pay attention to detail, even to think when you are not in good physical condition. The same situation occurs when you are on the job. Your physical fitness contributes to your job success. Physical exercise, enough sleep, the right foods, the right weight — all of these make up the physical fitness block in your success pyramid.

Ability to work under pressure

The next block is made up of the factors that contribute to your mental health — the ability to work under pressure on abnormal conditions. This means you are able to meet deadlines, keep three or four jobs going at once, do extra work without panic. Of course, you will be better able to work under pressure if your physical health is good, but there is an added factor. Can you remain calm in a crisis? One way to build this added factor is to learn to control your emotions, as has been discussed in this chapter. Sometimes when pressure mounts it will help to stop for a moment, especially when you feel your muscles tightening up, and take a few deep breaths. Other times you may find it helpful to do a relaxing

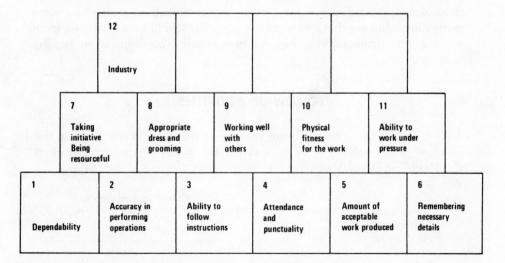

Figure 4-1. Third Phase of Success Pyramid

exercise — swinging your hands at your sides and dropping your head forward. Relaxation, of course, is the key; and many of us must train ourselves in relaxation. If you can find time outside your work to do some of the things you enjoy, you will be better able to work under pressure when the need arises.

Industry

The twelfth success block is industry. What is industry? Is it busy work? Most of you have had all you want of this kind of activity. Or is it rather a drive within yourself to get things done? How can you acquire this drive if you do not possess it now? Review the discussion of needs and motivation at the beginning of Chapter 1 and you will see that as needs change, the spark that motivates you will change also. Right now, you may be working for grades — a passing grade or a high one. Or you may be interested in the approval of someone whose opinion is important to you. Or you may aspire to the honor roll. All of these motivating influences are what we call "external" or "extrinsic" ones. This means that the spur to achieve comes from the outside. In time, this external motivation may be partly replaced by "internal" motivation, the kind that comes from within, with the satisfaction that comes from doing a good job.

When you are internally motivated in most things, you will find accomplishment much easier. Most of us, however, never quite reach the point where we care nothing for the praise or commendation of others. This stage of need fulfillment is sometimes called "self-realization." Consider it an ideal that, some day, you may attain. In the meantime, try to find some motivating influence that will work for you, that will help to keep you from wasting time, from making excuses to yourself — in short, from lacking in industry.

FOLLOW-UP ACTIVITIES

1. If the items listed below bring you joy or pleasure, check them in the appropriate column. Next, make a list of the items you checked "Much" or "Very Much."

	Extent of Enjoyment		
	Some	*Much*	*Very Much*
1. Listening to Music			
a. Popular			
b. Folk			
c. Rock			
d. Rhythm and Blues			
e. Show Tunes			

Extent of Enjoyment
Some   Much   Very Much

   f. Jazz _____
   g. Country Western _____
   h. Classical _____

2. Solving Problems
   a. Working on a Car _____
   b. Doing Crossword Puzzles _____
   c. Building Models _____

3. Eating
   a. Candy _____
   b. Ice Cream _____
   c. Cookies _____
   d. Fruit _____
   e. Nuts _____

4. Beverages
   a. Coffee _____
   b. Tea _____
   c. Soft Drinks _____
   d. Milk _____
   e. Beer _____
   f. Wine _____
   g. Cocktails _____

5. Animals
   a. Dogs _____
   b. Cats _____
   c. Horses _____
   d. Other Pets _____

6. Participating in Sports
   a. Football _____
   b. Basketball _____
   c. Baseball _____
   d. Tennis _____
   e. Golf _____
   f. Swimming _____
   g. Track _____
   h. Bowling _____
   i. Other Sports _____

7. Watching Sports _____

8. Reading
   a. Newspapers _____
   b. Magazines _____
   c. Adventure _____
   d. Mystery _____
   e. Love Stories _____

Extent of Enjoyment

Some   Much   Very Much

    f. Sports _____

    g. Humor _____

    h. History _____

    i. Travel _____

9. Outdoor Life _____

    a. Camping _____

    b. Hiking _____

    c. Bicycling _____

    d. Motorcycling _____

    e. Skiing _____

    f. Boating _____

    g. Fishing _____

    h. Hunting _____

    i. Walking _____

10. TV, Movies, Radio _____

11. Concerts, Theatre _____

12. Dancing

    a. Discotheque _____

    b. Ballet or Modern _____

    c. Ballroom _____

    d. Folk _____

    e. Square _____

13. Playing a Musical Instrument _____

14. Painting or Modeling _____

15. Sewing _____

16. Shopping _____

17. Sleeping _____

18. Talking with Someone You
    Like or Love _____

Most Enjoyable Activities:

    1.

    2.

    3.

    4.

    5.

2.   B E H A V I O R   C O N T R A C T

    I,_____, do hereby enter into the following agreement with myself. I will perform the behavior stated below for a period of _____ days. In return, I will receive the rewards listed below.

    BEHAVIOR _____
    REWARDS _____

    If I fail to live up to this contract, these penalties will take effect.

    PENALTIES _____

                                                            _____
                                                            Signature

3. Choose some way in which you want to change, to improve. You may decide to study more industriously or to do a better job in your work. You may decide to work on an emotional or a physical fitness problem. You may decide to diet. Whatever improvement you choose, fill in the contract shown in Follow-Up Activity 2. Write your name on the first line of the contract. Fill in the number of days in which the contract is to be in effect. On the line beginning BEHAVIOR write the one change you are going to work on. On the line beginning RE-WARDS list one or more of the activities you checked in Follow-Up Activity 1 as being the most enjoyable to you. On the line beginning PENALTIES list one or more of the enjoyable activities you will give up if you do not live up to your contract.

4. *Token Rewards.* Another way of giving yourself rewards is by the token system. With this system you give yourself a check mark for each hour or day that you live up to your contract. Then you give yourself the reward when you have earned a certain number of check marks. No penalty is needed when you use the token reward system; you will need a calendar or a progress chart on which to record the check marks you earn. With the token reward system you will fill in the contract in the same way, except that you list the number of check marks you must accumulate in order to earn the reward.

5. Take a destructive emotion, other than worry, that you have been or are troubled with. Describe it, show what it does to people, give an example, and then list as many ways of controlling it as you can.

6. Make a list of the groups in your community that offer opportunities for regular exercise. Find out the benefits of each group you are eligible to join, the membership dues, the obligations, and other information.

7. Draw up a schedule showing the amount and the kinds of exercise you have had in the last two weeks. What plans have you for following a regular schedule of time for exercise?

8. Make a selection of lunches appropriate and accessible for a salesperson in a downtown store. Tell what foods are to be avoided (a) if a person is overweight due to overeating, (b) if a person is underweight and undernourished, and (c) if a person is of normal weight.
9. If you are worried about a test or an interview, how do you cope with your anxiety? Is some fear natural and normal?

CASE PROBLEMS

1. Self-Confidence?

Maria Lopez was employed by Andrew Kline's clothing store immediately upon graduation from business college. She is proud to have been chosen from the many graduates in fashion merchandising to work in such an exclusive clothing store. After five months at work Maria is having difficulty getting along with her fellow workers and her superiors. She cannot understand why they are not impressed with her accomplishments. On several occasions she has reminded the other sales staff that she graduated with honors and was second in her class. One day Maria said to her supervisor, "Isn't it about time I left the sales floor and started doing something I have been trained for in business school? Being a salesclerk is just not giving me a chance to use my talents and abilities."

1. Why do you think Maria acts the way she does?
2. How would you answer Maria's question if you were her supervisor?

2. Nerves — Your Friend or Your Enemy?

Jane Allison has been working for Corliss Associates, a public relations firm, for three years and has done good work. In her ratings every six months there is only one negative criticism that can be made. Jane puts too much nervous energy into ordinary jobs; and, when one of high pressure comes along, she gets too nervous, works too fast, does work over, and generally does work below her usual standard.

The personnel manager is looking for a private secretary to the head of the firm, Mr. Harvey Corliss. Mr. Corliss wants a girl with energy and initiative, one who can take care of clients when he is away from the office. This is an important factor, as Mr. Corliss travels a good deal. In looking over the ratings of the girls in the office who might be promoted to the job as his private secretary, Mr. Corliss is impressed with Jane's credentials. She scored the highest of any applicant on the intelligence test that is given to everyone who is considered for employment; her skills are excellent; she is a graduate of a good junior college where her grades were all A's and B's. Mr. Corliss interviews Jane and is even more favorably impressed. He tells the personnel manager that he would like to have Jane as his private secretary. He adds that the vacancy will not materialize for two months and suggests that something might be done to help Jane overcome her nervousness. If you were the personnel manager, what would you do? Follow the problem-solving method given in Chapter 3 in arriving at your decision.

3. "Moonlighting"

Ray Benton works as a junior accountant in the accounting department of a large firm. Ray is ambitious and particularly anxious to make more money than his salary as a beginner pays him. To augment his salary, he keeps books for a number of small firms, doing the work at night and on weekends. He also makes out income tax returns for both these companies and the individuals working in them. Because he wants to keep up with his field, he reads the accounting periodicals at night before going to sleep.

All this activity naturally interferes with his rest; also, he has not taken a vacation in three years, preferring to catch up on his outside work during this period. There is an opening for a senior accountant, and Ray is being considered for the position. Mr. Henry, the controller, has noted Ray's tenseness, his look of fatigue, and his apparent lack of interest in his work. He asks one of Ray's friends if he knows of anything that could be wrong. The friend tells Mr. Henry that Ray is overworking. Unable to understand how this could be so, as Ray's work load in the company is only average, Mr. Henry calls Ray in and asks him what work he is doing. Ray tells him that he wants to make more money and what he is doing to earn it. What would you do if you were Mr. Henry? Follow the five-step problem-solving plan to arrive at your decision.

4. A Time for Decision

Sara Rice, an attractive black girl, has been dating a college friend, William Andrews, whom she would like to marry. She has refused to date other fellows because of the way she feels toward William. Her feeling is obviously not returned, however, as William goes out with a number of different girls and continues to treat Sara merely as a friend. This has been going on for a year, and Sara's work is beginning to suffer. There are also symptoms in Sara's looks and manner that indicate she is suffering from anxiety.

1. What does the term "mental health" imply?
2. Is emotional strain as harmful as physical strain?
3. Do you think Sara might work out a solution to reduce the conflict she feels?
4. Even if problems cannot be solved rapidly, can a plan of action be followed to prevent the ill effects of worry?
5. Have you discovered a way to reduce the anxiety you have felt at some time?

chapter 5

what about this dress jazz?

It has been said repeatedly that you can't legislate morality. It seems that the 1970's have taught us that you can't legislate fashion, either. The day is apparently over when Paris or Savile Row can turn the American buyer into an obedient sheep. Men, women, and children are developing minds of their own in the matter of what they should wear. Of course, the fashion designers and the school administrators are still trying. The designer continues to bring out new models, only to meet continued resistance. School administrators continue to try to enforce dress codes, only to meet the same kind of resistance in young people (and, frequently, their parents). Since the author does not have a crystal ball handy, no attempt will be made to predict what the future will bring. The day may come when we can wear anything. In the meantime, however, let's imagine some happy medium between complete freedom to wear whatever you wish in the business world and the strict "thou shalt nots" of ten years ago.

The best advice to the beginning worker may be this: Before you go for an interview to a particular firm, "case the joint" first. Make an excuse to visit one of the offices. Notice what the executives are wearing. Observe the dress of the secretary to the boss. You may be in for a big surprise. If you have visualized the business office as one vast gray flannel suit, you will see much more color and dash in men's clothing than you expected. On the other hand, the top secretaries may surprise you with the expensive look, the smoothness of line, the restrained good taste of their choices of clothing for the office. Some women may wear pants suits; others may wear hats and the latest extremes in fashion. It all depends on where you are located, what kind of business you wish to enter, and when you apply for your job. Some parts of the country are still quite conservative in business dress. Some businesses are casual; others are strictly conservative.

Winter clothing may be more conservative than that worn during the summer months. In any case, it is better to err on the side of being too conservative at first. Remember that bosses are of the older generation (with which you may have been experiencing a generation gap). Your boss may have the same old-fashioned ideas that your parents have. So don't be the *first* to try the latest fad. Wait until the shock has worn off. When the top executives or secretaries have adopted a fashion, it is safe for you to follow suit. This "wait and see" attitude sounds spineless, perhaps, but there are two reasons why waiting is best for the beginning worker.

First, clothes cost money and fads don't last long. A beginning worker usually does not have that kind of money to throw around. Second, the beginner who calls attention to himself or herself by his latest fad clothes may incur the jealousy of other workers and even of supervisors. A beginning worker doesn't have that kind of security to throw around, either. Examine your present wardrobe and plan new items to fit with those you already possess. Of course, business clothing is more subdued than the clothing you have been wearing in school or college, yet attractive, colorful selections are welcome in the business office.

DESIGN FACTORS IN CLOTHING SELECTION

When you buy clothing for the working world, train yourself to be aware of design. The design factors will help you create an image that is interesting and appealing. The design factors most important to you are proportion, balance, center of interest, harmony, color, silhouette, and texture.

Proportion

Proportion is particularly important in design. The relation in size of sleeves, collar, pockets, bows, and buttons to the total article of clothing must be pleasing. Your own size must be taken into consideration as well. For example, if you are large (and most young people today are larger than their parents), you should avoid small collars and small hats. If you are small, you will look all wrong in a large wide-brimmed hat and huge patch pockets.

Balance

Balance refers to making the various parts of the article of clothing balance with one another. A large shawl collar, for example, should

be balanced by a plain skirt. The visual attractions of the outfit should
be equal. Dark and bright colors carry the most visual weight; they are
best kept at the bottom half of the figure.

Primary Center of Interest

The most successful dress or suit will have a primary center of interest.
You will do well to have an interesting color, shape, space, texture, bow,
tie, collar, yoke, or jewelry so placed as to call attention to a part of your
figure that is most pleasing. For business wear, there should be only one
primary point of interest in any one outfit.

Harmony

Any outfit that is pleasing also shows harmony. The colors, lines,
shapes, and textures go together. The result is neither monotonous nor
"busy."

Color

The increasing use of color in men's clothing has caused men as well
as women to become more color-conscious. When choosing the colors
for your clothing, consider your age, your coloring (skin color rather than
eye or hair color is most important), your figure type, your personality,
and where you are going to wear the outfit. In the past few years, "men's
liberation" has been most noticeable in their color sense. Colored shirts,
brilliant ties, suits made of colorful double knits — all of these and more
are making the male of the species as style conscious as the female.

Silhouette

Careful selection of silhouette, or shape, of the outfit you purchase
is important. Two people with completely different figures will make
the same style look like two different items. In women's clothing, check
carefully the skirt fullness, the shape of the sleeves, the length of the skirt,
the placement of the waistline, the design at the shoulder. In men's clothing, check the width of trouser legs, shoulder width, size of lapels, and
particularly the length of the suit coat. You can be in fashion and still
choose the silhouette most flattering to your figure. The best choice will
draw attention away from your defects and emphasize your good points
to create the illusion of a perfect figure.

Texture

When you are choosing texture, you must first consider where you will use the outfit. If you purchase a slack suit strictly for casual wear, you might consider durable and sturdy fabrics, such as denim, sailcloth, or tweed. Such fabrics as polyester or jersey can be dressed up or down to serve several functions. You are safe in choosing contrasting textures in an outfit only when both have the same feeling and function. The pattern of the texture you use is also important. Prints, especially, should be chosen with care. Small prints look best on a person who is small. Bold patterns are quite dramatic — but you must be the dramatic type to wear them successfully.

RECOGNIZING SUITABILITY AND PROPER FIT

In addition to design factors, you must consider whether the outfit you wish to buy is suitable to your needs and whether it will fit your figure type. Both men and women should ask themselves these questions before they buy:

1. Is the article suitable to my needs?
2. Will it be durable enough for the use it will receive?
3. Does the article have enough "look" appeal, and is it sufficiently in fashion?
4. Do I need an item that has more than one use and that can serve for two completely different occasions?
5. Am I interested in comfort as well as in style?
6. Are price and the value I get for my money of prime importance?
7. Is it important that I buy an item that requires little care (no iron, drip dry, machine washable)?

Recognizing Proper Fit in Women's Clothing[1]

Certain general points should be kept in mind when testing for correct fit in women's clothing. They are the following:

1. The garment should fit smoothly all over, with no wrinkles, bulges, or obvious points of strain.
2. Side seams should hang straight.
3. Bustline darts should be aligned with the crown of the bustline.
4. In sleeveless garments, the armhole should not fall more than one inch below the armpit.
5. Back darts should stop short of the hip's fullest point.
6. Shirts should not fit too snugly over the hips and should not bag in the back.
7. Shoulder seams should not extend over onto the arm.

---

[1]Eleanor Wanty Mullikin, *Selling Fashion Apparel* (Cincinnati: South-Western Publishing Company, 1971), pp. 56-60.

8. Collars and necklines should lie or drape smoothly.
9. Sleeves should hang straight, and long sleeves should not extend over the wrist.
10. Garments with fitted waistlines should strike the individual just at her natural waistline.

The normal figure type is of medium height and is well proportioned. In addition, there are four other basic types: short and heavy, short and thin, tall and heavy, and tall and thin.

Short and heavy figures. The short and heavy girl or woman should look for the following flattering designs in making purchases, rather than ruffles, boxy jackets, very full or very straight skirts, wide belts, and contrasting skirts and blouses:

1. Slightly curved, vertical, or diagonal lines.
2. Simple designs.
3. Narrow belts of same material as rest of garment.
4. Shirt with front panel and slight flare.
5. Full-length coats.
6. Dull-surfaced, flat fabrics.
7. Grayed colors.
8. Medium to medium-dark color values.
9. Flat furs.
10. Jacket dresses rather than suits.
11. Set-in sleeves.
12. Medium-size accessories.

Short and thin figures. The girl or woman who is short and thin will find the following designs more flattering than large prints, straight, narrow skirts, and sleeveless dresses:

1. Soft, lightweight fabrics.
2. One-color costumes.
3. Small prints.
4. Flat furs.
5. Full-length coats.
6. Princess lines.
7. Short suit jackets.
8. Height in hats.
9. Small jewelry and accessories.
10. Blouse bodice styles.
11. Eased or full skirts.

Tall and heavy figures. The tall and heavy figure should avoid sleeveless dresses, wide or contrasting belts, bulky fabrics, excessive fullness at bustline or hipline, and short skirts. Instead, the following designs will be more flattering:

1. Vertical and diagonal lines predominating but with some horizontals to break up large areas.
2. Simple styles.

3. Fairly large accessories.
4. Medium-scale design detail.
5. Dull-surfaced fabrics.
6. Grayed intensities in colors.
7. Medium-dark color values.
8. Medium-size prints with little color contrast.
9. Flat furs.
10. Shirts with panels and a slight flare.

Tall and thin figures. Tall and thin figures will not look well in clinging fabrics, V-necklines, vertical lines, fussy clothes with small design details, low, bare necklines, and sleeveless dresses. Instead, the following designs will be more flattering:

1. Contrasting jackets or blouses.
2. Full sleeves.
3. Wide belts.
4. Contrasting belts.
5. Longer suit jackets.
6. Boxy rather than fitted suit jackets.
7. Large collars and patch pockets.
8. Double-breasted suits.
9. Three-quarter or seven-eighths length coats.
10. Rough, heavy fabrics.
11. Bold prints.
12. Tunic and peplum styles.
13. Full skirts.
14. Unfitted waistlines.
15. Blouson styles.
16. Horizontal design emphasis.

Recognizing Proper Fit in Men's Clothing[2]

A man's suit should fit comfortably and should provide room for movement; however, it should not appear so loose as to look sloppy. Check the following points to make sure that the fit is correct for you.

1. The collar should hug the neck closely and should show about a half inch of shirt collar.
2. Shoulder line should be straight from the collar line to the tip of the shoulder.
3. There should be fullness over the shoulder to allow freedom of movement.
4. Lapels should lie flat and not bulge outward.
5. Armholes should be comfortably full.
6. Sleeves should allow at least a half inch of shirt cuff to show.
7. The suit coat should cover the seat of the trousers.
8. Trouser legs should break slightly over the instep and should hang straight in the back.

---

[2]Mullikin, *op. cit.*, pp. 73-86.

The proper selection of clothing should make a short man appear taller than he actually is. An important principle is not to cut your height with contrasting colors in jacket and slacks. Vertical lines should be predominant in the design of each garment selected.

The tall-stout build requires a long suit coat or sport jacket; the short-stout build needs a length that elongates but does not cut the leg length. Single-breasted jackets are a must for the short-stout figure; the tall-stout figure may consider either a single-breasted jacket or a double-breasted jacket with a narrow, low-buttoned lapel. Sleeves should be tapered to slenderize, and patch pockets that add bulk should be avoided. Cuffless trousers give a longer look to the leg. Neither the jacket nor the trousers should be extremely tight-fitting; for if they are, excess bulges are going to be accentuated.

Men who are tall and thin should choose clothing with horizontal design lines to give the impression of more weight. Double-breasted suits and wide lapels are generally considered to be quite desirable for this type of figure.

Color and Pattern in Men's Clothing

With colors becoming more popular in men's clothing, particularly bright colors for shirts, the following combinations can be used as guides to the attractive use of colors available in men's clothing.

COLOR COMBINATIONS FOR MEN'S APPAREL

Color of Suit	Color of Shirt and/or Tie	
Blue	Red	Orange
	Gold	Green (certain shades)
	Gray	Yellow
Brown	Red	Green
	Copper	Orange
	Gold	Ivory
	Blue	Yellow
Gray	Red	Yellow
	Blue	Orange
	Green	
Green (bluish or grayish)	Tan	Ivory
	Gray	Copper
	Red	Yellow
	Brown	

In addition, the following table gives a summary of men's clothing that is suitable for business wear and casual wear. In many localities, of course, casual wear is acceptable for business.

SUMMARY OF APPROPRIATE BUSINESS AND CASUAL WEAR

ITEM	BUSINESS WEAR	CASUAL WEAR
Jacket	Single- or double-breasted	Single- or double-breasted
Jacket fabric	Cheviot, flannel, tweeds, worsteds	Cashmere, cheviot, flannel, gabardine, homespun, shetland, tweeds
Trousers	To match jacket	Match jacket, or separate slacks. Wool, cotton, blends
Shirt	Batiste, broadcloth, chambray, oxford, madras	Broadcloth, flannel, gabardine, knits, mesh, oxford cloth
Tie	Four-in-hand, bow. Stripes, figures, plaids	Smooth or rough-textured fabric
Hat	Homburg, snap-brim	Snap-brim, rough felt, porkpie, or Tyrolean
Gloves	Capeskin, chamois, mocha, pigskin	Deerskin, goatskin, knitted, pigskin
Shoes	Black or brown calf. Wingtip, bal, plain	Blucher, chukkas, full brogue, moccasin, monk-front, slip-ons
Outerwear	Cashmere, cheviot, covert, fleece, tweed	Camel hair, corduroy, covert, tweed

Certain rules for combining patterns may help you select the proper accessories to go with your suit or jacket. They are:

1. Use a pattern in no more than two major apparel items in any one outfit. With a patterned sport jacket and patterned shirt, for example, use solid-color slacks.
2. Patterns should not be placed on top of one another. With boldly striped shirts, for example, solid ties usually look best.
3. Do not combine patterns that are similar to one another. A tie with a narrow stripe should not be worn with a pinstripe suit.
4. Contrast within one basic type of pattern — such as combining bold stripes in one item with small stripes in another — is often acceptable.
5. Don't have an outfit consisting entirely of one pattern, such as all stripes or all plaids.

SENSIBLE BUYING HABITS

Whether the economy is up or down, the wise beginner in business will form the habit of thrift. Thrift does not mean miserliness; nor does it mean denying yourself the things you need and want. Thrift simply means that you learn to buy sensibly.

In Buying Clothes

Because one of the easiest ways to be a spendthrift is in buying clothes, a discussion of thrift is appropriate in this chapter.

One way to practice thrift is to take advantage of sales for buying staple items. Such articles as hose, underclothing, raincoats, shirts, blouses, and shoes do not show radical changes in style. Buying these articles at a reduced price is, therefore, a thrifty habit. It is not thrifty to buy extremes of color or style after the season of their popularity is past.

In Other Activities

Did you ever stop to think of the number of other ways in which you can be thrifty? One way is to be saving in the use of your employer's time and supplies. Typing accurately and making out sales slips carefully saves your employer money. Developing a speedy routine in handling repetitive jobs is another way of being thrifty.

There are a number of practices that should be avoided if you wish to develop the habit of thrift. These include such things as keeping people waiting on the telephone, making personal telephone calls during office hours, and spending too much time in the lounge. You should never take any supplies belonging to the office for personal use.

The final suggestion for developing the habit of thrift is a savings account. The first paycheck should start you on your saving habit. The first step is crucial: Take out a small sum for savings *first*, then pay your bills, make your purchases, and so on. If you wait until after you have taken care of these obligations, you will find you have nothing left for savings. If you have never saved any money, you may prefer to start by saving *for* something — a long vacation trip, for example. This kind of saving is less painful for the beginner. After you have established the habit of saving, you should begin to save for future security. When you have accumulated a reasonable amount, you may wish to invest some of your savings in safe bonds or interest-bearing securities. This kind of financial reassurance gives you greater poise and peace of mind; you will have purchased not only financial security but emotional security as well.

YOUR SUCCESS PYRAMID

The remaining three blocks on the third phase of your success pyramid are made up of personality — cheerfulness and/or charm; neatness and orderliness in maintenance or arrangement of physical surroundings, such as desks, files, and floor; and not losing excessive time in personal telephone calls, talking with fellow workers, going to the rest room, and the like.

Personality — Cheerfulness and/or Charm

The thirteenth block in your success pyramid is made up of your personality, and personality is made up — partly, at least — of your cheerfulness and charm. Actually, this block is the result of being able to accept yourself and to accept others. When you can take off your mask, when you can be your own self, you will have no need for the defenses you have built up to hide your real self from the world. When you accept yourself, you also discover that most of your troubles happen because of what *you* do. When you can change, when you can become more cheerful, you will be able to think of other people more, and less of your own shortcomings. You may find that a light touch helps you get over the negative habit — the opposite of cheerfulness and, more or less, the opposite of charm. You take things hard when you are concerned too much with yourself. Cultivate the light touch; learn to be cheerful. It only takes practice.

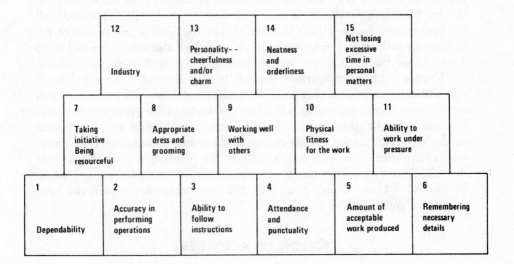

Figure 5-1. Third Phase of Success Pyramid — Completed

Neatness and Orderliness

The fourteenth block is made up of all kinds of neatness and orderliness. In this chapter the importance of careful buying of clothing is discussed. You must also form the habit of being neat and orderly with your clothing. But there is a need for neatness in your work station, as well. Your work must be neat; your desk or counter must be orderly. One way of keeping your work in order is to keep everything you work with in a certain place, where you will be able to find it when you need it. The office worker who constantly borrows tools from other workers soon finds he or she is losing friends and alienating people. Neatness may not come easily to you, but it is a habit worth cultivating.

Not Losing Excessive Time in Personal Matters

Most employers will rate the fifteenth block in your success pyramid as important. If you are interested in reaching the top of your success pyramid, you will take care of personal matters on your own time. When you are at work, you will give your time and your attention to your job. One particular personal matter that should be considered is personal telephone calls. Your company may have strict rules regarding personal telephone calls during working hours but, even if it does not, you should make it a practice to refrain from talking to family and friends during your working day except in cases of emergency. If a friend calls you at work, tell the friend you will call back on your first break or during your lunch hour. If you are a working mother, you may find it necessary to take a personal call if it has to do with your child's welfare. When the need arises, however, try to keep the call short. It is better to leave your desk and return the call from a pay phone than it is to tie up the business lines with personal matters.

Visiting with other workers should be discouraged, too. Of course, you will be friendly and pleasant. You will greet other workers when you come to work in the morning and when you leave in the evening. But talking over last night's date or your favorite recipe should wait until lunch time or during your break. Some companies permit smoking at your desk; others have a rule that you may smoke in the rest rooms only. Whatever the rule, do not spend too much time away from your desk for any reason. You would not take money from the cash register; neither should you take time from your working day.

FOLLOW-UP ACTIVITIES

1. If you have not yet begun your career in the business world, what changes in your present wardrobe will you make when you go to work?

2. What will you wear when you are interviewed by a prospective employer?

3. What preparations for your appearance will you make the evening before an employment interview?

4. What source of information regarding clothing, color, line, design, and fashion are available for study? Books? Magazines? Shops? Others?

5. What accessories should be worn with a navy knit suit?

6. What variations of accessories would you like to have to wear with the navy suit?

7. What lines of costume are most becoming to a short, stout woman? What lines are most becoming to you? Have you noticed also the effect of the lines of a coiffure on the shape of your face?

8. What lines of costume are probably most becoming to a tall, slender man? Would the lines of a suit be influenced by the style of the day?

9. Jim Austin has light red hair and a fair complexion. He has just purchased a dark brown suit. What color should his ties and shirts be to harmonize with the new suit?

10. Make a checklist of duties that should be performed regularly in order to maintain a neat, clean wardrobe.

11. Frank Ross wears his shirts two days before sending them to the laundry. Dave Brown questioned this practice, but Frank said that he did not have enough shirts to wear a clean one each day. Is there a better solution than the one that Frank uses?

12. Hazel Abbott likes drop earrings and bracelets that jangle. Her employer mentioned that he finds them distracting. Hazel later tells you that she considers her clothing her own affair and does not welcome such criticism from her employer. What would you tell Hazel? Why should Hazel be concerned about her employer's statement?

CASE PROBLEMS

1. Drifting

There was not enough work in the real estate office to keep Elsie Marsh, a general clerk, busy all the time. During the dull hours she often sat and looked out the window, building air castles for the future. Her employer found her so occupied one day and severely reprimanded her for wasting time. She told him that she had all her work completed. He insisted, however, that Elsie find some constructive work. "Make a record of the supplies on hand," he said, "or a list of the telephone numbers we use frequently, or arrange our listings by streets. Use your time to some advantage."

1. Why should Elsie have had no idle moments in the office?
2. Suggest other activities for her.

2. Take Up the Slack

Lisa Brady and Marian Stuart are employed as billing clerks by a merchandising firm. When Lisa is asked for certain invoices, she has to rummage through her files before she can find them. She does, however, make out all invoices neatly and accurately. Marian, who occupies the next desk and does the same kind of work, uses a system. She makes notations about invoices that cannot be completed at once and is constantly trying to find shortcuts and timesaving devices.

Lisa is always joking with Marian about the latter's "efficiency." Lisa tells Marian that she really does not produce any more work than she, Lisa, does. However, Marian is promoted to the bookkeeping department to a position that has more responsibility. Lisa believes that favoritism is being shown.

1. What businesslike attitudes does Marian show that she possesses?
2. In what ways does Lisa show that she is not businesslike?

3. Wisdom in Spending

Margaret Grover is fortunate in obtaining summer employment in a large office. There is a possibility that if she makes good, she may obtain permanent work later in the same office. The other girls in the office dress better than Margaret does, and they spend more money for recreation and entertainment. Margaret has been trying to save for further study, but wonders if she should not spend more on her clothes to impress her employer favorably so that she may be considered for a permanent position.

1. If Margaret decides to spend all or most of her money now, how will she benefit?
2. If she decides to save her money, how will she benefit?
3. What would you do in this case? Why?

chapter 6

that clean and shining look: good grooming

Whether you are in high school, in college, or have reached that "over thirty" barrier, you cannot be a success in business if you persist in defying the rules of good grooming. Free expression is fine; the author is all for it. But, for the business girl or man, free expression in dress and grooming must be done on your own time. Business, in order to exist and continue to hire beginning workers, must project an image of dependability, of solidity, of trust. Those managers and owners who hire beginning workers believe that such an image is destroyed if the employees of the business firm present a picture of unkempt carelessness.

Someone has defined a youthful leftist as a young person whose rightist father sends him a monthly check. When you take a job in business, however, you must change sides. You now belong to the group that pays the taxes, that keeps things going, that gets things done. To live up to your new image, to play the part you are assigned, you must pass the test of the clean and shining look.

BODY CLEANLINESS

Nothing makes one less popular either in business or in society than unpleasant odors. It is a fact of life, however, that we may be all too aware of the problem in others yet unaware that we, too, may be at fault. A daily shower or bath plus the use of a deodorant is usually adequate for safety; however, if special body odors are a problem, you should consult a doctor and follow his advice. Also, in this matter, you must be your own detective; truly, your best friend won't tell you. Sometimes more than one bath daily is required. Sometimes the problem is not body cleanliness but the habit of wearing a shirt or a blouse more than one day. Men in business can wear a shirt only one day; it must be laundered before it is worn again. The best policy for blouses is the same rule: wash after each wearing. Cottons and other washable dresses should also be washed after each wearing. Woolens and knits should be sent to the cleaners frequently, perhaps after three wearings; these wearings should be separated by several days of airing, however. Perfumes and colognes are acceptable if the fragrance is not too heavy, but Tabu in the office is taboo!

Before putting away clothing that has been worn, expose it to fresh air. An outdoor clothesline is ideal for periodic airing. If such a luxury is unavailable, however, let clothing worn during the day air elsewhere.

Everyone is aware that soiled hands must be washed immediately. Fingernails must always be clean. The use of nail polish is approved, but light colors are much more fashionable and in better taste. The use of colorless polish is a wise decision. The absence of color eliminates the problem of chipped polish, yet the nails present a cared-for look. If you work with duplicating machines, or if your hands become smudged from carbon paper, special creams and liquids will remove all but the most stubborn stains.

Hair must always be clean, and this means frequent shampoos. The frequency of the shampoo may vary but should never be less frequent than every ten days. Most women prefer the weekly shampoo and set. Dandruff should be controlled by daily brushing and by the use of special shampoos. If you have special problems with your hair, such as excessive oiliness, dryness, or dandruff, it may be wise to consult a dermatologist.

The Skin

Nothing contributes so much to an attractive appearance as healthy, glowing skin. Such a state of affairs involves more than health. The avoidance of certain rich foods is necessary in many cases. Plenty of fresh fruits, exercise, vitamins — all of these will affect your skin — plus sufficient rest. In addition to these factors there is cleanliness. Your skin must be clean! This means the removal of all makeup before retiring. It means soap-and-water cleansing in some cases and cleansing cream plus astringents in others. Whatever your skin type, you should never permit an oily, smudged look. If your skin is oily, eliminate most fats from your diet and wash your face with special soaps several times a day and follow each washing with the use of an astringent.

If ordinary cleanliness, diet, and rest do not care adequately for your skin, consult a dermatologist. The time and money invested in such professional help will be worth it to you in improved appearance and freedom from worry. If you have acne, the help of a dermatologist is absolutely essential. Today even scars resulting from bad cases of acne can be helped.

If you possess a clear and attractive skin, count your blessings. Then start a regimen that will keep your skin attractive. The same rules should be followed: adequate rest, sensible diet, perfect cleanliness, and exercise. One word of caution must be given: never squeeze a blemish that appears on your face. Wash your face carefully and cover the offending blemish with a medicated ointment. It will take care of itself in a short time, but any tampering with it may result in disaster.

The Hair

The importance of keeping your hair clean and shining has been discussed. No matter how beautiful the curl, how luxuriant the growth, or how modish the style, you cannot have attractive hair unless it is clean. One successful buyer in charge of ladies' ready-to-wear in a large shop said to the women employed there, "If your hair is clean, your face looks cleaner." The hair does create an illusion either of cleanliness or untidiness.

An old and tested way to care for the hair is to brush it one hundred strokes a day. At first, such brushing may make the hair oilier, and more frequent shampoos will be required. After a few weeks, however, you will notice a new shine to your hair, a cleaner look than you had before. Such brushing also improves the health of the scalp. Every day or so it is helpful to wash your brush and comb; a bit of ammonia in the water will make the task quick and easy. A clean brush and comb will help to keep your hair cleansed as it is brushed.

Hair styles for men have changed radically in the past few years, and they may change even more radically in the future. It is a good plan, nonetheless, to avoid extremes. At present, hair styles for men in business are shorter than those in vogue in school or college. A young man who is planning to go into the business world should observe the hair styles of young executives in a firm of the type he wishes to enter. Whatever the style, the hair should be clean and smooth. Hair dressings should not interfere with the natural look.

Women's hair styles also show great variety. However, as in the case of men's hair styles, extremes in hair styles should be avoided. Long straight hair that must be pushed back from the face at frequent intervals is not an asset when working with business machines. Whether long or short, however, hair should be kept sparklingly clean. Some girls wash their hair every day; others feel a weekly shampoo is better for their hair. The degree of oiliness in the hair should be the deciding factor as to frequency of shampooing.

Just as good points can be accentuated and bad points minimized by careful clothing selection, so can your hair style flatter your face, give an appearance of height, or call attention to your least attractive feature. It is advisable to consult a good hairdresser as to the most becoming hair style because hair arrangement can give illusions that change the shape of your face and that minimize or magnify either good or bad features. The way you wear your hair can also make you look taller or shorter. With the general features of a becoming style in mind, you can modify the hair style that is in fashion to suit you. It is unwise to go on wearing a favorite hair style long after it has passed into the out-of-date category.

Young girls will likely prefer simple styles that they can care for themselves. They do not need elaborate styles, permanents, and so on to look attractive. Hair that is clean and arranged in a simple style to show off a good feature is usually sufficient.

Women who do have permanents will probably continue with them about once every four months. A weekly visit to a beauty salon is no longer considered an extravagance, but careful brushing and (perhaps) resetting are necessary between such visits. One disadvantage with elaborate hair styles is the tendency to try to keep them intact for several days. A simple style that can be brushed each day is preferred.

A wig or hairpiece has proved to be a boon to the businesswoman in recent years. You may prefer a wig that matches your own hair; however, it is no longer considered particularly daring to invest in a wig wardrobe including one that is "tipped" in a lighter shade or one that is a different color than your own hair. If you do buy a wig, be sure it is becoming, that it is easy to care for, and that it is fitted properly. Many girls and women in business enjoy the convenience and attractiveness of wigs and hairpieces.

Makeup

The best guides for up-to-date developments in cosmetics are fashion magazines. New ideas are constantly pouring forth, and these magazines are mines of information. Another possibility is the cosmetics counter in the better department stores. For an expert opinion, you may want to consult a cosmetologist. Some of the latest discoveries in cosmetics are preparations that cover blemishes, scars, and birthmarks. Also most welcome are the "moisturizing" preparations that reduce the tendency of the skin to dry out as the years go by.

Like other fashions, styles in makeup change from year to year. One year heavy eye makeup will be fashionable. Another year may bring the bronzed look into vogue. Regardless of the current trend, the businesswoman should strive for the natural look. It must be admitted, however, that we become conditioned by what we see on all sides. A completely natural look does *not* look natural if we have grown accustomed to certain cosmetic aids. A case in point is eye shadow. A few years ago eye shadow worn during the day was considered to be in very poor taste. Now we see it on many women whether morning, noon, or night. Perhaps the key word in the use of cosmetics should be discretion. The woman in business should not look conspicuous — whether from too much or too little makeup.

The businesswoman should take the time to select the best shades and brands (for her) of foundation, powder, lipstick, and eye makeup. Books and magazines on grooming will prove helpful. Beauty salons and department stores frequently employ experts to help with these decisions. Many schools and colleges have classes in which the subject is studied. Some schools have style centers where individual help can be obtained. Some manufacturers of cosmetics provide free color charts indicating shades of makeup becoming to individuals with certain coloring. A little study and experimentation should provide the right answers. When a reliable and becoming brand has been chosen, it is wise to continue with it.

Applying makeup is an art, and skill in any art requires practice. It will pay you to take the time to master the lipstick brush, for example. Another skill requiring practice is the subtle use of an eyebrow pencil. Eyebrows should never be drawn on the face, although eyebrow pencil may be applied to darken brows or to emphasize their shape. Care should be taken to apply the pencil (sharpened to a fine point) in short hair-like strokes. If mascara is used, the lashes should then be brushed with a clean brush so they will not stick together and look spiky. And if you wear false eyelashes, make sure they do not look too artificial. The natural look is possible if care is used in selecting and applying the lashes.

Lipstick, nail polish, and rouge must be harmonized with coloring, face makeup, and costume. If rouge is worn at all, it should be placed high on the cheekbone and used sparingly. If a favorite brand of lipstick is drying, you might use lip foundation creams both at night and during the day.

TESTS FOR GOOD GROOMING

To simplify the grooming process, it may be helpful if one has some sort of yardstick to measure the extent to which one has achieved it. Just how well groomed should a young man or woman in business be?

Tests for Men — Brushed and Shined

If you are a young man planning to enter the business world, you should take the problem of grooming seriously. In some kinds of work, to be sure, the problem is not so crucial. Auto mechanics do not have to worry about how they look on the job. In business, however, everyone you meet will be judging you and your firm by your appearance. Your co-workers, too, will be affected by the care you take with grooming yourself. Each day you should mentally check off the following:

A man is well groomed when
His body and his teeth are clean and free from odor
His skin is clear, not oily, and he is freshly shaven
His hands have a cared-for look
His hair is neatly trimmed, clean, and combed
His underwear is clean
His shoes are shined
His socks are clean and not allowed to wrinkle around his ankles
His shirt is fresh daily
His suit is pressed; the trousers are well creased
No spots stain his clothing
His tie harmonizes with his shirt and suit
His clothing fits the occasion and is odorless
His beard and/or moustache are neatly trimmed

Tests for Women — The White Glove Look

A young woman who plans to work in business must be extremely serious about the problem of grooming. Unfair though it may seem, a man may be excused for certain violations of the "brushed and shined" look, while a woman will not. The reason may be that femininity is partially dependent upon the grooming shown by a girl or woman. Whether you have the money to spend on your wardrobe is not particularly important. You *must* spend time and money on grooming, however, if you are to succeed in business. Each day you should check off the following statements:
A woman is well groomed when
Her body and her teeth are clean and free from odor
Her skin is clear and well-cared for
Her hair is clean and attractively styled
Her clothing fits properly and suits her personality
Her clothing is appropriate for the business hours
Her shoes give an air of refinement and comfort. They are dust
     free and polished. The heels are straight, and the toes unscuffed.
Her makeup is not obvious; it is never applied in public
Her clothing is clean, pressed, and free from odors
Her underwear is fresh daily
Her hoisery is fresh daily and free from runs or holes
Her legs and underarms are free from hair

THE HABIT OF PERSONAL NEATNESS

Emerson once said, "I have heard with admiring submission the experience of a lady who declared that the sense of being well-dressed gives a feeling of inward tranquility which religion is powerless to bestow." Neatness and grooming are important, not only because they indicate orderliness and good taste, but also because of the feeling they give you. If you picture yourself and feel that others picture you as an example of a poised, well-groomed businessman or businesswoman, you will find it easier to play that role. The self-confidence that comes from feeling that your appearance is right makes it easier to give your entire attention to the tasks before you.

If your clothes are appropriate for office wear, if you do not wear the same ones every day, and if your shoes are polished and in good repair, you have attended to surface necessities only. Then get at the fundamentals. Your teeth are to be cared for; your skin and hair are to be kept in good condition; body odors are to be avoided; and your hands are to be well groomed. The cumulative effect should be one of good health, cleanliness, and tidiness. These matters are to be taken care of at home. In the store or the office, toilet articles are to be kept out of sight.

If you eat in the office, remove all evidences of the noonday lunch from your desk. Tidiness demands that you keep your desk clear of all unnecessary papers, that you put away equipment and supplies you have used, and that you pick up papers which someone else may have dropped carelessly. Be careful to throw wastepaper *into* the wastebasket rather than *at* it. Place things where they belong in or on the desk or in the files. Perform such housekeeping tasks each morning as the office or the store regulations permit.

If your duties are clerical, you are to keep neat reports and records, to keep the files in perfect order, to fold letters and insert them into envelopes carefully, to arrange all material systematically before giving it to your employer, and to send out only typewritten work that is mailable — that is, letters that are attractively arranged and free from carbon smudges, fingerprints, and visible erasures.

A young woman, sent to interview an employer about a prospective job in the stenographic department, reported a successful termination of her call. After her employment she was told that she had been selected from many applicants because she displayed traits which the company thought important. During the interview when she was being considered for the position, the personnel director had dictated some letters for her to transcribe. When she went to the typewriter to transcribe, she removed the cover from the machine and hung it over the back of her chair. When she erased, she was careful to avoid erasure crumbs falling into the typewriter mechanism. She moved the carriage all the way to one side so that the crumbs fell on the desk where they could be brushed away. When she completed her transcription, she covered the machine and moved the chair close to the typewriter table.

"Because of these indications of neatness," her new employer told her, "I selected you."

YOUR SUCCESS PYRAMID

The fourth phase of your success pyramid is made up of Blocks 16, 17, and 18. These blocks include the ability to make judgments or decisions quickly and accurately; natural aptitude and attitude for the job; and the acceptability of your work—within acceptable work standards for your particular job.

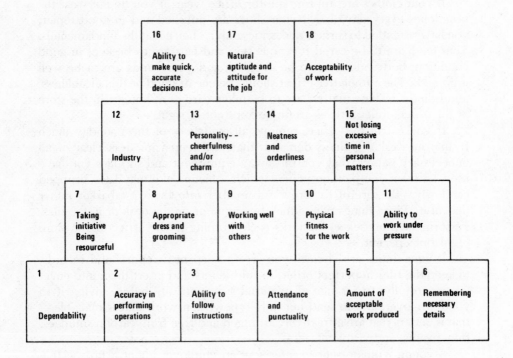

Figure 6-1. Fourth Phase of Success Pyramid

Ability to Make Judgments or Decisions Quickly and Accurately

In Chapter 3 a decision-making process was described. Throughout all of the chapters of this book, however, you have been given case problems in which to develop your decision-making ability. Nothing can slow down your efficiency and thinking ability so much as the inability to make up your mind. If you can develop the ability to make quick and accurate decisions, your productivity will be greatly increased. As was stated in Chapter 3, it helps to practice making quick decisions in minor matters. If you can't decide between the blue and the green shirt, for example, set a time limit: one minute to make up your mind. After you have made the decision, abide by it. Forget the alternative. Just this one skill can save you countless hours of pondering, of wondering, of worrying, of regretting the past. Really work on eliminating the wishy-washy side of your character. You will be amazed at the change this one improvement will make in your life.

Natural Ability and Aptitude and Attitude for This Job

Testing services have sprung up all over the world in which workers, both beginners and veterans, are helped to find the work they can do best. You can make some simple tests yourself that will help you find the work best suited to you. If you like detail, you will do well in clerical work of all kinds. If you are naturally orderly, you will have another clue that clerical work is best for you. If you like to solve problems, to take machinery apart to see what makes it go, you are better suited to problem-solving tasks, to mechanical jobs, to management and supervisory jobs in production work.

Another side of natural ability and aptitude is concerned with people. Are you more comfortable with a certain age group? Do you like to work with older people, younger people, or people your own age? Find the age group that suits you best. Try your hand at a number of different kinds of work to see which fits your hand best. These simple tests will help you find work that brings you satisfaction. If you can find happiness in your work, you will be far ahead of the vast majority of human beings: You will be happy eight hours a day!

Acceptability of Work — Is Within Acceptable Work Standards For This Job

Another test for natural ability and attitude for a certain job is your willingness to keep at it until you get it right. Willingness to take pains with your work is not spread equally over all different kinds of tasks. For example, you may be happy to retype a page in order to make it neat and free from smudges and noticeable erasures. This same desire for perfection, however, may not work for you when you are asked to go through the files and discard papers that have outlived their usefulness. You may do a slapdash job if you have to clean up the duplicating room. Every job has some drudgery in it. You must be willing to take the drudgery with the satisfactions. Be sure you have what it takes to become quality conscious in your work. Pride in your work can be developed; however, it helps if you can find the kind of work where you *want* to take pride in it, where quality is important to you.

FOLLOW-UP ACTIVITIES

1. Suppose you have been hired to work as a dental technician. You must wear plain white uniforms for work, but they may be of any material you prefer. Investigate the cost, upkeep, and wearing qualities of three different fabrics commonly used for such uniforms. Which one would you choose? Why?

2. You are a young man recently hired to work in a large office. It is necessary that you wear a fresh shirt each day. Your salary is not large, and you find washing and ironing extremely burdensome. See if you can find a drip-dry shirt that looks as neat as regular cotton shirts. What is the difference in cost? Which would you purchase? Why?

3. Janet Wells has just taken a position as typist in a small office. The ventilation is inadequate and there is no air conditioning. Janet's superior is Mrs. Christensen, who has a desk very close to Janet's. On a particularly hot day, Mrs. Christensen has the janitor move her desk into another corner some distance away. Should Janet consider this a reflection on her grooming? If you were Janet, would you say anything to Mrs. Christensen? If, so, what would you say?

4. Do you think a person's weight has any effect on his grooming requirements? If you were your present height and 30 pounds heavier, what additional grooming precautions would you need to take?

5. From your own experience, can you think of an application of the importance of neatness? Write the situation down and use it for class discussion.

6. You are a young man working in the data processing division of a large firm. All of the men in your division wear white shirts but remove their coats during working hours. What type of suit would you buy to wear to work? How often would you have it cleaned?

7. Do you take regular exercise? If you do, list the kinds and the frequency of each. In what ways could this list be extended? It is said that five minutes of exercise each day is better for you than two hours once a week.

8. It has been said that "your best friend won't tell you" that you are troubled with body odor. To whom can you appeal if you honestly want to know?

CASE PROBLEMS

1. Cluttered Desk

Joyce Matsura has a basket on her desk marked for incoming work. Joyce has asked her boss several times if he would please place any work for her attention in this basket, since her desk tends to get cluttered because of her many interruptions through the day. Nevertheless, her boss repeatedly comes in asking for work he has given her that she has never seen. When Joyce looks through the accumulated piles of paper on her desk, she finds the requested item.

1. Do you think Joyce handled the problem correctly? Why or why not?
2. Can you think of another way of handling the problem?

2. Samples From the Stock Room

Jim Thurman worked for the shipping department of Hogles Company. He hoped to become a salesman for the firm someday. After two years, however, he was neither given a raise nor promoted. Other men who were no older were transferred to the retail sales department. Finally, Jim became discouraged and decided to quit. Before he left, he asked his employer why he had never been promoted. The answer was that when Jim reported to work his hair was not neatly combed, his shoes were not polished, his clothes were not pressed, and his nails were not clean. Jim left feeling that his employer should have told him previously that his appearance was not measuring up to the firm's standards. Yet he could not see why it should have been necessary for him to be neat in the shipping room.

1. Do you think Jim was right in thinking that neatness did not matter in the shipping room?
2. Do you feel Jim's employer should have mentioned Jim's lack of neatness when it was first noted?
3. Do you think a person's work can be predicted from his personal grooming?

3. Prepare for the Day

Sam Cohn and Donald Huff worked in the same office. Both were good workers and were looking forward to being sent out on the road to sell the products of the company. It was a big moment when they received a notice to report the following morning to the sales manager's office for an interview. Sam looked over his clothing that night and saw that everything was clean and well pressed. Donald was going out and did not have time to see about his clothes. The next morning he overslept and had to rush to be on time for his appointment. On his way to the office he noticed that his shoes were in need of polishing and that he had on the same shirt he had worn yesterday. He felt, however, that he would pass inspection. He was interviewed first, and the sales manager missed no detail of his grooming. Sam was interviewed next, and he received the promotion.

1. Do you think it was fair to judge Donald solely on his appearance?
2. Would Donald's attitude toward his appearance be indicative of his attitude toward his work?
3. What effect might Donald's appearance have had on his attitude during the interview?

4. Constructive Criticism

Lester McAfee was the bookkeeper for the Worth Mercantile Company. As he was working he would often run his hands through his hair, leaving it mussed and untidy. Lester's desk could be seen through a window by the customers as they came into the notions department. The head of this department, Mr. Cameron, although not connected directly with the bookkeeping department, spoke to Lester about his habit and told him how untidy it looked through the window. Lester replied, "I've had the habit for years. I do it without thinking when I'm working."

1. Was Mr. Cameron justified in criticizing a worker in another department?
2. Should Lester have paid any attention to Mr. Cameron, since he was in a different department?
3. How would you have reacted to this criticism if you had been Lester?
4. Mr. Cameron might have gone to Lester's superior with his criticism. Would this have been preferable? Why or why not?

5. Your Best Friend Won't Tell You

Peggy Springmeyer works in a stenographic pool. One day four of the girls whose desks were near Peggy's made an appointment to talk with the supervisor, Mrs. Washington. Mrs. Washington asked the girls to stay a few minutes after work. When the meeting was held, the girls told the supervisor they would all like to have their desks moved away from Peggy. When asked their reason, the girls said they couldn't stand Peggy's disagreeable body odor. Mrs. Washington thanked the girls and promised to do something about the problem.

1. Assuming you are the supervisor, Mrs. Washington, how would you handle this problem?
   a. Would you tell Peggy that the girls had complained? Why or why not?
   b. Would you begin your conversation with Peggy with a question or with a statement?
2. Discuss the matter with four of your classmates. After you have agreed on a solution, write the exact words you think you would say to Peggy.
3. As an alternative to writing Mrs. Washington's conversation with Peggy, perform your version of the solution to this problem as a role-playing assignment.

part
three

personality is what you hear

chapter 7

communication — your lifeline

Suppose you are trapped in a giant plastic bubble. No one can hear you; you can hear no one. Then another bubble comes into your vision. Someone else is trapped in a bubble just like yours. Can you talk to that other person? Can you become friends? No, you cannot. If you are having trouble talking to other people, if you get stage fright when you have to talk before a group of people, if it is hard for you to say what you feel, you are trapped in just such a psychological bubble. Unless you do something about getting over your shyness, your communication difficulties, that plastic bubble of yours will get thicker every year.

Recent studies have shown that babies who are not communicated with by being held, talked to, and loved, frequently die within a year. You may have a relationship with someone in which you are having trouble getting through to that other person. Your relationship will die if you let things go on the way they are. Communication is, literally, a lifeline.

THE POWER OF WORDS

Even when you are communicating fairly well, you may still be encased in a bubble of sorts. Good communication has another ingredient. What you say and write must mean the same to your listener or reader as it does to you — and that isn't easy. You must get *through* your bubble by speaking and writing in ways that will make the plastic thin down. When you do that, the plastic in the other fellow's bubble will thin down, too, and he will be able to get what you are trying to say or write. The first step is to use *words* that will not be misunderstood. Secondly, those words must have the same feeling tone to the other fellow as they do to you. With some words there is no difficulty. A word like *slimy*, for example, has the same feeling tone to most of us. But other words, such as *left, right, establishment*, and *liberal* may be considered either good words or bad words, depending on a person's background and experiences.

It would be so simple if all emotionally charged words were reacted to by everyone in the same way. You could then deliberately avoid using "dangerous" words; but such a simple solution is out of our reach. You say what you say because you are the kind of person you are. In other words, you speak through your plastic bubble — some authors call it your *filter*. Furthermore, you hear what the other fellow says through that same filter. Someone else, with a different makeup and different experiences (and thus a different filter) will pick out different meanings from those same words. If you are suspicious by nature, you think other people are suspicious, too. You read into any statement made to you some part of your own characteristics.

Another barrier to good communication is that most of us want to skip the unpleasant things in life, particularly if they are a threat to the way we like to think of ourselves, our beliefs, and our prejudices. Each of you has had the experience of trying to persuade a friend to abandon his foolish ideas in favor of your sensible ones. The friend resorts to a simple and effective counter: He does not hear your arguments. We all have equal access to this device, by the way. We read what we want to read; we hear what we want to hear.

AIDS TO COMMUNICATION

When you talk with a friend on the telephone, you may either talk or listen. When you listen, you are the receiver. When you talk, you are the sender. The following aids to effective communication apply specifically to the activity of sending. You *send* the communication process when you speak or write.

Be Specific

In either speaking or writing you will *send* more effectively if you deal in specifics, if you avoid generalities. General statements are uninteresting mainly because they are hard to picture in your mind. If you are writing of your own school, for example, you might picture a red brick building covered with ivy and think "Central College." If you wrote "Central College," the reader would probably get the same picture in his mind. What will your listener or reader picture, however, if you write "college"? He may picture his own alma mater and the words "Yale University." The word *college* is not so concrete as the name of the specific college. Such a departure from concreteness is called a level of abstraction. If you say "school," you are still more abstract, since your reader may visualize his elementary school. If you write "institution," you climb to still another level of abstraction, since your reader may now visualize a hospital in his hometown.

The way to avoid abstract words is to ask yourself one or more of the five W's — Who, Where, When, Why (or How), and What. If you are tempted to say "charitable organization," you would ask yourself, "*What* charitable organization?" and your answer might be the Red Cross. The listener certainly gets a clearer picture from *Red Cross* than he does from *charitable organization.*

Be Clear

To communicate clearly means that the reader or listener gets the message you send. He will get your message without fail only if you make your statement or request so clear that it cannot be misunderstood. Following are three devices that can be recommended with confidence to help you speak or write clearly.

Brevity. The reader or listener will understand five words better than he will understand ten words. He will understand ten better than he will understand twenty. In the same way, he will understand a two-syllable word better than he will understand a six-syllable word. A paragraph containing six lines will be easier to understand than one containing twelve lines. Brevity must not be overdone, of course, since your communication must be grammatically correct and courteously phrased. Within these limits, though, your communication will be clearer if you use short words, short sentences, and short paragraphs.

Variety. Your communication will get attention if you avoid sameness, such as several sentences beginning the same way. Another way to put variety into what you say or write is to avoid using the same words or phrases over and over. Watch, too, a tendency to write several sentences in succession that all start in the same way, as well as that of having all of your sentences the same length. Interest and clearness will also be improved if you have variety in the way you make up your sentences.

Itemization. Clearness is improved if you itemize any sort of list that you wish to communicate. Notice how hard it is to understand the following written instructions:"Will you please go to the files and find the letter we wrote to Mr. J. K. Bliss last Monday and then make two Xerox copies and send one of them to the auditing department and the other one to the central filing department, and to the one to the filing department attach a copy of the contract signed by Mr. Bliss in October of last year."

By itemizing these instructions, their clearness is improved, as follows: "Will you please (1) make two Xerox copies of the letter sent to J. K. Bliss on Monday, October 5; (2) make a copy of the contract signed by Mr. Bliss in October of last year; (3) send one copy of the letter and a copy of the contract to the central filing department; and (4) send the other copy of the letter to the auditing department."

The instructions are even easier to understand if the writer lists the items one below the other, as follows:

"Will you please take care of the following:

1. Make two Xerox copies of the letter to J. K. Bliss on October 5 of this year.
2. Make a Xerox copy of the Bliss contract signed in October of last year.
3. Send one copy of the letter and a copy of the contract to the central filing department.
4. Send the other copy of the letter to the auditing department."

Be Positive

You have learned how important it is to be positive in earlier chapters. As you will see, it is just as important to write or to take care of business matters over the telephone in a positive manner. In other words, it is better to say what you *can* do instead of what you *cannot* do. When you must say "No," however, one of the following ways will help you.

Imply the negative. If someone asks you, the secretary of a mail order company, if you will let him have copies of your sales letters, you might answer, "Since our business depends wholly on sales and collection letters for its business, they are for our use only." Such an answer strongly *implies* that the answer is "No," yet it does not actually say "No."

Say what you can do. Another device for handling negatives is to avoid the "No" by saying what you can do. For example, a customer may call you to ask if his Christmas order can be moved forward and shipped on December 1. Instead of answering that early shipment is impossible, you might say, "We'll have your order to you by December 15 — with seven shopping days still remaining before Christmas."

Use sentence structure. If you must say "No," the sting can be removed somewhat by putting the "No" in the dependent clause of the sentence, the part of the sentence that cannot stand alone. Instead of saying, "You failed to send the catalog number of the camera you wanted," you would say, "If you will give me the catalog number of your camera, I'll send it right out."

Impersonalize the negative. Your "No" answer will be more acceptable if a *thing* (rather than the person) is the subject of your sentence. Thus, if you say, "The shoes had scuff marks on the soles and cuts on the heels," the listener will accept the statement. But if you say, "You obviously wore the shoes outside the house," your statement sounds accusing and your listener will not accept it. Still another way to impersonalize the negative is to put the listener or reader in a group. If you want to tell the new file clerk to sort the papers before she files them (perhaps for the third time), you might say: "We've found that most of our new girls want to skip the sorting step, but they find they take more time to file than they save by not sorting."

SPEAKING BEFORE GROUPS

If you are given an assignment to speak to a group — a committee, a club, an organization — your procedure will be similar to that used in writing. You collect your thoughts in written form; you organize them, you write and rewrite your outline. But there is a difference. When you prepare a talk, it is usually best to stop at the outline stage. Some good speakers, it is true, write down their speeches and memorize them. But those who speak frequently seem to do better if they first outline their thoughts carefully and then speak from the outline. One reason for this is that effective reading is even more difficult than effective speaking. Unless you have been trained in reading aloud, you will give a dull and uninteresting presentation if you rely on reading alone. If you are a "just starting" speaker, the following tips may be helpful.

Notes for Speaking

Type your notes on 5" x 8" white cards instead of on regular sheets of paper. Cards can be handled so that the audience is less likely to notice them. Sheets of paper will be noticed as you turn the page. If you use stories, dramatic statistics, or other examples (and they are good to use), type them on yellow cards of the same size. The use of color signals the fact that the example is coming up and helps you get ready for a change in your approach. It is also a good idea to write on the back of each example card the date and title of the talk in which it was used so that you can avoid using the same example before the same group later.

Tips for Improving Your Speaking

To improve your speaking ability, two attributes are needed: relaxation and practice.

Relaxation. Learn to relax your throat. Yawn. Notice how your throat feels. When you yawn your throat is open. Try to keep this feeling when you are speaking. If you learn to relax, you will benefit in another way, since the nervous speaker punctuates his remarks with "uh" and "er." To break the "uh-er" habit, in addition to relaxing, you should just stop speaking when you are at a loss for a word. Pause, look pleasant, and no one will know the difference. In fact, a pause is actually helpful, since many of us speak too fast; but the "uh-er" habit is deadly.

Practice. Take advantage of every opportunity you have to talk with others. *Want* to share, to communicate. Next, listen to a recording of your voice. You may not recognize what you hear as belonging to you, but you will probably note certain faults that you can improve. Some possible faults are these:

Do you project your voice? If you want to be a good speaker, you must "push" your voice to the person farthest away from you. Learn to speak directly to the ones in the back row.

Do you speak with your best pitch? There is a simple test for finding your best pitch. Go to a piano and sing "ah" down the scale to your lowest comfortable pitch. Then sing back up four whole notes. This level is your best speaking pitch. Most of us speak with a higher pitch than is pleasing.

Does your voice sound alive? If you are interested and enthusiastic about what you are saying, you will be interesting — and your voice will sound vibrant and alive.

Do you speak your words clearly? Speaking clearly results in proper articulation. This quality is improved if you pronounce your consonants sharply.

Do you look at your audience? Your listeners will be much more interested in what you have to say if you look directly at them. Looking at your audience is called "eye contact." It means that you look at someone's face in the center of your audience for a short time, then at someone's face on one side of your audience, then at someone's face on the other side. Never devote all your attention to just one part of your audience, since this makes those in the other areas feel left out (and they will tune *you* out). Also remember that looking at the wall above their heads will not do. And *never* look out of the window while you are speaking.

Improving Your Feeling Tone

It isn't what you say; it is the *way* you say it that sometimes makes the difference. If you are to improve *tone*, or the way you say it, you must develop the traits of empathy and tact. You may think there is no place in the business world for empathy, but this is not true. What you will find is too little time for the expression of empathy. In any case, you should be concerned with being empathetic yourself, not with having others empathize with you. Your employer is working under a much greater strain than you are. You should be empathetic to his problems and understanding of his impatience and irritability.

Empathy. You will have many opportunities to show understanding and empathy, which is feeling *with* someone. If you are sensitive to the feelings of others, you will try to make them feel at ease. This ability to make others feel at ease is an important factor in getting along with others. If you are relaxed and natural yourself, it is because you are able to think of others instead of yourself.

In addition to putting others at ease, you will be careful to treat others as you would like to be treated. Nothing has ever made the Golden Rule obsolete. You will speak in a friendly manner to new employees; you will take the trouble to be kind to those who are in trouble; you will be sensitive to moods and not infringe on another's desire for privacy. The human touch is not absent from business entirely. Flowers are sent to those on sick leave; visits are paid to old, retired employees; donations are made for wedding gifts and anniversaries.

But, in the matter of empathy, it is better to give than to ask. You must not exploit empathy. You should not ask that exceptions be made for you because of bad luck. You should not be so noble that you become a martyr in order to get more empathy from your co-workers. If you are ill and must ask for time off or decreased duties, do so. If you injure your health in attempting to carry too much work and cope with trouble at the same time, your problem will be aggravated.

Another way of exploiting empathy is in expecting raises and promotions because you have responsibilities or heavy expenses. Promotions and raises are not based on need; they are based on what you can offer your employer. If you describe in an employment interview the many misfortunes you have experienced and the burdens you carry, you will place yourself in a dubious role. Your interviewer will hesitate to employ or promote you, fearing you will continue to ask for favors and exceptions because you are troubled. Business is interested in the happiness and comfort of employees, but wise employees will not take advantage of this interest by exploiting it.

Tact. Tact is a sixth sense that makes us aware of what would be fitting to do or say at a given moment. It puts us in the other fellow's shoes. If you are tactful, you will make life infinitely easier for yourself and those around you. Tact involves understanding the other person's needs and wishes. There is hardly a situation in business that cannot benefit from a tactful approach. The following list of such situations should be studied carefully. Describe how you would use tact in each of them.

1. Maintaining any business relationship on an impersonal basis.
2. Handling a telephone communication in order to facilitate the smooth operation of the business situation involved.
3. Dismissing unwanted callers.
4. Making visitors feel at ease if they are kept waiting.
5. Answering questions about the office that are asked by outsiders.
6. Avoiding being pumped by outsiders for information about the business.
7. Ascertaining a caller's business before disturbing your employer.
8. Giving a caller the impression that, no matter how trifling the interview may be, your employer will be glad to see him if possible.
9. Keeping annoying, disturbing, or trivial matters from your employer's office, especially if he is already irritated.
10. Reminding your employer of work still to be done.
11. Knowing when and how to enter your employer's office or to withdraw from it.
12. Making executives of the organization feel comfortable and secure in their own self-esteem.
13. Being the scapegoat for the employer's mistakes, if necessary, when outsiders are concerned.
14. Suggesting improvements to be made, equipment to be installed, and supplies to be furnished.
15. Asking for a promotion or a raise.
16. Finding ways of putting the dictation of the employer into good English without offending him.
17. Listening with interest to the jokes your employer wishes to try out on you.
18. Finishing work that the employer has left undone.
19. Accepting your employer's ideas on unimportant matters about which you may disagree.
20. Reminding the employer of an appointment.
21. Asking the employer for information when he is busy.
22. Suggesting a new method of doing work so that your employer will not think you are trying to run his office.

23. Suggesting to your employer that you keep his desk tidy.
24. Making your employer think that your suggestions are his ideas.
25. Responding pleasantly and courteously when you have been spoken to in a rude manner.
26. Putting people at ease.
27. Taking care of an unpleasant situation so that those involved will be spared embarrassment.
28. Making necessary criticisms of other people in such a way that you will not hurt their feelings unduly.
29. Being considerate of subordinates.
30. Complimenting a fellow worker on a job well done.
31. Dealing with adverse criticism. Thank the critic and show an eagerness to improve.
32. Settling a difference of opinion among fellow employees.
33. Disagreeing with another without being offensive.
34. Remembering the names of people for whom and with whom you work.
35. Taking the initiative.
36. Sending a salesman away satisfied with the interview, though he has made no sale.
37. Dealing with an angry customer.
38. Collecting an account.
39. Explaining to a customer, without losing her trade, why she cannot return an article.
40. Explaining to a dissatisfied customer why her order was not sent on time.
41. Arranging an appointment with an important customer when the employer is not in the office.
42. Appealing subtly to the hobbies of the people with whom you come into contact.
43. Replying with enthusiasm to a tiresome, oft-repeated question.
44. Accepting casually the idiosyncrasies or the physical defects of others.

LISTENING TO COMMUNICATE

Of the three ways of sending and receiving communication discussed in this chapter — writing, speaking, and listening — the most difficult is listening. Yet good listening is a useful art and one that can be practiced every day. If you want to improve your listening ability, you should (1) concentrate on the speaker, (2) take well-organized notes, and (3) avoid the stumbling blocks of good listening.

Concentrate on the Speaker

In face-to-face listening you may find yourself planning your reply instead of concentrating on what the speaker is saying. This same tendency may be your downfall when you listen to a lecture. Instead of concentrating on the speaker, you may find your mind wandering to personal matters where, indeed, you plan what you are going to say. To avoid such distracting thoughts, listen for hints as to the speaker's organization plan. He may tell you his title (or it may be listed in the program). Write down the title. Now certain main divisions may seem logical to you. Write these divisions down, numbering them with Roman numerals about a half page apart. Then if the speaker does not follow a logical plan, you will have one made for him.

Take Notes in Outline Form

One of the common fallacies of note-taking is that you feel you must take down nearly everything the speaker says. A better plan is to listen a lot and write a little. Remember: Listening is the receiving part of communication. Understanding is the key. Understand the main points of what the speaker is saying. If you spend all your time getting down words, you will be sure to miss some of these main points. Under your main divisions, then (numbered with Roman numerals), you will write subdivisions (A, B, and C). Leave plenty of space between these subdivisions. You can then put the speaker's afterthoughts in their logical place.

Avoid the Stumbling Blocks of Good Listening

You must be mentally alert if you are to get the most out of your listening practice. To "stay on the beam" with the speaker, you must avoid the stumbling blocks of daydreaming and paying attention to distractions.

Daydreaming. The enemy of daydreaming is activity. When you feel your attention wandering, begin to write industriously. Look at the speaker; anticipate what he will say next; think of possible examples he might use to underline the points he makes.

Attending to distractions. Your surroundings may distract your attention: noise in the corridor, street noises, latecomers, whispering in the audience. Moreover, the speaker may distract you: his appearance, his pronunciation, his voice. To all these distractions, you must turn a deaf ear. Concentrate on the content of the talk. Let all unimportant matters go. Remember, too, that listening is work. Be sure to work at it when you listen.

YOUR SUCCESS PYRAMID

The fifth and last phase of your success pyramid is made up of two blocks: ability to organize work, and ability to suggest improvements in work techniques and operations. These blocks are crowned with your objective — success.

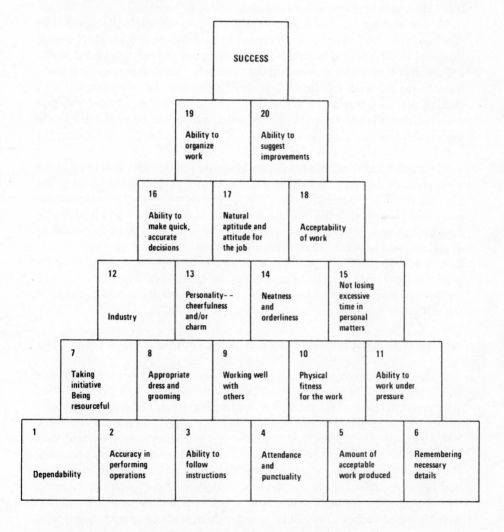

Figure 7-1. Your Completed Success Pyramid

Ability to Organize Work

The next-to-the-last block in your climb to success is the ability to organize a task into manageable units, to see that if Job A and Job B are needed in order to do Job C that Jobs A and B are done first. Organizational ability becomes more important as you rise higher in your work level. When you take your first job, it is usually a routine one. Someone else tells you what to do, checks your work, and suggests improvements. As your ability increases, however, you will find that you are trusted more and more to take care of the total job, to decide how you are going to attack the problem. Here is where organizational ability will be needed.

Much of what has been discussed in the preceding chapters will help you become better organized: learning to make decisions quickly, seeing that your work output is high, developing accuracy in your work, and working within the acceptable standards of your job. Now, however, you must learn to do the hard job first. You must eliminate the common habit of putting off until tomorrow what should be done today. Secondly, you must see that all of the papers, drafts, tools, and so on, needed for a single job are kept in one place so that you will not be wasting time looking for the things you need when you start work on that job.

Organizing your work also means planning your work. You must make a plan before you start. If organizing is new to you, you should write your plan down. First comes the due date. Write down when the job must be completed. Next, divide your task into parts and set a date when each one is to be finished. Third, make sure all of the supplies, papers, answers to questions, and needed calculations are at hand. Then get to work. Don't be a pencil sharpener. A pencil sharpener is someone who spends all of his time getting ready to work but never actually gets going. See that you work on the task the number of hours necessary each day in order to complete the job when it is due.

Ability to Suggest Improvements in Work Techniques and Operations

The last stepping-stone in your climb up the success pyramid is one that must wait until you have established yourself in your job. Even then, it is wise to make suggestions for improving work techniques tactfully. Reread the suggestions in this chapter on *tact*. When you can make suggestions without offending other workers or your supervisor, you will have become a real asset to your company. New ideas are always welcome; the danger lies in suggesting your new ideas with a "know-it-all" attitude — and before you have really learned how to do your job efficiently. Remember, though, that business needs new ideas, new techniques, new ways to save time and money. Be willing to offer them without expecting anything in return, and you will truly be ready for that top step — success itself.

FOLLOW-UP ACTIVITIES

1. Make a list of ten words you use occasionally that have an unpleasant emotional connotation or coloring. Next, see if you can find a synonym for each of the ten words, each synonym to have a pleasant connotation. Try to make the pleasant words a part of your vocabulary, at the same time eliminating the unpleasant words.

2. Assume you have been promoted to supervisor. One of the girls with whom you formerly worked is now working under you. This girl, Kay, is habitually late for work; she is doing a good job otherwise. It is your duty to talk to Kay about her tardiness. What will you say to Kay? Write down your exact words.

3. To increase your vocabulary, try the following plan of learning a new word each week.

   a. Choose a word from your daily reading that you do not know.
   b. Place this word, including pronunciation and meaning, on your bulletin board, a chalkboard, or attach it to your mirror, where you will see it several times a day.
   c. Involve your family or roommates in the activity.
   d. Use the new word in your speaking; perhaps others will use the word, too.
   e. Remember: Each week choose a new word — but don't forget the new words you learned earlier. Keep a list of all the words you have worked on, and make them a part of your daily speech.

4. Listen to the radio or television speech of any well-known personalities and bring to class a list of their colorful words, of their specific words, or of the words they pronounce differently from the way you are accustomed to hearing them.

5. Locate an article in a current newspaper or magazine bearing on a current problem, and underline the words that give the article color and life.

6. Substitute more colorful expressions for these trite ones:

pale as a ghost	busy as a bee
green as grass	sweet as sugar
pure as snow	white as a sheet

7. Reread the first four suggestions for eliminating faults in your speaking: (Do you project your voice? Do you speak with your best pitch? Does your voice sound alive? Do you speak your words clearly?) For one week spend 10 or 15 minutes a day on *one* fault that is most serious for you. For example, if you lack projection, count from *one* to *ten* aloud, starting softly on *one* and increasing your projection until it is at its strongest point on the count of ten.

8. Practice the suggestions given in the Listening to Communicate section in this chapter in one of your lecture classes. Do you think that this method of taking notes has helped you? Discuss.
9. Begin a conversation with someone whose remarks usually irritate you. Let the other person talk; you listen. Do not interrupt for at least three minutes. See if you can detect *why* he believes as he does, if there is some logical basis for his point of view. Now, answer with a temporizing statement, such as, "You do have a point there, but what do you think about . . . ?" Ask an intelligent question, one that shows you were really listening. Did this activity improve your relationship with this particular person? Discuss.
10. Write down five negative statements you have made recently. Rewrite these statements, using one of the four suggestions for handling negatives given in this chapter. Do you think a more positive approach would have improved the situation? Discuss.

CASE PROBLEMS

1. Yeah

Lena Washington, a recent high school graduate, thoroughly enjoys her first job as a salesperson in the Foss Drugstore. She is efficient and keeps herself busy tidying up the shelves when business lags. Nevertheless, the store manager, Mr. Valdes, is sharp with Lena, especially when she talks to him. He is friendly and sociable to Nancy Knight, the other salesgirl; and this fact is disturbing to Lena. Lena likes Nancy but finds she must often help her out of careless mistakes. One day Mr. Valdes listens in on Lena's conversation over the telephone with a customer.

Customer: "Do you carry Acme travel clocks?"
Lena: "Yeah, we have it."
Customer: "Do you have it in blue?"
Lena: "No, just groovy green."

Customer: "What is the price?"
Lena: "Ten bucks."
Customer: "Thank you. I'll try another store."
Lena: "Sorry."

Later, Lena approaches Nancy in tears, explaining that Mr. Valdes called her in his office and curtly told her to let Nancy answer the phone from now on. Nancy answers that Mr. Valdes probably objects to Lena's way of speaking.

1. Assuming you are Lena, solve this problem using the five-step method explained in Chapter 3.
2. Why is it Lena's problem, rather than that of Mr. Valdes?

2. Word Lack or Judgment Lack?

Alice Curtis took dictation from Mr. Grayson, the head of the advertising department. Mr. Grayson was a rapid speaker and occasionally slurred words to the point that Alice could not understand them. One day during dictation, Mr. Grayson used the word *hybrid*, but Alice heard the word as *high-bred*. Not getting the idea, Alice interrupted, "Do you mean high-bred?" Mr. Grayson was annoyed at losing his train of thought. "Use better judgment," he said, "and don't interrupt."

1. Assuming that Alice had been working at this position for more than six months, is there some way she could have avoided this situation?
2. How should Alice have reacted to this reprimand?
3. What clues should she have had from the context to help her in deciding which word was intended?
4. Is there a grammatical rule that might have helped her in this case?
5. Some dictators prefer to be interrupted during dictation. What personality clues would help you in deciding when to ask and when not to ask a question during dictation?

3. Use of Initiative

Frank Zwiefelhofer has just completed a report that must be sent out in the afternoon mail. His employer intends to send a letter with the report, but he is called out of the office just before closing time and without having been able to dictate the letter. He says nothing to Frank before leaving. Frank knows, however, that the letter will be similar to the one sent the previous month. He decides to type the letter and sign it with his employer's name and his own initials.

1. What would you have done in Frank's position?
2. Which would be more serious, sending the letter without being told or sending the report without a covering letter?
3. If you were Frank's employer, how would you react to having an employee act in this way without instructions?

4. A Place for Sensitivity

Ann Madison is a secretary in a large plastic surgery clinic. Her task is to fill out routine records concerning patients for the files. The data are of a factual nature and contain no medical information. When talking with a middle-aged man, she observed that he was embarrassed by having to supply such information as his name, age, address, and business. When she had recorded these answers, Ann said to the patient, "And now will you tell me why you have come here?"

"Look, young lady," he answered, "is it the practice for a patient to have to give you that kind of information?"

Ann answered, "I'm sorry, sir. I'm only doing my job. My instructions from Dr. Reynolds are that I must get this information."

1. Do you feel that Ann was sensitive to the needs of others?
2. About what types of needs or feelings are some people very sensitive?
3. Should Ann have insisted that the man answer her question? How would you have handled this situation? Why?

chapter 8

your voice with a smile

In Chapter 7 you read of the importance of what you say, the words you use. In this chapter, you will discover the importance of *how* you say these words. In some businesses, the personality you hear is far more important than the personality you see, since many of these business dealings take place over the telephone. How do *you* sound when you speak? Does your voice sound warm, friendly, interested? You will need these three qualities in your voice if you are to develop a pleasant telephone personality. In fact, businessmen everywhere are searching for workers who can project a positive image of their company over the telephone. They know that when someone calls their business firm and a worker answers the telephone, that worker *is* the company to that caller.

A good telephone personality demands more than a friendly voice, however. In addition to sounding friendly when you speak, you must become a friendly listener. You may wonder what a friendly listener could possibly be; it is just this: If you do nothing more than remain silent while someone else speaks, you are a passive, or unfriendly, listener. Instead, you must listen actively. To be an active listener, you must do the following:

1. Think hard about what the other person is saying. Don't pay any attention to his voice mannerisms; concentrate on what he says.
2. Repeat to yourself the key words the speaker says. If the caller says, "My navy jacket was supposed to be altered and delivered yesterday. It hasn't come yet and I have to wear it tonight," think of these words: "navy jacket," "delivered," "today."
3. Put everything out of your mind except the speaker's words. Avoid daydreaming, planning your own activities, thinking up alibis.
4. Put yourself in the other person's shoes. Feel with the speaker. This is called empathy. If you can listen with empathy, you will be an active, friendly listener.

5. Listen positively. Look for points you can agree with. Don't argue mentally with the speaker. You will usually find the points you look for. If you look for positive ideas and suggestions, you will find them. If you plan your own defense as the other person speaks, however, you will not be paying attention to *his* points. The key idea in friendly, active listening is to think about the other person's point of view.

As in face-to-face communication, your telephone communication consists of both sending and receiving. Keep your voice warm and friendly when you send; listen actively when you receive. These two qualities are the foundation of all telephoning in business.

TELEPHONE TECHNIQUES

How is your telephone personality evaluated? The only medium available to the caller is your voice. By your voice the customer or client will form his opinion and be influenced in his future dealings with the firm. You have heard the expression "The voice with a smile." This slogan should guide you in using the telephone in your work. Confidence can be established and friendliness can be maintained if your voice carries enthusiastic interest in the affairs of your business as well as personal attention to the affairs of the customer or client.

The telephone directory should be studied; it contains information with which you should be familiar. For example, you should not guess about a number. If there is any doubt in your mind, refer to the directory for accurate information. When calling long distance, know when to dial direct and when to dial person-to-person. Know the likely charges before you begin to speak. Know when and how to reverse the charges and how to make collect calls. Learn to use coin telephones and telephones connected through private branch exchanges. There are definite techniques you should master both in answering the telephone and in placing calls.

Answering the Telephone

The most important factor in answering the telephone is promptness. Always answer the telephone on the first ring if you can. The customer or client who places the call is always critical about a delay. Your firm may have an approved form of greeting that you must use, but you can make that greeting a cheerful one. The approved greeting may be, "Good morning," followed by your identification. This is important. Always identify yourself immediately; that is, give the name of the business or the department, or your title or name. A slight rising inflection when giving your name or title is a tactful way of suggesting to the caller that you would like to help him. Depending upon the circumstances, you will use one of the following means of identification.

Name of the company. You will identify the name of the company when you answer the outside line, as in a small office. In a small real estate firm, for example, you would give some such identification as the following: "Good morning. Becker and Forest Company." The caller would then talk to you or ask to speak to someone else in the firm.

Name of the department. You will identify the name of the department if the company has a private branch exchange (PBX) and you are one of a number of workers in that department without a particular title. If you were a clerk in the accounting department, for example, your caller would reach you by telling the switchboard operator he wanted to talk to someone in the accounting department. Giving him this information, therefore, would enable him to go on from there, either by speaking to you or by asking for someone by name or title. In answering the phone in this situation, you would say, "Accounting Department," because the name of the company and the "Good morning" would already have been given by the PBX operator.

Your name or title. You would identify yourself by your name or title if you were the assistant to an executive. Your choice would depend on the circumstances. In a small town or city you would probably give your name, as you would if you worked in a school office. If you are well known by name, you should give your name. If your firm is located in a large city, on the other hand, it would usually be more helpful to your caller if you were to give your title. In this instance, you would say, "Mr. Henry's secretary speaking."

You should always keep a pad and pencil near the telephone so you will have something to write on and something to write with when messages need to be taken down. Never trust to memory about numbers, addresses, or the time for appointments. A pad of telephone message blanks (similar to the model on the next page) makes it easy to report messages that are taken for others in their absence.

Your enunciation is important when telephoning. In face-to-face conversation, facial expression helps to make your message clear. Over the telephone there is nothing to help you but the way you speak. Always speak clearly, slowly, courteously, and directly into the mouthpiece of the telephone. Be sincere; then your voice will sound sincere. Develop a listening ear along with your sincere voice. Concentrate on what is being told you or asked of you. Some voices over the telephone are hard to understand; some use gutteral tones, some speak with accents, some use whispers, some crack against the eardrums. Concentrating on what is being said with your listening ear will help you to understand the speaker.

Be courteous, too, in your choice of expressions. For example, it is more courteous to ask rather than demand, as "Will you wait just a moment, please?" It is also more courteous to use the person's name, as "Yes, Mr. Jones." Slang expressions are taboo in business telephoning; be sure to avoid them. If you do not understand the speaker and must ask to have something repeated, be sure to assume the blame yourself. If you say, "I can't understand you," the

MEMO OF CALL
To _Mr. Roberts_
From _Mr. Allison, Western Const. Co._
_311_   _872-2368_   _—_
AREA CODE   TEL. NO.   EXT.

- [x] Telephoned
- [x] Please call
- [ ] In response to your call
- [ ] Will call you later
- [ ] Called to see you
- [ ] Wishes to see you

Message _Wishes to discuss_ _Richmond bid with you._ _(file attached)._

Received by _C.B._ Date _3/9_ Time _1:10_

caller will take it as criticism of his enunciation. But if you say, "Would you mind repeating that name? There is quite a bit of noise in this office," the caller will be free of any blame and will probably be glad to help you.

Transferring a Call

It is annoying to a caller to be transferred from one telephone to another. If you can take care of the call yourself without transferring it, you should make every effort to do so. If you are unable to take care of the matter, be sure to use the utmost tact in transferring the call. Tact requires the following steps:

1. Give whatever information you have; then *ask* if you can transfer the caller to another department or individual. You might say, "I'm sorry, but we don't have that information. I believe the Accounting Department can help you. May I transfer you?"
2. If the caller objects to being transferred, you may ask if he would like you to give a message to the other department or individual and have him telephone the caller. You might say, "The Accounting Department should have that information. If you will give me your number, I'll have them call you back in a few minutes."

Placing a Call

You must learn how to place a telephone call for your employer. Men of importance have prerogatives that should be respected. It is a matter of business etiquette to know which person is to be kept waiting, if only for a few seconds. For example, you should get an outside man of lesser rank on the line before you call your employer, but you should get your employer on the telephone before a man of equal or greater rank is called to the telephone at his end of the line. Never place a call for your employer until you make sure he is available to take the call when it comes through.

Direct dialing. Since the advent of direct cross-country dialing, telephone numbers have changed from prefix letters and numbers to all numbers. The local telephone number will consist of three digits, then a hyphen, followed by four more digits. When dialing direct, you must first dial "1" for long distance station-to-station calls. This is followed by the area code, such as 204. After this, you dial the seven digits of the number desired. If dialing person-to-person, collect, credit card, and other calls, follow this same procedure except dial "0" first instead of "1."

If you do not know the telephone number of the party you wish to dial direct, simply dial 1-(the area code desired)-555-1212. You will be asked the city desired. Give the name of the city promptly. When that operator answers, give the name and address of your party. This service is given without charge.

Local dialing. When dialing a number in an office having a PBX, you may call out by first dialing 9. You then listen for the dial tone (a steady humming sound on the line). In some recent installations, there is instant outside dialing. You dial 9 as before; however, there is no change — no dial tone is heard — but an outside line is reached instantaneously. You now dial the number you wish. A short wait follows before the ring is heard. If you should get a busy signal (a rapid "buzz-buzz-buzz" sound), hang up and dial again later. If you interrupt someone else's dialing on a party line, say you are sorry and hang up. If someone else interrupts your dialing on a party line, tell that party about the matter in a pleasant tone.

Telephone Judgment

You must use judgment in telephone matters. One tried-and-true statement, for example, is being dropped by many executives. So many secretaries and clerks have used the sentence, "Mr. Blank is in conference," to get rid of an unwanted caller, that the response is now suspect. Now, rather than using this sentence, you should say, "Mr. Blank is in a meeting. May he call you after 3:30?" when he is in a meeting. If your employer is away, you should give this information; but you should make the statement neutral as far as giving additional information goes. That is, you do not say,

"Mr. Blank has gone to San Francisco," as this may be information that a competitor can use to his advantage. Merely say, "Mr. Blank is out of the office until next week," or some equally noninformative statement.

If your boss is talking on another line, you should say so. It is discourteous to say, "Mr. Jones is busy." Instead, say, "Mr. Jones is talking on another line. Will you wait?" If the caller agrees to wait, you should check back after a minute or two. You might say, "Mr. Jones' line is still busy. May I take a message?"

It is good telephone judgment to follow disappointing answers with an offer to help. If someone asks for your employer and he is away, you might say, "Mr. Blank is out of the office this week. May I connect you with Mr. Clarke? He is handling Mr. Blank's accounts until his return." If there is no other person in charge of your employer's work during his absence, you should ask if you can help.

In answering telephone calls, it is good judgment to attend to as many details as you can without calling anyone else to the telephone. Try to become conversant with as many details and policies as possible, as you will need to answer many questions. If you work in the office of a retail store, for example, you may be called upon to know at what time the last delivery leaves the store, what the sales specials of the day are, or at what time the store post office closes. The more diversified the duties of your job, the wider is the field from which you are expected to draw your information.

Remember that at your end of the line you are the agent representing the business; that your voice and manner reveal desirable or undesirable traits and attitudes; that, invisible though you may be to the person at the other end of the line, and unimportant though you may be in the organization as a whole, you are a powerful influence in business affairs when you use the telephone.

Telephone Systems, Instruments, and Services

Systems, instruments, and services connected with the telephone change and improve so rapidly that a business worker who has been away from his or her job for ten years would have a great many new telephone techniques to learn. For example, a new concept is the Centrex service. Centrex is an adaptation of the PBX or switchboard service. Centrex additions include DID (direct inward dialing), whereby incoming calls can be dialed direct to an individual user. DOD (direct outward dialing) is also provided, whereby all local and long distance calls can be dailed direct to the user.

Some of the recent additions to telephone instruments include the Card Dialer, whereby specially punched cards are inserted into a slot, a special start bar pushed, and the number is dialed automatically. Another instrument is the Rapidial, in which up to 290 names can be handled on a small index accompanying a push-button telephone. Still another instrument is the Call Director, whereby a small desk switchboard is capable of handling up to 29 lines.

Recent services include the Conference Call Service, whereby, through appointment calls, several people can talk together from any set of locations. Telephone dictation is possible by dialing a certain number on a regular telephone and being connected to a central dictating machine. Wide Area Telephone Service (WATS) permits unlimited long distance interstate calling. The user of WATS service pays a monthly rate for a special telephone line.

TELEPHONE AND EVERYDAY COURTESY

Courtesy is based on respect. If you respect a person, you will show this respect by treating him as you would like to be treated. You will do nothing to make his work more difficult; you will do nothing to offend his dignity or to make him lose face. Although you may not respect all people in your work, you must treat them as though you do.

You should learn the language of dignity and respect. In such language you do not use slang, profanity, angry words, or verbal attacks, even though others may occasionally use these methods in speaking to you. Do not criticize religious faiths, political parties, or personal tastes.

Always call your employer by his last name and Mr., Doctor, or some other title of respect, even though he may call you by your first name or even a nickname. The use of last name shows respect for his position, an important factor in business. Other important factors are knowing the names of customers, clients, or callers, and receiving callers pleasantly, and determining the importance of their calls. A sense of courtesy helps you to know how to congratulate others on honors they have received, how to avoid unnecessary noises that disturb others, how to dispatch desired information when it is needed.

Simple courtesy is involved in the habit of saying, "Thank you," and "Please," "Good morning," and "Good night," to your office associates. The same habit of courtesy will help you to refrain from excessive borrowing from others, from laughing at their mistakes, from being curt or ungracious to business inferiors. A lack of courtesy is shown in slamming doors, banging the receiver of a telephone, interrupting office routine or business conversations unnecessarily, and tactlessly correcting another's mistakes. Behavior like this will soon win hearty disapproval for you among your office co-workers because it indicates that you lack a feeling of consideration for others.

FOLLOW-UP ACTIVITIES

Dramatize the following situations. Make use of the suggestions given on the preceding pages. If it is possible to have three telephones connected on a battery, two to be used by students and the third by the teacher or another student who listens in for the purpose of offering criticism, these practice exercises will be most interesting.

Some of the following exercises require the addition of the telephone conversation of the person at the other end of the line. As such exercises will require time and careful consideration, the missing conversation should be provided in home preparation. In school you will dramatize the situations and discuss the techniques employed.

Answering Telephone Calls

The telephone rings.   One student, who represents a salesman of the Brown Drug Company, answers the call. The customer is Mrs. Jones, a part played by another student.

SALESMAN. "Brown Drug Company. Mr. Walters speaking."

MRS. JONES. "This is Mrs. Jones of 202 Broad Street."

"Good morning, Mrs. Jones."

"Is Blossom soap on sale today?"

"Yes, our sale price on Blossom soap is 12 cents a bar, one dozen to a customer."

"What about Luster soap? Is it on sale?"

"No, there is no sale price on Luster soap."

"I think I'll come down to the store to decide."

"We also have other standard articles on sale. You may be interested in them."

"I'll wait until later. Thanks."

"You are welcome. Call again. Good-bye."

"Good-bye."

. . . .

The telephone rings. One student, the cashier of the Orpheum Theater, answers the call. The conversation of the inquirer is to be supplied by a second student.

CASHIER. "Good morning. Orpheum Theater."

INQUIRER. "_ _ _ _ _ _ _ _ _ _ _ _."

"The feature picture is on at 3:15."

"_ _ _ _ _ _ _ _ _ _ _ _."

"You're welcome. Good-bye."

"_ _ _ _ _ _ _ _ _ _ _ _."

Placing a Local Call

One student is Roberta Jones of the Cinnamon Inn Restaurant. The other is Karen Holmes of the Hales Bakery.

ROBERTA. (Dials 721-4499)

KAREN. "_____."

ROBERTA. "This is Miss Jones at the Cinnamon Inn Restaurant. I would like to know what happened to the bread order that was supposed to be here at ten o'clock. It's over an hour late already!"

KAREN. "_____."

ROBERTA. "If it left an hour ago, then something has happened. What are you going to do about it?"

KAREN. "_____."

ROBERTA. "You'll have to do more than check the route. We must have that order here by 11:30. Can you send us a duplicate order with a special deliveryman?"

KAREN. "_____."

ROBERTA. "Well, I guess it will be all right if you check the route first. But we're expecting a big crowd for lunch today; the order *must* be here before noon. Will you call me at 683-4444 by 11:20?"

KAREN. "_____."

ROBERTA. "You're welcome. Goodbye."

KAREN. "_____."

Placing a Long-Distance Person-to-Person Call

One student is John Evans, the bookkeeper of the Emerson Wholesale Grocery, Cincinnati, Ohio. The answering conversations of the Operators are to be supplied by other students.

JOHN. (To reach long distance directory assistance he dials "1" then the area code "601" (which is listed in the front of the telephone directory as the area code for all locations in Mississippi) and then "555-1212." (The number "555-1212" is used when you do not know the number of the party you are calling.)

FIRST OPERATOR. "_____."

JOHN. "Longview, Mississippi."

SECOND OPERATOR. "_____."

JOHN. "May I please have the number of the Mississippi Mercantile Company."

SECOND OPERATOR. "_____."

JOHN. "Thank you." (He then dials 0-601-538-9605. If it had been a station-to-station call, he would have dialed "1" first instead of "0.")

THIRD OPERATOR. "_____."

JOHN. "Yes, please. I would like to speak person-to-person with William Brown.

SWITCHBOARD OPERATOR. "_____."
THIRD OPERATOR. "_____."
(John should have at hand all invoices, letters, or other materials that may be needed for his conversation with Mr. Brown.)

Taking an Order over the Telephone

One student, who represents a clerk of the Home Grocery Company, answers a telephone call. A second student, as Mrs. Williams, places an order.

CLERK. "Good morning. Home Grocery Company."
MRS. WILLIAMS. "_____."
"Yes, Mrs. Williams?"
"_____."
"Peaches are a dollar a dozen. They are very fine and large for the early crop."
"_____."
"One dozen? Anything else?"
"_____."
"Best creamery butter is 80 cents a pound."
"_____."

"Two pounds? How about some fresh cottage cheese? We have just received today's order, and it looks very appetizing."
"_____."
"Thanks, Mrs. Williams. Your order will be delivered this morning. Call again. Good-bye."

Taking a Call for Your Employer

One student, as the stenographer, answers a telephone call. A second student is the client calling.

STENOGRAPHER. "Shore and Silver's office. Miss Whitney speaking."
CLIENT. "_____."
"Mr. Silver is very busy. Perhaps there is something that I can do?"
"_____."
"An appointment for Friday? I can arrange an appointment for Friday afternoon at 3:00 P.M."
"_____."
"Thank you very much. Good-bye."
"_____."

In case arrangements that satisfy the client cannot be made, any one of the following conversations may result:
"I am very sorry, but Mr. Silver is out for lunch now. Would you like to leave a message?"
"_____."

"Shall I call you when he returns?"

"——————————."

or

"I'm sorry, but Mr. Silver is out of town for the week. This is his secretary speaking. Perhaps I can help you."

"——————————."

"In that case may I call you when Mr. Silver returns to town?"

"——————————."

"I am very sorry. Good-bye."

or

"I'll connect you with Mr. Silver." (To Mr. Silver the following announcement is made.) "Mr. ——— is on the telephone, Mr. Silver, and wishes to speak with you."

Answering the Telephone When the Wrong Number Has Been Called

You are a busy clerk, one of whose duties is to answer the ring of the telephone.

"You have the wrong number. This is 871-7100."

Notice that you give politely what information you can, even though you are busy.

Answering the Telephone When the Call Is for Someone in Another Office

"Miss Dobbs is not in this office, but you can reach her at 541-4348."

In a courteous manner give what information you can.

Receiving a Telegraph Message Over the Telephone

"Dr. Walker's office."

"——————————."

"Dr. Walker is not in, but I am his secretary and will take the message."

"——————————."

"Let me read the message back to you to see if I have taken it correctly."

By giving her position, the secretary indicates her right to receive such messages as this. The accuracy of the message should be checked to avoid an error.

Making Use of the Telephone Directory

Make a list of the telephone numbers you might need in your home. Include the number of a grocery, a drugstore, a doctor, and a dentist, as well as the numbers of other businesses and persons near your home.

How do you report a fire by means of the telephone?

In case of trouble how do you notify the police by telephone?

Choose a particular business, and make a list of telephone numbers that you might need if employed as a bookkeeper or clerical worker.

CASE PROBLEMS

1. The Seamy Side

Louise Ryan is the secretary to a small-town welfare association. Her work is to keep the unemployed individuals satisfied as far as possible and to try to create a feeling of goodwill between the association and those on relief. One day, when she answered the telephone, a man's voice demanded to talk to the head of the association. Louise replied that he was not in the office and asked if she could help. The man answered in a loud voice, using abusive language. Louise had never heard language like this and she put the receiver down with a bang. The telephone rang for some time, but she refused to listen again to such talk.

1. What is the correct attitude toward difficult individuals in social work situations?
2. Was Louise behaving in an objective manner?
3. Why do you think Louise acted as she did?
4. What might Louise have done that would have served the association in a better way?

2. The Customer is Always Right

Louis Welti works in the office of the sales department of a coffee company. He keeps the records of the men who are on the city routes. His books show the supplies the salesmen take out of stock and their returns in cash and merchandise. Louis is exceptionally efficient. If there is a mistake in the record of a route man, Louis always catches it; if there is an argument about reports, Louis can offer the needed facts to eliminate further talk. Louis does have one fault; he has not developed a courteous telephone technique. The manager has had a number of complaints from customers who are annoyed at the way Louis handles situations over the telephone. Typical of Louis' conversations:

An irate customer says, "But I told the salesman I wanted a light roast and he left a package of dark roast." Louis answers, "Why don't you give the dark roast a try? It's one of our best sellers."

A dissatisfied customer says, "I just received my bill and you have charged me $10.16 for Saturday, November 18. I did not place or receive an order on that date." Louis says, "You must be mistaken. The bills are checked most carefully before we send them out."

An angry customer says, "I asked that my orders be delivered on Saturday morning, and this is the third time it has been sent out on Monday." Louis says,

"This is the first time I have heard about it. Are you sure you told the delivery-man?"

When the office manager speaks to Louis about the complaints he has received, Louis defends himself vigorously. He knows he is right; he says he is positive the customers are mistaken. The next time the office manager has to come to the rescue to keep a battle from developing he resolves to tell Louis what he should have said in each of the cases cited. Assuming that you are the office manager, how would you have answered each of the three customers?

1. Why does Louis talk as he does? Do you think he may be covering up a lack of confidence?
2. What personal techniques should Louis develop in addition to keeping records?

3. No Personal Calls

Ruth McDonald is busy with her work when she receives a personal telephone call from her friend, Harriet. Harriet wants to find out about a weekend trip that is being planned. Harriet is working at her first job; Ruth knows she does not realize that the office is no place for personal calls. Ruth doesn't want to hurt Harriet's feelings, so she tries to be tactful. Finally, she says, "Harriet, I must go now. Mr. Maxwell is buzzing me. See you Friday."

1. Do you think Harriet was made aware that she should not call Ruth during office hours?
2. Should Ruth have been more honest with Harriet so she would understand how to behave in the future?
3. Can you think of a tactful way that Ruth could have informed Harriet of the general rule regarding personal telephone calls during business hours?

4. To Screen or Not to Screen

Mr. O'Rourke, your boss, comes in from lunch and tells you that he does not want to be disturbed for any reason. He must finish up a complicated report that must be ready for a board meeting at 2 p.m. He tells you to take care of all telephone calls. It is now 1 p.m.

a. You are extremely busy typing the completed section of the report. At 1:15 the telephone rings. When you answer, giving your name and position, the voice says, "Put me on to Pat, will you?" You answer that Mr. O'Rourke cannot be disturbed until four o'clock because of an important meeting. The voice says, "Just tell him it's old Jack from Miami. He'll be glad to talk to me." What will you say now?

b. At 1:30 the telephone rings again. The voice is that of Mr. O'Rourke's wife. She is extremely agitated and explains that she is calling from a public telephone, that she has locked her car keys in her car and wants Mr. O'Rourke to bring his spare set to 4879 Collette Drive to unlock the car. Collette Drive is five miles from your office. What will you say?

c. One of your friends, Mary Jane, rings at 1:45 to tell you some important plans about the dinner she is giving this evening. Mary Jane talks fast and is hard to interrupt. What will you say or do?

d. The telephone rings at 1:50. It is Richard Van Der Berghe, the production manager. He says, "Put me on to your boss right now. The foreman just knocked one of the men down. He's unconscious. Hurry! This is an emergency!" What will you say or do?

chapter 9

What is your greatest social fear? Wearing the wrong clothes? Probably not. Most people are much less concerned over fashion than they were in the past. Table etiquette? No. The casual mode of entertaining has almost eliminated worry about which fork to use. The one fear nearly everyone has is that of carrying on a conversation with someone who is not a close friend or member of the family. The difficulty arises when we must talk with those we know slightly, or perhaps not at all. You may be fearful, ill at ease, afraid you will be judged by what you say. How can we overcome fear of conversation?

Actually, the secret of success in oral communication is one that has been mentioned before — just being yourself. Part of the strain that causes feelings of uneasiness stems from trying to impress others with a false personality. But if we pretend to be what we are not, we must be constantly on guard. The other person can feel this guardedness. To him, however, it is a defense against him. He judges our attitude as an attack against some weakness in himself of which he is aware. He may defend himself with similar pretenses. This vicious circle can produce nothing but disaster.

DON'T JUST STAND THERE. SAY SOMETHING!

You have already learned that the human element is the most important one in business. If you can get along successfully with others, you will have many of the qualities you need for success. Most of "getting along with others" involves conversation. You must ask others to do things for you; you must express appreciation for a kindness; you must persuade a sales prospect; you must put your customer or caller at ease. All of this involves conversation. The importance of the ability to establish friendly relations with others cannot be overemphasized. Much of your success and happiness will depend on it. Some of the specific areas in your business life where conversational skill will help you are discussed in this chapter.

Improving Personal Relations

You will improve your relations with others if you improve your conversational skills. The secret lies in making your listener feel important. If you talk about yourself and your own accomplishments, you will be considered a bore and a braggart. If you talk sincerely about the accomplishments of your listener, you will have a fascinated audience. Everyone is interested in himself; no one feels he is properly appreciated. For example, the story is told of a man who picked ten names at random from the telephone directory and sent them telegrams with a one-word message, "Congratulations." He signed his name and address to the wire and awaited results. Nine of the ten individuals wrote him warm letters of thanks. All of them stated they had not been aware that anyone knew of their recent accomplishments. Only one person wrote to ask, "Congratulations for what?"

Getting and Giving Information

Another way conversational skill can aid you is in giving and getting information. The teacher, the supervisor, the foreman, and the head clerk must have the ability to talk conversationally to those whom they wish to instruct. Getting information is involved here, too; it is a two-way process. If you can ask pertinent questions, if you can show with a nod or a smile that you understand, you will be using your conversational gifts to advantage. Knowledge can be pursued in several ways, you see. Some get their knowledge from books; some go on to higher and higher levels of education; but one of the most effective ways to learn is by listening to those who know. Intelligent conversation can bring you the twin rewards of interest and information.

Getting Things Done

Conversation is also an aid to getting work done. If you can write conversationally, you will be able to persuade through letters. If you can lecture conversationally, you will be able to get large groups to do your bidding. If you can talk to your staff conversationally, they will be more likely to follow your suggestions. A good conversationalist has a friendly interest in others. This interest is contagious. If you can express it, you will be more likely to receive it in return.

"TEN EASY LESSONS" IN CONVERSATION

It is all very well to say you should be able to converse with others with ease. But such a statement is certain to bring the question "How?" The following paragraphs will tell you how; after that, you need only practice.

You Must Like People

If you don't like people in general, this will be your first task. It is helpful if you realize that *everyone* is insecure to some degree. So if you feel insecure about liking others, you are not the only one who feels as you do. One of the best ways of starting on your "people-liking" campaign is to act "as if" you did. You will be surprised at the reaction of others. You may even begin to like them!

Don't Talk Too Fast

Good conversation should be relaxing, so if you talk too fast, you will find your feeling of tenseness spreading to your listeners. A good way to slow your speaking tempo down is by frequent pauses. Don't be afraid of silence. Constant chatter can be extremely wearing, and an occasional pause will point up what is said afterward. Clear enunciation is important. If you speak with a relaxed manner and with clear enunciation, you will find others listening to you. Your words will take on a new importance from your method of delivery.

Learn To Listen

One of the hardest lessons to learn is that of listening, but it is one of the most important. If you will think of your conversational group as a basketball team, for example, it may help you see the necessity of giving each player a chance at the basket. Throw the conversational ball to others; listen with concentration; show your interest in your face. Learning this one lesson well can make others think you are a gifted conversationalist. You won't need to say much yourself if you can make the conversation of others seem more important. A good listener must keep out all feelings of criticism, too. If you think, "This fellow is stupid," you may show it in your manner and thus defeat all you have been trying to accomplish.

Avoid Flat Negatives

If you want to become extremely unpopular, all you need to do is speak out flatly for the viewpoint opposite to that expressed. When you contradict the speaker, you are guilty of being rude. Even more unpleasant, however, you will usually stop the conversation dead. A mild response is much more effective, even if the speaker has made a foolish remark. "Do you really think so?" may sound spineless to you in such circumstances, but it is better conversational tactics than a flat contradiction. You should eliminate all feelings of competitiveness in conversation. There is no winner or loser; there should be, instead, a feeling of friendliness in a group who are talking together.

Don't Be Backward

If you are excessively shy, you may worry about yourself; yet you may never have considered the effect of your shyness on others. For the "backward" conversationalist makes the others feel too forward. By fading into the background, you create an unnatural atmosphere that makes normal talkativeness seem excessive. Another difficulty with being overly shy is the tendency to appear cold and unfeeling to others. This makes people uncomfortable in your presence. You can see that shyness, which may appear to you to be based on feelings of inferiority, will impress others as being based on selfcenteredness. It is much better for you, and for the group in which you find yourself, to make an effort to be interested in others. If you start with showing interest in what others say, it won't be long before you will be able to say something now and then.

Don't Hold Center Stage Too Long

If you tell a story, make it short. If you explain the way you think about something, hit the highlights only, leaving out the details. You must do this in order to leave space for others to talk, too. If you monopolize the conversation more than a moment or two, you will seem to be seeking the spotlight. This should be avoided, especially by the beginner in the game of conversation.

Watch Your Eye Contact

A very important part of talking in a group is looking at all of the members of the group. This makes them feel included; again, it builds up the other person. If you look at just one person as you speak, the others will feel excluded. It is hard to tear your eyes away from someone who seems to be responding to you; but if you are to converse well, you must make the effort to do so. Try looking first to your left, then to your right, and then straight ahead. As you look in each direction, focus your eyes on some feature of one of the persons in that area. It *is* hard to look listeners directly in the eye; but you can fake this look, and no one will be any the wiser, so long as you look at the person's face.

Keep Your Statements Positive

When you first start playing the game of conversation, you should avoid unpleasant topics, criticism of others, sarcasm, and pessimism. In fact, it would be a good idea to avoid them entirely. It is especially important, however, for the beginner to refrain from derogatory remarks. In the first place, few people admire the person who makes them. In the second place, they destroy the spirit of comradeship that is built up by good conversation.

Make Yourself Talk

The conversational beginner may have some trouble getting started. It is a good idea, therefore, to have some plan ready before you begin. You may decide to compliment one of the speakers; this is always a good approach. Just saying, "How interesting. I had never thought of that," is really praise of the other person's remarks. Or you can say, "Do you really think this will happen?" This is complimentary to the person speaking because it shows you are thinking about what he has said. Another opener for the beginner is a question. The speaker is always glad to have a question because this gives him a chance to talk to a definite point. If someone has been talking about his painting hobby, for example, you might ask, "How long did it take you to learn the technique of oil painting?" A question is another sincere form of flattery. It is an easy way, too, to get started.

Avoid Laying Down the Law

A good conversationalist keeps a tolerant attitude. If you preach, if you hand down judgments, you will not be listened to with pleasure. The secret is to keep an open mind. A conversation should be a free exchange of ideas. No one person should try to dominate it. Avoid, then, giving the final word on any subject. This will permit another person in the group to add what he thinks. This is one way of keeping the conversational ball rolling.

WHAT TO SAY WHEN

Many of us have no difficulty carrying on a conversation after it has been started, but we do have some trouble starting it. Is there any rule to help get that first minute of conversation under way? Think for a moment of the most common subject of casual conversation: the weather. Why do strangers who must say something to each other resort to, "Is it hot enough for you?" The reason is that, banal though such a remark may be, the other person is certain to have something to say on the subject. When starting a conversation, then, it is best to begin with something about which everyone has an opinion.

When you use a question as a conversation starter, be careful to choose one that cannot be answered by a flat *yes* or *no*. Instead of the question asked in the previous paragraph, which would be almost sure to be answered, "Yes," you might say, "How long has it been since we had a good rainstorm?" This is no more sparkling than the previous question, but it does require some thought and a more or less complete sentence in reply. Asking a question that requires a statement in answer will keep the conversation going for a time, at least.

Some questions should be avoided. These include personal questions, particularly those involving health and money. If you are in doubt as to whether a question is too personal, put yourself in the other person's shoes. Would you like someone to ask you why you are limping? Would you like someone to ask how much you paid for the suit you are wearing, or how much your car cost? It is also wise, when starting a conversation, to avoid emotionally tinged subjects, such as religion and politics.

Talking With Superiors

Beginning workers are frequently ill at ease when talking with their superiors. A good tip to remember is a single word: *follow*. In most cases, it is better to let your superior lead the conversation; and you should listen more than you talk. If your boss is thinking about something or is deeply engrossed with his work, don't disturb him except for important matters. On the other hand, if your boss is in a humorous mood, follow his lead — laugh at his jokes. If your boss asks your opinion on something, give it promptly, tactfully, and confidently. If you follow your boss' lead in all oral communication, if you develop the skill to pick up clues to his feelings by paying attention to his facial expression, his gestures, and so on, you will have no trouble. These clues are called nonverbal communication. They will often tell you more about a person's feelings than the words he speaks. One final point: Listen actively when talking with your boss.

Talking With Your Workers

When you are promoted to a supervisory position of any kind, such as foreman, supervisor, chief clerk, or executive assistant, your role is reversed. Now it is important that you put your staff members at ease. Of course, the best way to put another person at ease is to feel relaxed yourself. Even when you have started up the ladder of success, you should still be yourself. You should not try to imitate the speech, the mannerisms, the style of someone higher up the ladder than you are. Remember, too, the importance of a positive attitude toward those whose work you supervise. If you honestly like your staff members, they will know it. Your communication will be easier. In addition to feeling positively toward your staff members, you should tell them you appreciate their good work. Everyone needs recognition; give it when you can.

When it is necessary to make a comment about work that is not good, try the device of getting the worker to talk. Ask questions about his work. If your feeling is positive, if you have given praise when it was deserved, your task of constructive criticism will not be so difficult. Always remember, however, that criticism must be for the action, not for the person himself. You never say, "You are dumb not to follow these simple directions!" Instead, you might say, "Did you understand the directions for making out the sales slips? If you did, I must ask you what happened with these slips that were filled out yesterday." Notice, in the latter example, that the slips become the villain — not the worker. This point is an important one. Avoid direct accusations. Saying *you* when you praise and not saying *you* when you give blame is a skill worth cultivating.

Talking With Complainers

You may have one communication problem you could do nicely without. You may be the kind of person to whom everyone complains.

It is a compliment when others come to you with their troubles, but you'll be tempted to minimize the other person's troubles by saying, "Don't take everything so hard." Such remarks are not appreciated by the complainer, and he now has something else to complain about — your heartless attitude. One technique has proved to be effective. You merely repeat what has been said to you, but in different words. If a co-worker comes to you and says, "I hate that Miss Brown! Just because she's the supervisor doesn't give her the right to treat me like dirt," you answer, "Miss Brown has made you angry." Statements of this kind help the complainer to begin to calm down.

The same technique can be used with your own children or with your brothers or sisters. All the technique amounts to is putting the other person's feelings into words. By doing this, you say to the child or the co-worker that you understand his feelings. You do not condone his violent outburst, but you understand. If you have a rebellious teen-ager in your family, do not preach to him about his expressions of anger. If he says, "I'm quitting school. What good is it — all that book stuff?" You might answer, "Something has happened to upset you."

The reasoning back of the "repeat" method of communicating with complainers is that such a device eliminates the so-human tendency to give advice, to preach, or to defend yourself against an implied criticism. The "repeat" method, on the other hand, seems to draw out some of the negative feelings and makes it possible for the speaker to pause, take stock of the situation, and think it through. The same technique is especially effective when the angry person is aiming his anger at you. The same kind of response is the best one. When a co-worker yells at you when you knock some papers off his desk, "How can you be so clumsy," you answer calmly, "I don't know. I just seem to be awkward." If your husband says, "Can't you ever have meals on time around here," your response is, "I'm not very efficient, am I?" Admitting your own faults to the accuser is almost guaranteed to eliminate the anger in the accuser. The only problem is that you must keep all traces of sarcasm from your voice as you give your calm reply. You see, bad feelings and crossed wires between people don't just happen; they are caused. Without knowing it, you are usually part of the cause. If you can take the giant step of admitting your part of the cause of the trouble, you will help the other person take an equally hard step of admitting his share of the blame. Just take your share of the blame and see what happens.

Creative Listening

In Chapter 8, active listening was discussed in connection with telephone techniques. In face-to-face communication, listening is just as important. In fact, listening now becomes a creative process. To develop the skill of creative listening, just follow these steps: First of all, you should watch the person who is talking; there is much to be learned from his expression. If you mentally put yourself in the place of the speaker, you will gain even more because you will know how he feels.

The second part of creative listening is to organize in your mind what the speaker is saying. If you are being told something that you are to do, it is better if you can take notes. If this is impossible at the moment, however, you can gain considerably from mentally putting the important statements made by the speaker in logical order.

The third factor is interest. You should show that you are interested in what is being told you. An alert expression will follow suit if you *are* alert. This expression will tell your speaker more than words could tell him. If you are interested, however, you will also want to say something to further the statements that are being made. Such responses as, "I see," "That's a good suggestion," and "I'll get right at it," will help the speaker and also help you. In all aspects of conversation, whether of speaking or listening, success depends on cooperation.

FOLLOW-UP ACTIVITIES

1. Conversation can be changed by associating what has been said. Suppose you were in a conversation with several co-workers at a coffee break. Someone has just said he can't stand Mr. McFarland, the supervisor. Realizing this is not the kind of talk that should continue, you decide to change the conversation. What would you say? How would you include the previous speaker so he would not be offended?

2. You have been asked to show a new clerk around the office. As you start back to your floor, you have an opportunity for conversation. You know the new worker is keenly interested in bowling. How would you start a conversation on this subject?

3. You have a friend who is extremely interested in current politics. In order to converse with him, go over one of the newsmagazines for this week. Choose five topics that might interest your friend and learn something about each topic.

4. Humorous stories, particularly if they are brief, add interest and emphasize certain points of view in conversation. Go through some of the latest magazines and collect five stories that you could use in ordinary business conversation.

5. The next time you are talking with a friend, try this experiment: See if you can remain silent exactly half the time. When your friend is talking, you may need to spur him on with such remarks as, "And

then what happened?" See if you are talking too much or too little as a general rule.

6. The way to avoid arguments is to *relax* and wait for the whole story. The next time you are tempted to argue with someone say nothing. Just wait and listen. Write down the result of your experience. Did you accomplish anything? Do you feel this is a helpful solution for you?

7. Choose someone in your place of business who seems aloof and with whom you do not ordinarily talk. Then deliberately start a conversation with him or her. What opening remark did you use? How did the conversation go? If your opening statement was not successful, can you see why? What other statements do you think might have been better?

CASE PROBLEMS

1. Shyness is Selfcenteredness

George Holmes, a young black bookkeeper from a small southern town, has found no friends in the office in the city where he is employed. He has been away from home for three years, but he is still homesick. He is very lonely and does not know whether to stay in the city or go back to his hometown. It seems to him that everyone in the office shuns him; they have never asked him to join in any group activities.

1. Is it possible that George is to blame for the attitude of others toward him?
2. Assume that George has talked to you about his problem. What would you advise him to do in order to break out of his shell? Be specific.

2. Keeping Distance

Irene Mears has worked for the ABC Company for five years and has just been promoted to office manager. Jane Harrison has been working in the same office for just two weeks. Her job is in the stenographic pool. Jane and Irene were in high school together. At noon on the first day after Irene had accepted her new job, Jane asked Irene to go to lunch as her guest to celebrate the promotion.

1. If you were Irene, what would you say to Jane?
2. What would be the best attitude for Jane to assume toward Irene in the future?
3. What would be the effect on the office force if Irene were to accept?
4. What attitude should Irene have toward all her former co-workers — and Jane?

part
four

psychology and the group

chapter 10
personality, psychology, and selling

chapter 11
group psychology and the office

chapter 12
**psychology of relationships:
        his, hers, and theirs**

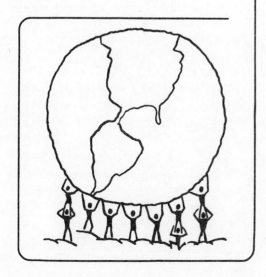

chapter 10

personality, psychology, and selling

The most successful salesmen are those who create a personal relationship with their clients. This statement seems to work even when the selling is done by mail. The selling letter that is friendly, that offers to help fill a need in the reader's mind, that is conversational and persuasive, is a better sales letter than one that is stiff, formal, emphasizes how good the product and company are, and virtually demands that the customer buy. Personality has always been a factor in successful selling, even when the actual salesperson seems to be missing. Displays are arranged, advertising is planned, and packages are designed to appeal to the personality of the buyer.

Why do people behave as they do? In other words, why do people act like people? Many laymen believe they know. They have watched television shows; they have read popular articles; they can tell you all about inferiority complexes, overcompensation, and so on. Most psychologists, however, believe they are still learning about people. They dislike giving the impression that human nature is an open book. Still, research continues at an ever-increasing rate, and more and more of the complexities of people are being understood. We do know some of the factors causing behavior. Some of them are conditioning, or building up habitual responses to certain words, rules, and other stimuli; illnesses, particularly those affecting the nervous system; conflicts, both conscious and unconscious; and the pressures exerted by the different groups that are active in a person's life.

Such knowledge of psychology is helpful in understanding ourselves and others. A beginner in business is making a wise choice when he enrolls in courses in psychology. Although a discussion of general psychology is beyond the scope of this book, some psychological principles and techniques that are particularly useful in business will be mentioned.

BEHAVIOR PRINCIPLES TO HELP YOU

A principle is a rule that is reached through research and thinking. A great many principles have been derived from research in the sciences that deal with the way people behave. Only a few will be given here, but additional help can be found in the list of books given at the end of this text.

"Yes" Works Better Than "No"

If you want to persuade someone to do something, you will be more successful if the discussion (the transaction, the dealing) is positive or pleasant. If your customer likes you as a person, he will be more willing to listen to what you have to say. The best way to keep your dealings with your customers as pleasant as you can is to look for "yes" situations and to watch out for the things that have unpleasant consequences.

Make the Other Fellow Feel Tall. You will not succeed if you build yourself up at the expense of your customer. If you boast about how well you are doing, you will make the other person feel doubtful about his own success. If you treat your customer as if you were on a higher plane than he, you will again make him doubt his own value. For example, if you say, "You may not understand this, but . . . " you will make your customer feel smaller. Another statement that causes your customer to feel small is to say, "It ought to be perfectly obvious that . . . " The way to make your customer feel tall is to ask his advice, to get his point of view, to make him a part of any decision you make. Look for opportunities to give recognition to your customers, to build them up, to make them feel ten feet tall.

Ignore the negative. When your customer complains about your product, your service, or your presentation, let him talk. Remember the section in Chapter 9 about active, creative listening. You may learn something that will help you if you will just listen attentively. As you listen, ignore the part of the conversation that sounds as if it is directed to you personally. Negative statements of this kind are best forgotten. Just concentrate on what you can learn and give the customer the opportunity to say what he has to say.

Reward the positive. When your customer says something positive about your company, or your product, or you, respond warmly. Such a response is rewarding to the other person, and you have learned from previous chapters that rewarded responses are more likely to be repeated than those that are not rewarded. Most of us have trouble, however, in accepting compliments.   Practice saying something warm, something "giving" back to the person who compliments you. Instead of saying, "Oh, it was nothing," show the other person how the compliment made you feel. If you say, "That makes me feel good to hear you say that," you are giving the other person warmth in return for his kind words to you. Accepting compliments warmly *takes* practice, and it is never too late to begin.

Acceptance: the First Step in Change

The hardest lesson to be learned in selling, as in living, is that change can come only through the wishes of the person involved. You may see someone acting foolishly, making mistakes, or taking the wrong turn. You may have made some of the same mistakes yourself, and your natural tendency is to point out to the person the error of his ways. You will learn, however, that you cannot change another person through pointing out his faults.   In fact, such a step usually makes matters worse.   Change comes because the person himself wants to change — and through no other way. The principle involved in changing someone is *acceptance* — acceptance of yourself and acceptance of others.

Accept yourself. What does "Accept yourself" mean? Simply this: Work every day — for just a few minutes at a time — to accept yourself the way you are. Don't dwell on your faults; just accept them. Say to yourself, "Yes, I know you put things off until the last minute. I know you are sarcastic whenever you are afraid someone is going to hurt you.   I know you are afraid to take the first step in getting acquainted with another person. But I like you anyway." Do you know what happens when you accept yourself the way you are? With acceptance comes the ability to change. As long as you defend yourself, make excuses, blame your troubles on others, you will be unable to change. You will have a sort of mental paralysis that literally keeps you from getting rid of any of the qualities within you that are hurting your chances for success and happiness.

When you take that one hard step of acceptance, however, you seem to release a brake inside of you. No longer will you be driving yourself with your brakes on. You will be free from the drag of that nonacceptance brake. With that brake released, you will find it easier to change. Don't forget, though, that accepting yourself is not easy. It is, in fact, terribly hard. Don't try to build self-acceptance too quickly. Just work at it for a few minutes at a time. One psychologist has mentioned five minutes as the goal you should set. For five minutes at a time, look at yourself square-ly. Say, "Yes, that's the way I am. But I'm still O. K."

Accept others. The second step in acceptance seems to follow the first one naturally. After you have learned to accept yourself, you can begin to accept others. When you have learned to look squarely at your own faults, without criticism, you can look at the shortcomings of others without trying to change them. The "brake release" effect seems to work with others just as well as it does with you. When you can look at your bullying customer and say, "He is angry with me, but it may be caused by something else. Even though he is saying things that are unkind, he is a good guy underneath," you will release your customer's brake. Another psychologist has written a book called *You Are Not the Target*. This book says that most of the cruel things said to others are not really directed at them. The "picked on" person may have just been around when the speak-er defended himself or herself by lashing out at the closest person. When *you do not defend yourself* but merely accept the person for what he is, your attitude will tell that other person that you are still his friend. When he feels your accepting attitude, in spite of what he has said or done, he will be able to release the brake that is holding him back. He will be able to change.

SOME HELPFUL TECHNIQUES

A technique is a small part of an activity; it may be in line with a certain principle. If we wish to succeed in business, we will develop good psychological techniques.

Techniques in Selling

You have been using techniques in your work and in your play all through your life. You have learned that some techniques are effective and that some are not. At the age of three or four, you may have tried the tech-nique of lying on the floor and screaming to get your own way. You may have discovered, too, that this didn't work too well at nine or ten. In this same way, you may have tried and discarded many techniques of behavior. If you should decide to try for a career in selling, you should sharpen up some techniques you now use and perhaps become familiar with some en-tirely new ones.

Develop a friendly attitude. A friendly personality is an asset any-where; in sales work a friendly attitude is essential. If you were born with a liking for people, you should do well in selling. If strangers make you hide in your shell, don't give up. Some of the greatest salesmen of all time achieved their status through long, hard hours of working and improving. The technique of courtesy is a good place to begin working on creating a friendly personality. Sometimes it is easier to learn a form, a technique of manners, than it is to *feel* friendly. Memorizing rules like standing when a woman enters a room (applying to men) or when an older woman enters (applying to both men and women) is not difficult. After you have followed the rules for awhile, you will actually *feel* more friendly.

The following illustrates how a friendly attitude pays. One afternoon when the weather was dark and gloomy and business was bad, a drab little woman, modestly dressed, came into a furniture store. One of the older salesmen said, "Don't spend any time with her. She'll look and look and never buy anything." But one of the younger salesmen stepped forward with a friendly greeting. He showed the woman furniture for the rest of the afternoon. Then, as the older salesman had predicted, she left without buying anything. A few weeks later, however, the young man was pleased and surprised when he was asked to help decorate the new mansion of the Andrew Carnegies. The woman whom the salesman had helped so patiently was Mrs. Andrew Carnegie.

Know your merchandise. The young man in the foregoing story had a second valuable technique. He knew his merchandise and could show it intelligently. If you are to persuade, you must be able to inspire confidence. You will inspire confidence in others if you have confidence in yourself. To develop self-confidence you must build it on a solid foundation of knowledge. Learn everything you can about the merchan-dise you sell. If you are working in a dress department, you can build assurance by studying the fashion magazines. If you are selling sporting goods, read the sports news and sports magazines.

Be enthusiastic about your merchandise. Enthusiasm is contagious. Know the "talking points" of everything you sell. The ability to answer objections, to supply necessary details, to give information — and all with the point of view of the customer's needs — is a skill required by those who would succeed in the career of selling.

Help your customer feel important. An important technique in selling is learning how to play second fiddle. This may seem an odd way to make a sale, yet it is an effective one. Your customer is the one who must be built up. His self-esteem should grow during the selling conver-sation. If you watch successful salespeople, you will notice their easy, relaxed manner. This manner sets the stage; it provides the kind of atmosphere needed in selling. If this atmosphere is friendly, if the customer feels important, and if the salesman can explain the product and answer questions intelligently and courteously, the customer will feel free to choose but will be much more likely to choose in favor of the salesman. If the atmosphere is friendly, the salesperson will present facts in a nonargumentative style; yet he will still be able to meet objections accurately and honestly.

The biggest reason for making the customer feel important is the help it will give you when you deal with the "difficult" customer. Most customers, of course, will be pleasant and courteous; but many, in the frenzied rush that accompanies shopping, show dispositions that require the use of tact to insure smooth going. It takes practice to serve those who are irritable, inconsiderate, talkative, or snobbish. It requires skill to satisfy the suspicious type of buyer or the close buyer. It calls for patience to deal with the "smart-aleck" customer. It may take pressure to close a sale for a timid buyer. Yet all these tasks will be easier if you have given the customer a feeling of importance and worth.

Study the art of selling. How can you best learn the art of judging people? Formulas may be learned, but their success in your case will depend on you — on your own personality — and on the effect of your personality on the customer. If you have the native qualities this work demands, a friendly spirit, an innate enthusiasm, a charm of manner, an attractive appearance, a quick intelligence, you should by all means take courses that will prepare you for selling.

No matter how much you learn in school, however, you will find that selling requires that you learn from experience. In your grandfather's day they called it learning from the "school of hard knocks." But, whatever you call it, experience will help you learn what to do and what not to do by trial and error. Eventually, you will discover the traits and attitudes that are so vital in dealing with the public.

ETHICS AND VALUES

No matter how skillful you are in the art of selling, how deep is your knowledge of the psychology of changing others, you will need still other qualities in order to help build up the image of your company. If a business enterprise is to survive today, it must be served by workers who build, not destroy; who believe in service to customers and the community; who have, in short, a sense of ethics and values. Some of the qualities you will need are the following: adaptability to change, cooperation and teamwork, generosity of spirit, initiative, and integrity.

Ability to Change

You are adaptable to change when you are able to adjust, to alter, to fit into or respond to changing conditions. Any kind of work in business requires this trait, but it is particularly needed in selling. Your first adaptation must be to your firm. You may have worn sports clothes most of your life, yet you must change willingly to tailored suits and even hats if your firm wishes it. You will adapt yourself, too, to your merchandise and develop an enthusiastic appreciation for what you have to sell.

Second, you will adapt yourself to your customer. You may be quick and alert in everything you do or say; yet you must talk slowly and adjust to long pauses if you wish to sell to someone who thinks, speaks, and reacts slowly. You will be tolerant of mistaken ideas, and you will refrain from criticism. One adjustment you will be sure to find necessary is that of talking and dealing with people much older than you. If you treat older customers with courtesy and respect, you will be successful.

A third adjustment must be made to changes in the business world. You will serve your firm best if you are constantly alert to changing routines, to changing conditions of the times, to the growth and progress of your business. Even the moods of your customers and the weather conditions may require that you demonstrate your ability to adjust. If you are set in your ways, if you cling obstinately to procedures and methods of the past, you will have failed to develop and practice adaptability. Furthermore, you will be less effective in serving your firm.

Cooperation and Teamwork

In this age of competition the ability to cooperate, or work smoothly with others, is in danger of becoming a lost art. But cooperation is like a bank account. It is an investment that may not pay immediate dividends. Yet, if deposits are made, the dividends will eventually become both frequent and of a high rate. Like a bank account, too, cooperation may demand the sacrifice of immediate conveniences for later reward.

You must earn the reputation for cooperation. You will earn it by thinking, not of your immediate comfort, but of the ultimate welfare of your firm and your customer. Cooperation is actually an expression of self-interest and unselfishness. It demands that you adjust your immediate pleasure to the best interests of others. Yet the reward for immediate sacrifices is a reputation for cooperation which will contribute to your success.

Cooperation may be a simple little act of sharing your materials or equipment with a co-worker. It may mean covering the territory of another salesman who is unable to do it himself. It may mean willingness to go out of your way to help a customer or co-worker. It may mean holding your tongue when you want to disagree, being a good sport when you have lost a sale, or showing tolerance in listening to the ideas of others when your own ideas seem superior.

If you are cooperative, you can still express your ideas; you should still make suggestions when you feel they should be made. You must use your good judgment in deciding when you should speak and when you should keep silent. In some cases you should protest, but you should also listen to the ideas of your superiors and your customers. If a decision is made and your ideas have been overruled, you must abide by the decision in a cheerful manner. There are times when a frank discussion may be required, but there are also times for cooperative submission to your firm or your customer.

Sometimes you may have to ask a subordinate employee to assume some of your responsibilities, but you should never take advantage of another or shirk your own work. When you do ask for help, you should speak well of the person who helps you. If you are cooperative, you will not place another worker at a disadvantage by calling attention to his faults or errors unless you are his superior and your work requires you to be critical. Even if such criticism is part of your work, you will show more cooperation if you point out inefficiencies in an impersonal way.

Teamwork in a business is founded on cooperation. Unless every member of the force practices it, there is a lack of unity of purpose; and the final results are likely to be ruinous. As a beginning worker, you will first cooperate by being loyal to the business that employs you. You will demonstrate your loyalty by following the suggestions and directions of your supervisor willingly and enthusiastically. You will abide by their decisions because they are made with the welfare of the entire organization in mind.

In every minute of your business life you will find an occasion when you are expected to cooperate. These occasions include keeping your office and belongings neat and tidy, assuming additional duties and assignments without complaint, and so forth. They include working overtime when there is a need and offering your services even when you are not obligated to do so. You will surrender your own ideas if they do not fit in with the policy of the organization. You will tell others of devices that may help them, showing unselfishness of action whenever you can. You will pass on your ideas and the results of your own experiences; you will listen when another tries to help you by giving his ideas and the results of his experiences. You will work harmoniously with others to advance the interests of the organization.

Another way of cooperating is by being on time for appointments. This shows your customer that you respect his time and his interests. You should also observe cheerfully all of the rules of the firm and work cheerfully with the fellow employee who has been promoted. You will go out of your way to help those who have not yet adjusted to their work. Keeping your reports up to date and turning them in on time is one simple but very effective way of cooperating that is greatly appreciated by sales managers.

Cooperate in maintaining good human relations. Do not criticize the business that employs you, your superiors, or your co-workers. If you possess business information that should be kept secret, you will not divulge it. You will never pass the buck when things go wrong, nor will you try to "get by" when heavy assignments are made. You will show consideration for others by feeling no resentment when you are called on to do extra work caused by the error of another worker. But you will try not to create extra work because of your own errors. You can see that the trait of cooperation covers a lot of territory.

Generosity of Spirit

Generosity is defined as liberality in spirit or act. It is as necessary a trait in the business world as it is in life generally. Business is not mechanized to the extent of excluding the personal element. On the contrary, business affairs are directed and influenced by the individual personalities of workers and superiors. As with the trait of cooperation, you will find many opportunities for showing a generous, unselfish spirit. When you acknowledge the ability of others, when you help other workers, when you help a new employee, when you lend your personal possessions to aid the work of another, or when you share office equipment, you will be demonstrating the trait of generosity.

Generosity is shown when you contribute willingly to worthy organizations endorsed by your business. You will add your mite to a joint office gift, not just for conformity's sake, but because of your unselfish desire to give. You will give a customer all the time and the attention he requires. You will give other employees the gift of being pleasant, one of the most welcome you have in your power to give. It doesn't hurt one's image as an above-the-crowd worker.

Generosity is best shown by overlooking the shortcomings of others and by praising others when praise is merited. Do not begrudge the time you give to your job; you are investing with the hope of future returns, but this thought should not be uppermost in your mind. You will show the trait of generosity when you refuse to listen to ridicule or gossip regarding your employer or your fellow workers. In the first place, this is a dangerous pastime. Repeated gossip (and it is sure to be repeated) will react most unfavorably against you. In the second place, gossip is unkind, ungenerous, and unworthy of the *best you.*

Initiative

Initiative has been discussed previously as a part of one of the blocks in your pyramid to success. That block was made up of "Taking Initiative and Being Resourceful." Initiative is so important in successful selling, however, that further discussion of the quality is given here.

Initiative means the energy or aptitude displayed in the action that tends to develop new fields; self-reliance; originality; enterprise; resourcefulness. You can hardly read such a definition without thinking of the selling field. The successful salesperson *must* have initiative. He must think of new methods of reaching his customers; he must sometimes seek out new customers; he must stress the new features of his merchandise. Initiative is a central trait in selling, but it is useful in all business jobs. When you are a beginner in an office, you do not find many important situations calling for the use of initiative. The first job calls for following orders implicitly, doing what you are told to do without question. In time, though, you will grow through experience and practice. You will then be given larger responsibilities and demands that call for independent thinking and action.

When to use initiative, as well as how much to use, calls for the use of your own good judgment. Again, put yourself in your employer's place. If you were he, how would you like your employee to proceed? The new salesman should not rearrange displays so they will look more attractive. This is showing too much initiative. On the other hand, failure to act in a crisis when there appears to be no precedent may be even worse. For instance, if a customer is upset because he received different merchandise than he ordered, the salesman or other employee should certainly show he is concerned. He should say that something will be done about the situation whether he had been previously instructed to do so or not.

You will be showing initiative by learning all you can about the business and your place in it. Initiative is also shown when you find additional tasks to do when your assigned work is finished, by taking courses to prepare yourself for promotion, and by going ahead with work that must be done even though it has not been definitely assigned to you. Initiative is displayed also by learning how to think and act swiftly in emergencies, by doing more than you are told to do. If new and unusual situations arise, aside from your regular routine, you should handle them.

You will show initiative if you are able to take another employee's place without detailed instruction. You should be able to apply information received in one situation to a similar situation. You will plan and carry out new duties with a minimum of help from others. You will attempt constructive creative work.

Learn to handle all telephone calls adeptly and to arrange conferences to the satisfaction of both or all persons concerned. Experience will enable you to determine whether your employer should be called at his home or at his club if an important customer appears unexpectedly.

If you are alert, original, and determined to see opportunity and to make the most of it, you will learn to take advantage of situations by a display of initiative. The person who is enthusiastic about putting new ideas into effect does not say, "It can't be done." Nor does he bother superior officers with trifling matters or wait to be told what to do. Nor will he need to have work laid out for him or to be told repeatedly how to perform a task. Do not let new and unfamiliar situations upset you. Through the use of initiative, let them be stepping-stones to greater efficiency.

Integrity

Integrity means straightforwardness and fairness of conduct and speech; it means honesty and truthfulness. Integrity is a quality you must have if you are to succeed in business. In selling, for example, you must be trustworthy; your total selling situation demands that you be believed. Business and personal friends will usually give you a second chance if you fail in most qualities; they are most unwilling to do this after you have proved to be dishonest.

Businessmen and women are expected to keep their word. When you make a promise, it must be fulfilled. If you make an error, you must accept the responsibility. Because you are honest, you will never shift the blame for your errors on an innocent person; neither will you accept credit or praise for something you have not done. Instead, you will indicate the person who should receive the credit.

When you are called upon to state your opinions, you should do so frankly and honestly. You need not go out of your way to be tactless, to give opinions you know are painful to your listener, especially on controversial subjects like politics or religion. If you are asked, reply correctly and honestly, but apologize quietly if another's statement is being contradicted. If you should be questioned about another's dishonesty, you must give honest testimony. In the matter of expense accounts, handling money, and keeping records, show by your honesty that you are worthy of responsibility. You must work an honest day for a day's pay. Your working hours do not belong to you. Give your best to your job, not just your share.

It is disturbing to have to speak against someone, but when questions of fact are referred to you, do not try to deceive by understatement, by exaggeration, or by omission. You should never lie to avoid an unpleasant situation; neither should you try to smooth things over with half truths. Do not misappropriate funds by direct theft, by petty trickery, or with the intention of paying the money back. Honesty means you will never steal time, money, office materials, or another's ideas.

FOLLOW-UP ACTIVITIES

1. If you are selling shirts, you suggest the purchase of matching ties to your customer. If you are selling shoes, you suggest hosiery. What suggestions would you offer to customers who purchased:
   gloves   a toothbrush   a bar of soap   a sweater
2. How would you spend your time while waiting for customers:
   in a dress shop   in a bookstore   in a drugstore
3. In order to get along with all sorts of customers, you will need intelligence and tact. What would you say:

   (a) To an angry customer who says, "I thought you said this material was silk. It's marked synthetic blend." (You had made a careless mistake in stating facts.)
   (b) To a trying customer to whom you have shown the entire stock. She finally says, "I want to see the model on display in size 42." (It has an accordion pleated skirt and would be most unbecoming on the short, stout lady.)
   (c) To a customer who runs a large account who says, "I've worn these gloves only once, and look at the seams!" (You know that it took more than one wearing to get the gloves that color!)

4. What will determine your selection when the customer says, "I want to see a hat"?
5. What qualifications do you possess that you think will be needed in a selling position?
6. What disagreeable personality traits may cause a salesperson's discharge? Have you ever shown any evidences of possessing any of these traits?

CASE PROBLEMS

1. Job or Career?

Laura Montefiero is a salesclerk in a dress department. All the sales force in the store is paid a weekly salary. No commission is paid for the amount of goods sold.

Laura is very industrious and is usually the first to greet a customer. After serving her customers, Laura returns the dresses to their racks. She then keeps busy arranging merchandise or studying dresses that have been recently put in stock. She is always pleasant and courteous.

Carla Salizar, who works with her, tells Laura she is foolish to work so hard when she receives no extra pay. Laura knows that Carla's attitude is characteristic of the feeling of many of the members of the sales force.

1. Is it profitable for Laura to work as she does?
2. Do you feel that Laura may be rewarded for her work attitudes?

3. If Laura does not receive a promotion, can you think of any advantages her attitude would have?
4. Why do you think the other clerks feel as they do about their work?
5. If you were in charge of Laura's department, how would you handle this situation of indifference on the part of some of the sales personnel?

2. Is the Customer Always Right?

An irate customer enters a shop with a dress that she has purchased from a salesgirl who said the dress would not fade or shrink when washed. The customer has the dress and it is badly faded. The customer proceeds to vent all her anger on Dolores Gallegos, who is taking the other girl's place that day.

1. Is this situation a common happening?
2. If you were Dolores, what would you say to the customer? Would you try to handle the situation yourself? Why or why not?
3. Was the customer justified in her complaint?
4. If you had been the customer, how would you have handled this situation?

3. Hard, Not Heartless

Ida Meyerhoffer is feeling low. She has been at work only a week, and today Mr. Johnson, the floorwalker, spoke to her sharply because she spent half an hour showing dresses to a fussy customer who walked out without making a purchase. Ida is hanging the dresses back on the racks and trying very hard not to show how dark her world has grown because she knows the store is no place for the display of emotions. Mrs. Walton, looking across the store, notices Ida and remembers how she felt the first time she had been reprimanded. She decides to say something to Ida to help her to feel better.

1. How might Mrs. Walton help Ida over this episode?
2. Why does Mr. Johnson speak to his sales personnel as he does?
3. Should Mrs. Walton tell Ida not to worry about Mr. Johnson's reprimands?
4. What constructive suggestions could Mrs. Walton make?

4. Room at the Top?

Tad Ochi has obtained a subordinate position in an advertising firm. In high school Tad capably handled all the advertising copy for the various school publications. He feels, therefore, that his experience fits him for doing creative work, and he is not interested in the tasks assigned to him. He considers them to be prosaic, routine duties. The manager knows that because Tad cannot do the type of work he wants to do, he often neglects to do well the work he has to do. Tad's negligence also causes more work for others in the office. They, in turn, complain to the manager. When Tad is called to the manager for questioning, he explains that he does not like his present tasks and tells of his ambition. The manager does not seem to be impressed with his reasoning.

1. What is your opinion of Tad's attitude toward his work?
2. If you were the manager, what would you say to Tad?
3. Why did Tad's ambition fail to impress the manager?
4. Have you observed this attitude toward starting at the bottom in other lines of work? Explain.
5. Why was Tad's attitude not fair to the other employees?

5. Expense Accounts

Sam Cohen and Harry Dahl are salesmen for the Zimmerman Company. Their territories are adjoining, and sometimes it is possible for them to spend occasional weekends together in a middle-sized city. To have this meeting, it is necessary for Harry to go twenty miles out of his way. He reasons that the inconvenience caused him is compensated for by his not having to remain in a small town over the weekend. He feels, however, that the extra traveling expenses should be borne by himself. Sam tells him that he is a fool, that the company should pay all of his traveling expenses.

1. If you were Harry, would you charge such trips to your expense account? Why or why not?
2. What are the rules for charging expenses to the company?
3. What regulations does the federal government have on the matter of expense accounts?

chapter 11

group psychology and the office

In every office there are at least two people, and two people make a group. If you work, or plan to work in an office, you must learn as much as you can about the psychology of groups, what makes *them* tick. How does our group behavior differ from our individual behavior? Why is it so important? Group behavior is important because whatever you do affects the way someone else in your group feels. When your actions make another person feel positively toward you and toward the group, he is helped to do a more effective job. When your actions cause friction and bad feeling in one of the group members, he or she will be held back from doing his best work. Thus, your actions will diminish the effectiveness of your group. The problem, then, is to work on yourself, to create the kind of person who brings out the best in people in the group, not one who contributes to the problem that so often exists when people work closely together.

Even if you do not contribute to the problem of anyone else in your group, do you do anything to *help* the problem employee, the group member who drives everyone up the wall with his insecurities, his negativism, his closed mind? There are two things you can do to help the "odd one" in your group. First, you can tell about some problem you had when you first joined the group. You can go to the difficult group member and tell what a hard time you had in adjusting to so many different personalities. You can tell how inferior you felt, when everyone else seemed to be so much more competent than you. This is one sure way to help the difficult group member open up to you, to tell you some of his troubles in the group and thus make them less troublesome. The second thing you can do is comment favorably on something the other person has said or done in the group, something that made the work go more smoothly, that helped get things done. If you do this, you will be working to make the group a real one, because real groups are made up of real people. By showing another person the real you, you help that person become more real himself.

The theory behind changing a group so that it works better is called *shaping*. If you can get some of your office friends to help you shape the difficult group member, you can accomplish some remarkable results. Shaping means that you pay no attention to the irritating things the group member does; but you reward or praise him for the things he does and says that are helpful. Most of the difficulties people have when they become a part of a group are caused by lack of confidence. Praise is a good confidence builder.

The first step, though, is to be a real person yourself. You must be willing to feel real feelings. If someone says something to you that makes you feel happy, tell him so. Say, "That makes me feel wonderful." If someone says something to you that hurts you, you will be a real person if you can say, "I wish you wouldn't tease me about my weight. It is something I am a little too sensitive about." If you say something like this in a straightforward manner, without whining or accusing, you will show the other person a part of the real you. You will remove part of your mask; and, in most cases, the other person will respond by removing part of his mask, too. Of course, such real statements are hard to make. It is much easier to sulk, to go away, to refuse to talk to the other person. But these nonreal actions do nothing but make matters worse between you and the other person. Every bad relationship in a group hurts the group as a whole and makes it less effective in getting things done.

One thing about shaping and being real is that you must proceed indirectly. You cannot call all of your fellow office workers together and say, "Look. Let's all be real. Let's all try to accept one another." When you do something like this, the rest of the group will wonder what you are after. People do not like to be forced to do things — especially if they are for their own good. Shaping and being real work best when both of these techniques begin with you. When you are more real every day, that realness becomes contagious. Some of your fellow workers will catch realness from you. Someone else will catch realness from your fellow workers. In an organization where everyone is real, where no one needs to wear a mask to cover his or her real self, work no longer seems like work. Going to work then becomes a joyful activity.

YOUR POSITION ON THE TEAM

Think of yourself as playing a certain position on your office team. You may be keeping records. If you are, make sure that these records are accurate and thoroughly checked. If you are a shipping clerk, see that your position is filled perfectly; see that there is no slipup in your part of the team play. If you write the first draft of a report, check the information that goes into the report. Do your very best to see that the report is written as well as you can do it. But remember, like the player in a football game who throws a forward pass, you pass your part of the report to the person, perhaps your boss, who is going to write or dictate the final draft. Your boss will make the touchdown. You will be the team member who makes it possible for the boss to catch the ball and carry it over the line. You can see why the office worker *must* understand why people behave as they do. Facts and figures may be supplied by machines, but people still make the office go — or break down. One person in a large office can create enough friction to make it break down, too. You must make sure that *you* are not a behavior problem, but you must also learn to understand others when they are.

The successful office worker, first of all, uses his head. He follows the motto THINK. He does not let his feelings, his emotions, tell him what to do. But even the best of us cannot hope to be 100 percent objective — even part of the time. There is a good possibility that we do things, and say things, for an unconscious reason. The thing we must do is be on our guard for this possibility. If we are promoted to a new and difficult job, for example, we may find ourselves in a state of panic. If you should find yourself in this position, don't look for sensible reasons for your fears. They may be caused by an excessive desire to be perfect. Thus, you may be afraid of failure and not afraid of the job. The cure for your panic may lie in telling yourself that mistakes will almost surely occur at first. The expected, you see, is not so frightening as the unexpected, and you may find your fears disappearing.

An understanding of the possible reasons for behavior will keep you from hasty judgments of others. If the girl at the desk next to yours takes offense at everything you say to her, don't stop speaking altogether. It may be that your co-worker is extremely insecure. She may want to succeed just as much as you do, but she may feel inferior to the other workers. She may have no idea how to seek help for her real or imagined inadequacies. Try reassuring her now and then.

Sometimes unattractive personality traits cover up a tendency that is their exact opposite. Thus, the braggart may be doubtful of his worth; the girl who laughs too much may actually be shy; the excessively sweet girl may be covering up a real dislike of people.

You have read in Part 1 of this volume about the basic needs that are common to all of us. It will help you to understand your co-workers and your supervisors if you review what you have read. Everyone has these same needs. Your employer may seem to be the ultimate in success, yet he may feel completely unappreciated. In fact, the higher you climb the ladder of success, the more lonely you may become. It will help you and your firm if you take the initiative in the friendly greeting, the approving word. No one gets enough appreciation. If you are able to show your appreciation of others, you can make a good start in building a better psychological climate around you.

If you are committed to a greater understanding of others, of their quirks and foibles, the next step is to keep from being a behavior problem yourself. It is better to be positive, to be cheerful. Perhaps you have made great strides in eliminating the negative side of your personality. You have learned about clothes, about grooming, about speaking. Now, let's talk about *working*. Work in an office is made up of two factors: service with a smile and good work habits.

Service With a Smile

The office is the service hub of the company wheel. Everything that is done in the office is of service to some other department. Records are kept, papers are filed, correspondence is carried on, plans are made, all to serve the company as a whole. Any worker in an office, then, must be service conscious. He must be willing to do all in his power to make the company run smoothly. To fit into an office, you must be willing to serve. The office is no place for the temperamental person.

To recognize the importance of service in an office, imagine that you are a member of a "bucket brigade" engaged in putting out a fire. A long line of people pass the buckets along the line from the stream at one end to the fire at the other. Suppose you drop the bucket when it gets to you? What will happen to the group effort? This is how important each member of the office group can be. To carry your share of the office work, you must: (1) be willing to work, (2) be able to communicate, (3) know how to organize, and (4) be aware.

Be willing to work. It may seem redundant to explain that an office worker must be willing to work. But many office workers seem to spend their time in other ways. There are a number of clues to tell your supervisor or employer how willing a worker you are. You willingly perform the task that is assigned to you. After the assignment has been made, you arrange your duties so that the work is completed on time. Because mistakes can be as serious as dropping the bucket when you are putting out a fire, you take great pains to be accurate. You proofread *every word* you type; you verify every number that comes your way; you look up needed information in the files or in reference books. You take pride in your craftsmanship; the finished product has a careful, painstaking look.

Be able to communicate. Because office work is almost synonymous with paper work, the office worker must be precise in all written communication. This may mean a brushup on grammar and punctuation. Your use of these tools will "peg" you, as far as education goes. There are many inexpensive paperbacks to help you. If you have a little trouble with verbs and adverbs, for example, do some studying on your own. You communicate with arithmetic, too, so be sure that yours can be trusted. Always double check discounts and extensions, even when using calculators and adding machines. A reputation for accuracy in English and arithmetic is worth working for.

Know how to organize. You may have heard of Parkinson's Laws, one of which states that work expands so as to fill the time available for its completion. You know, yourself, that if you are invited to an exciting party and have just 30 minutes to finish up a task, you'll get it done in 30 minutes. If you have three hours in a lazy afternoon, somehow that same task will take three hours to finish. Knowing how to organize is the key to licking Parkinson's Law. It consists of nine steps. Let's take them in order. Say you have a big, difficult job to do. Here's how you go about it:

1. Get going right now. Don't wait until you can do a good job. Get started, good job or not, right now.
2. Give yourself a mental reward after your first hour of work. Say, "Hey, that's not bad." You know that praise is the best motivator there is; why not use it to motivate yourself? But keep it strictly to yourself.
3. Try being positive about the job for 10 or 15 minutes at first. Later, you can build your positive mental attitude to 20 minutes, then 30 minutes. Before long you will have developed a positive attitude toward the entire difficult task. Somehow, a positive attitude makes the job go faster and better.
4. Organization doesn't come naturally to most of us. We have to work at it. If you are the creative type, you will have to work harder. Have an exact place for everything with which you work, and put it back in that place as soon as you are finished with it. One trick is to have a cabinet with deep drawers into which you can put *all* of the papers, tools, references, notes, and so on that belong to one job. When you must go on to Job 2, put all of the materials needed for Job 1 in that deep drawer. When you are ready to return to Job 1, everything will be in one place.
5. Don't put off that hard job until a better day comes along. You may think that today is too hectic to start a big, important job; you'll put it off until tomorrow when things will be better. But tomorrow will not be better; it will be worse. You can play a trick on yourself by saying, "I won't do very much on this hard job today; I'll just get started." Somehow, the momentum builds up from getting started, and you may get a big chunk of the job finished the first day.
6. Don't be a pencil sharpener. The pencil sharpener is the one who wants everything to be perfect before he starts to work. The temperature must be just right. The light must be adjusted several times. You are thirsty and decide to get a drink of water. While you are up, you sharpen six or seven pencils so you won't have to bother sharpening them while you are working.

But you needn't have bothered. You will never get to work. There will always be something left to do so that the working environment will be perfect. Instead of being a pencil sharpener, start with a stubby pencil. Never mind the temperature or the light. Concentrate on your work and you won't notice them. Get a drink of water as a reward for your first 30 minutes of effort. Don't get ready. Get at it!

7. Don't do all the small, easy jobs and get them out of the way and then tackle the big job. You know what happens. By the time you get those small, easy jobs done you're tired — and it's time for your coffee break. Let the easy jobs go. Do the hard job first. Having it off your mind will release all kinds of untapped energy, and you'll be able to polish off those easy jobs in half the time.

8. Don't waste time making decisions over trifles. Learn to make decisions quickly. If the question is a minor one, flip a coin. Indecision is actually only a bad habit; yet it slows down the "getting things done" potential in all of us beyond belief. Elbert Hubbard wrote: "An executive is a man who makes lots of decisions — and some of them are right." By actual count, you make more right decisions if you make more decisions. Follow your hunches. They are actually signals from your unconscious mind. Trust them — and make up your mind fast.

9. Don't leave your workday to chance. *Plan* each day the night before. If you are the creative, disorganized type, you had better write down your plan. The mere act of writing something down is the first step toward doing it. Also, writing your plan for the next day just before you go to sleep gets your unconscious mind to help you. The next day you'll be ready to get at it. Don't think of the difficulties as you plan — how hard the job is, how tired you are, how little you are appreciated. This kind of thinking gets your unconscious mind on *their* side — working against you. Think instead about how you are going to do it; visualize yourself doing it.

Be aware. Awareness is a quality that is especially important when you work in groups. It means that you are aware of the feelings and personalities of the people who work with you. You know which areas can be discussed with your co-workers and which should be left alone. You know when your fellow workers would rather not be talked with and when they would welcome an invitation to lunch. If you are aware of others, you will spend more of your time looking out instead of in. Awareness grows as you become less self-centered. Awareness has another side, as well. Be aware of the flow of authority in the firm and particularly in the office in which you work. This means that you will "go through channels." You will take your questions and problems to your immediate superior; he takes them to his boss, and this boss takes his problems to *his* boss. If you should "go over the head" of your superior, you not only fail to show respect for his position, but you put him in a bad light. You should study the organization chart of the firm, which lists the officers of the company, the heads of departments, supervisors, and so on. You will then know how the whole organization works; you will also have a clearer picture of your position. You will know the path downward and upward of directions, information, suggestions, and grievances. It will also show you where your work ultimately goes, a knowledge that adds to your feeling of worth.

Awareness also means that you will become familiar with the flow of business papers utilized by your firm. You will know the purpose and the processing routine of these papers. It means you will become acquainted with your firm's policies and regulations. These can usually be found in office manuals or printed brochures about the company. Because you have respect for your firm, you know what information is to be discussed and where and with whom to discuss it. You will keep confidential information inviolate and share facts only with those employees who share responsibility for them.

Good Work Habits

If you have never worked or if you have never put in a full day's work for a day's pay, you will have little conception of what this means. Any job contains a certain amount of routine work, and most of this work is concentrated in the beginning levels. The way to emerge the victor over drudgery is to make your habits work for you. Work habits, like other habits, are built up day by day. It will pay you to form good work habits from the very beginning of your first job. The work habits you should form are habits of time, and habits of efficiency.

Time. When you work, you are paid for your time and the way you spend it. In business, of course, time is money; many of the good work habits you will need involve the proper use of time. For example, you will arrive at work on time — or even a few minutes early — every day. This habit cannot be overstressed. It is important because it shows others that you value your job, but the greatest value in arriving on time is its effect on you. This is best illustrated by what happens when you are late for work. Everything you do becomes shaded by the fact that you were late. You are behind with your work, so you hurry to catch up; because you hurry, you make mistakes; making mistakes causes you to become flustered, so you hurry faster. This circle of hurry and errors goes on all day. On the other hand, if you come to work early, you are relaxed when you start your first task. Relaxation helps you work rapidly and accurately. Working in this way brings you a feeling of satisfaction, and this feeling helps you with the next task at hand. The result is a circle of excellence that works for you all day.

Leaving early should be avoided. Clock watchers seldom get promoted, you know; and the person who starts to clear his desk *before* the

closing hour is advertising his clock-watching habits. Time that belongs
to the company is involved if you leave early for return late from lunch
and coffee breaks, or if you spend extra time talking in the washroom.
Time is involved in the rules that govern smoking in your office. Whatever the rule may be, whether smoking is permitted at the desks or only
in the lounges, you must abide by and not exploit the rule.

Efficiency. One of the most important work habits an office worker
can possess is efficiency. This means that, first of all, your desk is arranged
neatly. Study examples of neat, efficient layouts for desks. Notice how
supplies should be arranged for quick and easy handling. A neatly arranged
desk will make *you* more *efficient*. You will be ready to plan and organize
materials, supplies, and the work itself so that tasks can be completed as
rapidly and as accurately as possible. Efficiency also involves discovering
the work standards in your office and working hard to meet them. One
difference between actual office work and school assignments will soon
become apparent: Perfection is always desirable but sometimes must
give way to practicality. For instance, if a letter is not centered, you might
have to mail it anyway, because time and supplies might be more important than perfection. In other cases, such as a letter to an important client,
you will need to rewrite a letter that is improperly placed on the page.
Being efficient involves judging the relative values of tasks when measured
in terms of time, energy, and supplies. These judgments will vary, of
course, according to the needs of your particular firm.

"Don'ts" for the Office

Do you irritate your co-workers? If you have any of the following
negative habits, you probably do. Just as there are habits and techniques
you should cultivate for success in office work, so there are habits that
you should avoid. Unfortunately, most of these unwelcome habits never
slip into our awareness. We notice them in others, but we fail to recognize
that we may be guilty, too. Most of the following objectionable habits
come under the heading of bad manners. We can hardly be blamed if we
fail to realize our faults, but certainly we should make an effort to correct
any faults once they have been called to our attention. Ask a close friend
to check you against the following list — and you do the same for your
friend. Then make a sincere effort to eliminate any that you do — even
occasionally.

Drumming or tapping with fingers, toes, or a pencil
Humming or whistling under your breath
Sniffling or snorting
Breathing noisily

Blowing your nose noisily
Clearing your throat with a rasp
Sucking your teeth
Coughing or sneezing without turning your face and covering your mouth
    with a handkerchief
Coughing loudly
Fussing with your hair
Playing with rings, beads, or other jewelry
Adjusting your collar, cuffs, belt, or the like unnecessarily
Scratching your hair or picking at your face
Chewing gum
Yawning
Back slapping
Whispering
Drawing designs in your notebook as you wait for dictation
Wrinkling your brows
Slamming doors
Banging telephone receivers
Dashing in and out of rooms

Before beginning this improvement campaign, resolve to be objective
about the whole thing, and do not feel hurt when your friend checks an item
that is surprising to you. Remember, we are seldom aware of these habits.
When you know which of the objectionable habits are to be eliminated
from your habit structure, start on the first. When it is eliminated, go on
to the second. To eliminate an undesirable habit: (1) be conscious that
you possess it, (2) honestly desire to get rid of it, and (3) stop it *now*.

Use of Judgment in the Office

When a prospective employer talks about a potential employee, he
may say that he wants someone who can use his head, or someone who
has common sense, or someone with judgment. These are all names for
the same trait — and one that is missing in at least two out of three beginning workers. One reason for its scarcity lies in the word *beginning*. If
you have had no experience in a certain field, you will have few tools at
your command for making wise judgments. Perhaps the following situations will show you the kind of judgment that is needed.

It takes judgment, for example, to determine the importance of a
caller's business and his need for seeing your employer personally. In
placing a telephone call for your employer, it takes good judgment to
decide who will be called to the telephone first. You need judgment to
know when to take a message yourself and when to interrupt your employer. You must have judgment if you are to recognize the relative importance
of clients or customers when they call at the same time.

If you are able to evaluate the situation, you will use discretion in
dealing with an angry customer, receive complaints graciously (regardless

of their number), learn when to keep your eyes and ears open and your mouth closed, and how to discriminate in giving information of a confidential nature to those who ask for it. You will reserve judgment of one who seems to have committed an error against you. If you measure yourself by the same critical standards that you apply to others, you will become more liberal, less critical, and better able to evaluate justly.

Judgment implies that you will not discriminate between fellow workers because of personal like or dislike, but that you will learn to keep business relationships on an impersonal basis during business hours. Judgment also implies that you will not interrupt a conference unless it is absolutely necessary, nor will you refer questions asked over the telephone to your employer unless you cannot find the answer elsewhere. Good judgment must function as an outstanding quality in your business life.

YOUR STANDARDS OF CONDUCT

When you take your first office job, you will be working with a cross section of people. Some will be young; some will be nearing retirement. Some will be parents of children; others will never have married. Some will have an "anything goes" standard of conduct; others will be strict in their views of what should and should not be done. It will be up to you to set moral standards for yourself. Whatever they are, think them through; decide for yourself; then stick with them. Your morality will mean conformity to the standards of what *you* believe is right.

Some adults are concerned with the moral standards of young people. Many people are concerned by a lack of ethics and morality in business. Moral standards in business are certainly dispensed with by some firms. Because business is concerned with profits, because it is competitive, and because success is based on rivalry, the contention is sometimes made that business cannot be moral.

An ambitious businessman or woman, however, must look beyond the surface evidence and study the long-range results of morality in business. This scrutiny will reveal that companies that have become firmly established through years of service are more interested in protecting their good reputation than in making a single sale or in making transitory profits. Young firms, too, who want to establish lasting goodwill are more interested in their integrity than in the profit of the moment. In testing the effect of morality, it is well to examine the businesses that have stood the test of time with success.

The businessman (or woman) should guard his record of morality because it is a valuable possession. He should guard it because he is ethical, has faith, and because he has a sense of fair play and a social conscience. He should guard it for selfish reasons, also, because it is as valuable to him in business as capital or education. All businessmen and women should exhibit this type of selfishness.

Successful businessmen and women should also be interested, not in transitory praise or a moment of glory and success, but in long-range esteem and respect. Seldom are there any secrets in business. Even long after an incident of immorality, someone will remember. Facts can come to light in other ways, too, for there are many types of records. That a person did not make a sale, that a task was poorly completed, that an employee was promoted will be forgotten. But immorality will become a part of the record. If this record is not in writing, it will be whispered.

On many details of morality people do not agree, but some basic precepts are common to the consciences of all people. Other basic precepts in addition to those of all society are recognized by business people. The game is to be played fairly. All people have a sense of sportsmanship and justice. Nothing should be done outside of the office that would embarrass the firm. Feelings of others should be respected. In short, in business as elsewhere in life, " . . . as ye would that men should do to you, do ye also to them likewise."

The following should be considered rules of business and they should not be violated:

> Do not take office supplies for personal use.
> Do not show a too-friendly emotion toward your employer.
> Do not make unfair demands of subordinates.
> Do not take expensive gifts from customers or salesmen.
> Do not appear in public under the effects of alcohol.
> Do not repeat gossip about the private lives of your co-workers or superiors.

Your personal morality requires that you abide by ethical standards that you prize. You should not be unduly critical, however, of those whose standards are not the same as yours. This is an important point. Not only will the moral codes of other people differ from your own in some respects, but sometimes through thoughtlessness, stress, or grief some of your fellow employees or even your employers may violate their own moral codes. Whenever possible, be charitable toward these shortcomings. In similar crises, you may also err.

FOLLOW-UP ACTIVITIES

1. Interview an experienced private secretary or administrative assistant in your school or community. Ask her if she would be willing to discuss some of the incidents in her first year on the job that were critical or difficult for her. Report your interview to the class.
2. Practice the following suggestions for remembering names. Report whether the suggestions were effective for you.

a. When a person is being introduced, be sure that you not only hear the name but know how it is spelled. If there is doubt in your mind about the spelling, ask him to spell it; never ask the person who introduced you.

b. When you have the name, turn your attention to the face. Look at the person and in some way associate the name with the face.

c. File this association away in your memory, *knowing* that you will remember that person next time you meet him or her.

d. Whenever you meet a person, make it a point to address that person by name at the beginning of your conversation.

3. The following situations are presented for your decision as to how you would handle them. Write your exact words and the probable replies of the other person.

a. Your boss, Mr. Montesari, is away for a week on business. One of the managers comes in and demands that you call him long distance because of a personal conflict with another manager. You have Mr. Montesari's itinerary, but he asked you not to bother him with ordinary matters, since he plans to be very busy and seldom in one place long enough to take a telephone call. Mr. Nakamura, the assistant to Mr. Montesari, is handling routine matters.

b. A salesman, James Metzner, whose products are used by your company, comes in and asks to see Mr. Montesari.

c. Mr. Montesari returns from his business trip. The morning has been hectic. He has a board of directors meeting at 10:30. It is now 10:25. He says, "(Your name), are those reports ready? Where are the tables I gave you to type? Where did I put those statements? Did you call Mr. Olsen?" You have taken care of all of these details. How will you answer Mr. Montesari?

d. At noon, just as you are covering your typewriter before going to lunch, Mr. Montesari returns from his board of directors meeting in a bad mood. He says, "Where in thunder did you put that letter from Washington? I had it in my briefcase, but it isn't there now! Can't I keep anything around here without somebody running off with it?" Mr. Montesari had asked you to file the letter just after he came in that morning. What do you do or say?

e. At 3:30 Mr. Montesari is meeting in his office with the two vice-presidents on a serious matter. He told you as he went in to the meeting that he was not to be disturbed. An important client comes in on urgent business, something that cannot wait. What do you do or say?

CASE PROBLEMS

1. The Difficult Boss

Mr. Tims, a patent attorney, is struggling to build up his own business. To save money, he hires young and inexperienced stenographers. He is demanding and criticizes his employees angrily when they make any mistakes. He constantly reminds them how much work there is to be done and tells them they should work faster. An example of a daily occurrence follows:

Sheri, a conscientious beginner, presents a letter to Mr. Tims for his signature in which she has added an undictated comma; the rules of punctuation demanded the change.   When Mr. Tims notices this one change in an otherwise perfect letter, he calls Sheri to his desk, crosses out the comma, and writes "Retype" in pen across the top of the page. Sheri is upset; now she will have to retype the letter when she could have erased the offending comma.   Moreover, she feels she was right in her action.

Anne, who is a dependable and efficient secretary, has spent several minutes trying to find the correct spelling of a peculiar name in the telephone directory.   She finally turns to Sheri to see if she has any idea of how to spell it.   Before Sheri has a chance to reply, Mr. Tims (who has his desk in the same room as the girls) looks up and says, "Work on your own projects, girls."

Both girls find the work interesting, but they feel the only solution to the problem is to resign.

Solve the problem with the five-step method described in Chapter 3 from the point of view of the girls.

2. Delegating Responsibility

Jane Heiman was instructed by Kay Bishop to obtain some information for the latter to use in making out a report of customers who had overdue accounts.   By error Jane added the name of a good customer who had never been in arrears.   When the customer was approached by the credit collection bureau, he became highly indignant, called the general manager of Kay's company, and threatened to take his business elsewhere. The general manager called Kay into his office and reprimanded her. Kay insisted it was not her fault, that Jane had made the error.   The general manager said nothing to Jane, but persisted in blaming Kay.

1. Do you agree or disagree with the general manager?
2. What was Kay's responsibility in the matter?
3. If you delegate some of your responsibility to another, what must you be sure to do?
4. If you are capable of assuming responsibility, what would your reaction be to the reprimand from the general manager?

3. Time for Decision

Russ Palmer has been working in the programming department of White and Charters, Inc., since he graduated from junior college a year ago.   Since the time he began working with the firm he has received no raises in salary.   The work of the programming department, however, has increased to the extent that two new employees have been hired to help him.   This involves some supervisory work on his part.   In checking the salaries paid by other firms for similar work, Russ finds that he is not earning as much as most other companies pay. As Russ is debating what to do, a friend who is office manager of Hanson and Hanson Company offers him the same type of job at 15 percent higher salary. Russ likes the people in his department, as well as the other personnel of White and Charters. Hanson and Hanson do not provide the fringe benefits he is receiving.

1. What would you do if you were Russ?
2. If you decide to ask for a raise, would you tell your employer about the other offer?
3. Write down the "case" you would present to your employer in asking for the raise.
4. In accepting a position, what factors in addition to salary should be considered?

4. Should You Sleep on It?

Mr. Graham, Linda Rozow's employer, was infuriated because of a serious mistake in an order sent in by Mr. Yeoman, a salesman on the road. Mr. Graham immediately called in his secretary and dictated a letter discharging Mr. Yeoman. Because Mr. Graham had to leave at once for a meeting, he asked Linda to sign and mail the letter. Linda was aware that her employer was having an off day. Mr. Yeoman was a personal friend of hers, and she knew that up to this time he had been very efficient and well liked, both by his customers and Mr. Graham. Instead of transcribing and mailing the letter, she held it until the next day.

1. What do you think of Linda's action?
2. Should personal friendship enter a business situation of this kind?
3. What chance was Linda taking?
4. Do you think Linda might have been motivated by feelings other than friendship for Mr. Yeoman? If so, what were they?
5. In case Mr. Graham is of the same feeling the next day, what should Linda do?
6. Suppose Mr. Graham comes in the next morning and tells Linda he has changed his mind and that he is going to call Mr. Yeoman to see if he can talk him into staying with the company?
7. Can you think of a more straightforward way by which Linda could have accomplished the same result?

5. Taking Responsibility

Mr. Limmer, a division manager of a business that distributes its products nationally, has been out of the office for a week. He is in the hospital recovering from an operation and cannot be disturbed with business affairs. The operation was an emergency, and nothing was said about who should make the decisions. John Shafer has just received a large rush order over the telephone from a new local customer whose credit rating has not yet been established. It is the policy of the business that all orders from new customers must have Mr. Limmer's O.K. before being delivered.

John takes it upon himself to investigate the credit standing of this new company. He finds it to be excellent. John has three alternatives from which he can choose. He can (1) refuse the order, (2) call and ask if the company can wait for two weeks (when Mr. Limmer will be well enough to discuss business matters), or (3) approve the order in Mr. Limmer's name and have the goods delivered.

1. What is John's responsibility in this matter?
2. What is John's authority?
3. Which decision should John make? Why?

6. Set in the Groove

Neva Garcia, who has been transferred from the central office to one of its branches, finds it difficult to adjust herself to the new methods. She is continually referring to her old position: "Mr. Brown wanted letters written in this style." Some of Neva's ideas are good, and in time she may be able to contribute to the efficiency of office routine. At present, however, she annoys everyone else in the office. Unless Neva adjusts to the new situation, she is in danger of losing her position.

1. What should Neva's attitude be toward her job?
2. Why is it best for a newcomer to refrain from making suggestions about changes?
3. If Neva's ideas are good, how and when may she present them for consideration?
4. Is there a similarity with this situation and the common practice of saying, "This is the way my teacher in school told us to do this"?

chapter 12

The double role of worker/mother has its difficulties. From all sides we seem to hear that modern woman is destroying her home, her children, and herself; that she is frustrated; that she is a bundle of tensions.

Is all this true? Don't women get along pretty well as they juggle their various roles? Right here may be the difficulty, however. Instead of leading two lives, many women lead four, five, or six. And it is a plain fact that they can't star in all roles. The problem, then, is to decide which shall be starring roles and which shall be supporting roles.

If you are serious about your work, you want to make it a starring role; but in the early years of your marriage, while your children are young, your job will have to be the second lead role. Your home and family must come first. Save your ambitions to conquer new worlds until your children are more or less on their own.

Your supporting roles will differ, according to what you like best to do: church duties, civic duties, the PTA, hobbies, playing bridge, or visiting friends. The important decision you must make is which roles are to take on secondary importance? This will differ according to your likes and dislikes. A good rule, though, is to give slight importance to any activity that takes more out of you than it gives back.

STARRING ROLE: WIFE OR GIRLFRIEND

An important relationship for most women is with the man (if there be one) in her life. She may never understand her man fully, but there are important things that will put joy into that relationship. Here is a rule: Men like to be comfortable, they like to be praised, and they like to be free.

Men rarely love women because of their nobility. A wife may be a saint and still be unsuccessful in marriage. She may be self-sacrificing, thrifty, and hard working; but if she is possessive, all her virtues will go for nothing.

How do you combat this trapped feeling? First, you fight possessiveness. Your don't *own* your husband or boyfriend. You shouldn't even *want* to possess each other. But how do you fight it? You fight possessiveness by getting rid of its cause — fear. What do you fear? That no one will love you? Then practice being more lovable. That you are personally unfit for love? Then work to improve your personality. That your husband or boyfriend will leave you? Then work to make your home and yourself so pleasant and comfortable that he wouldn't think of such a thing.

What about incompatibility? One of the bits of advice that the working woman gets thrown at her is that she should join her husband's interests, turning herself into a carbon copy of him. Be true to yourself: Grudging "togetherness" is worse than none at all. Almost all couples are incompatible in some ways — partly because they are men and women, and partly because one grew up in one family and the other one grew up in another.

One woman worried so much about the great differences between herself and her husband that she sat down and made a list. She liked to talk things out; he hated postmortems. She liked to talk; he was the strong, silent type. She liked parties and dancing; he preferred reading and chess . . . and so on. When she finished, she thought, "But still, we love each other; we like each other." And that's the main thing.

If you and your husband are alike in most ways, it will be an easier marriage in the beginning. But what will it be like 20 or 30 years later? If neither changes, the marriage will become dull; neither partner will have grown as a person in order to understand the other. If neither person changes, the marriage will grow static; yet as soon as one of them does change, there are the makings of incompatibility.

If two people start out with tremendous differences and resolve them over a lifetime of living together, they have a bond that nothing can destroy.

STARRING ROLE: MOTHER

Just as you can't possess your man, neither can you possess your children. They are not *ours* to do with as we see fit. They are people that we are privileged to live with. It is our good fortune that we may help them to grow into happy, creative men and women. We love them, we help them, but we do not try to dominate them. We treat them as important individuals. We *listen* to what they have to say. We refuse to nag them—only to have them nag us as they grow into "know-it-all" adolescents. But that is the way. If we make them dependent upon us, we will be crippling them for adult life.

If you think of your children as people, not things, the right decision is much easier. For example, children need to be held and touched when they are babies and young children. A working mother must spend a great deal of her time with her children when she is home. She shouldn't try to make them self-reliant too soon. When you are away from your children during the day, you must have a capable substitute mother to take care of them.

Include the children in the household duties simply because they are members of the family. They should have money to spend for the same reason. One way out of the "to pay or not to pay" dilemma is to give each child an allowance—simply because he is your child—but to post a list of duties by which the child can earn extra money if he wishes.

There are few things more self-disciplining than working outside the home *because you want to.* You can't bewail your lot because the natural retort is, "Well, why don't you quit your job?" If you like your double job, you must take care of both sides of it with a smile. Just remember this fact: A working wife/mother has to be 100 percent wife and mother whenever she is home. A mother who spends only four hours each working day with her children must make every minute of those hours count in a positive way. One plan to make each minute count is to give out plenty of hugs and kisses to your family; another is to be honestly lavish with praise. The smallest of helping tasks must not be overlooked. Also, tell the family members how much you depend on them, how much you appreciate them, how wonderful he or she is.

The teen years will be the hardest for the working mother, but they are also the hardest for the full-time mother. If you treat your teen-agers courteously, if you listen to them, praise their accomplishments, attend as many of their school functions as is humanly possible, you'll probably be pleasantly surprised when these years are over. The problem children come from homes where no one noticed them, where nothing they ever did was good enough, where they were not listened to, where they were disciplined unfairly. If your home is a growth-producing environment and if you provide a happy climate, you may have fears, but they should be unfounded.

SECOND LEAD ROLE: OFFICE WORKER

When women first "invaded" the office back in the 1880's, everyone expected the heavens to fall. Ministers preached from the pulpit about destruction that was lying in wait for these young girls. Doctors predicted early death from working in poorly heated and ventilated offices. Now the whole picture has changed. About forty percent of all the people who work are now engaged in some form of business activity. One out of every three workers is a woman. Most of them are working in offices.

Are there any psychological techniques to aid us in this coeducational "rat race," the modern business office? There seem to be some, but all of them do not apply in all cases. There are techniques for male executives, for male workers, for unmarried girls, and for married women with families to look after. Suggestions will be made for each of these four groups, but they will be classified into two main divisions — his and hers.

Isn't That Just Like a Man?

The male executive in today's office may find that his troubles are mostly feminine! Whether feminine peculiarities are innate or learned, no one knows; but they seem to be there. For example, marketing research has shown that a woman's senses are sharper. Because of this, perhaps, they react to harshness (whether of voice, word, or surroundings) to a much greater extent than men do. Some psychologists even say that women are fifty percent more sensitive than men — or at least that many more of them are too sensitive for their own good.

If you are a male executive, then, you will need to treat your women workers with politeness. Gruffness, brusqueness, snapping remarks are all resented more deeply by women than are long hours and low pay. In fact, better work would certainly be better motivated if the supervisor or manager would just compliment good work now and then. This is another area where women workers are different. They are more deeply motivated by words.

As words are powerful in dealing with women, it is only sensible to use considerate ones whenever possible in dealing with women. If a mistake has been made, it must be pointed out — but not necessarily with hammer and tongs! In fact, any employer will get fewer errors in the work of women employees if he compliments the work that is errorless. Almost any woman will work her fingers to the bone for a word of praise. And 99 women out of 100 will think, "What's the use," and not even try if the typical reaction is fault-finding.

An admirable quality in male executives is a sense of fairness. When a man becomes an executive, he may be called upon to work overtime more and more. If it is necessary to have a secretary or clerk work overtime as well, the executive should not attempt to make the occasion a social one. An executive, too, receives a higher salary to compensate for longer working hours. The clerical worker, however, usually does not receive this kind of remuneration. It is only fair that such work be either infrequent or that it be remunerated with "supper money" or overtime pay.

If an employer should find that he must work late or on Saturday, he should notify in advance the employees who must help him. Girls may have dates, and they cannot always cancel these plans on short notice. The girl may not mind, but if her escort has purchased tickets to the theatre or for a sports event, he may hesitate to ask her again. Fairness on the part of the executive would make it optional for girls to remain after hours. Such questions as, "Would it upset any of your plans this evening, Miss Taylor, if you stayed until about 7:30 to finish this report?" leave it up to the girl. Also, in fairness, the employer should not be upset if Miss Taylor replies, "I'm sorry, but I do have a date. Would it be all right if I asked Marilyn if she is free?"

If late work seems to be required habitually, the employer and the staff should get together to discuss the matter and devise a plan that will be fair to all. It may not be possible to please everyone concerned, but at least everyone will have had a hand in making the arrangements. Under these circumstances, too, some kind of overtime pay should be given to those who work late. When such arrangements are made (such as time and a half for overtime), many employees welcome the extra work.

The unmarried co-worker of women in an office who wishes to ask one of them for a date should invite her for some social occasion. He should then call for her at her home. Social engagements are strictly for after hours, however. At the office, friends should treat each other with the same businesslike courtesy they show other co-workers.

If a young man should meet one of the girls from the office in a restaurant, he should be under no obligation to pay the check. Each one pays for his or her own lunch or snack. There are other social customs, too, that are not observed in the office. For example, a young man does not rise from his desk to carry a heavy ledger, nor does he open and close doors for her. This is because an office does not represent a social situation. Women in business should not expect special favors of men co-workers. They should accept the same conditions that men face. The rules of the game allow no exceptions. Women neither expect nor desire the chivalry that men accord them in the social world.

Isn't That Just Like a Woman?

The Cinderella story of modern times is usually set in an office, so many girls may look upon office jobs as the Royal Road to Romance. Of course, an intelligent, perceptive girl will know this idea is pure fiction. To her, the impersonal nature of business relationships is obvious. She will know that most businessmen are far too engrossed in their work to have time for flirtation. The perceptive girl will also be too interested in her job and in growing in her own capabilities to be interested in shallow relationships. Strangely enough, a girl is more attractive when she is deeply interested in something other than herself and her personal affairs.

Girls and marriage. Most girls have one or both of two goals. They want a successful career, and/or they want a happy marriage. Some years ago these goals presented more of a conflict than they do now. Still, many girls consider the business world merely as a stopgap until they get married. This attitude, however, is one that may spoil their chances in reaching either goal. Every girl should have some goal in mind, of course, and she should analyze the threat of "marking time" in an office to her own success.

You will improve your chances of career success if your attitude is entirely businesslike during the workday. Naturally, you will be flattered if you notice that someone in the office is attracted to you. The important point, however, is this: You should have or develop enough self-confidence so that you will not need this kind of flattery. A girl who is cool and business-like is more attractive than one who obviously tries to interest the men in the office. No girl should show how she feels before the man does. Some-times it helps to act a role. If you can't feel calm and cool, perhaps you can act as if you were.

The girl who is beginning her business career will do well to keep her former friends and to go out of her way to keep these relationships intact. The fact that you do have other friends seems to make itself felt. Others will be attracted to you because you don't need them. The psychology of not being too eager in any kind of relationship would make a fascinating study, but it is beyond our scope.

If you should become interested in one of the single men in your firm, your best procedure is to follow the rules of acceptable behavior. So many men are frightened of marriage responsibilities that, again, the light touch is much the best one. Don't be too interested. Let the man make the first move. If he is interested, he will invite you to dinner, to a movie, or to some other entertainment. And here we come to an im-portant point. If a man asks you for a date, you are his guest; you do not offer to "go Dutch." One of the undermining influences at work is the assault on a man's ego when his girl makes as much or more money than he does. This assault is aggravated by any aggressive display of money. It is much better to take a walk with a man than offer to buy theatre tickets and meals at restaurants. The one exception is when tickets are given to you. Be careful even in this instance, though. Don't go too far in taking the initiative. The rare occasion when you have been given tickets should be handled as follows: The man should call for you at your home; you should hand him the tickets; and from then on the evening is up to him.

Following the conventional ways is best. If you should decide to return the hospitality (and then only after a man has invited you several times), the best plan is to invite him to a small party at your home or apartment. When others are invited, too, it looks like what it is, merely a wish to be friendly and appreciative.

Women and emotions. A criticism commonly leveled at business-women is that they are too emotional. This criticism is actually based on fact. Women's emotions seem to be closer to the surface — whether by heredity or training. The best thing to do in business, however, is try to control them. A display of unpleasant attitudes or uncontrollable emotions is immature and definitely not one of the traits desirable in a business-woman. Emotional outbursts do not belong in the office — whether they be tears, angry words, or hurt feelings. Count to ten — or a hundred. Realize that your employer is under greater pressure than you are. Go bowling after work. But don't indulge in your emotions during working hours. Such indulgence is likely to alienate some of your co-workers.

Sex should also be kept out of your thoughts. You should get rid of those wishful thoughts that some day you will marry your employer — or his son. One help in this will be to interpret what your employer says to you as having a business meaning and nothing more. He is interested primarily in his business. Don't let your imagination create situations that do not exist.

What about invitations from your employer? The best rule here is to use your common sense. If the invitation to have dinner when you are working late is made casually, if the situation can be kept on a business basis, then you may accept. If the invitation has overtones of something more, however, you should make some excuse. This may be similar to walking a high wire in a circus. You must keep your relationship on a businesslike level, yet you must not offend your employer. The best excuse, again made casually, is that you are sorry but that you have a date. You do not want to become a target for gossip, and you do not want to make your office relationship difficult.

The best cure for possible or present emotional entanglements in the office is to keep a wholesome interest in affairs outside the office, in a circle of congenial friends. If you fill your days with work and your evenings and weekends with play and self-improvement, you will not look for a leading, romantic role during working hours. You will keep such situations from developing if you dress becomingly but appropriately, if your manners are serious and self-reliant, and if your work is done skillfully and competently.

SUPPORTING ROLE: HOUSEKEEPER

If you work, your role as housekeeper is only a supporting one. An orderly house is pleasant, but a scrubbed-within-an-inch-of-its-life house is actually intimidating. Lived-in houses are the nicest ones, both for your children and for your friends. One way to make your three lives easier to accomplish is to remember that you don't have to be a perfect house-keeper. Everyone is entitled to one failure. If housekeeping is your failure, see if you can possibly afford some part-time housekeeping help.

Women workers are increasing at twice the rate of men workers. One out of every three workers is a woman. In the 70's there are about 30 million women workers, more than half of them married, many of them with small children. How can the homemaker/office worker keep both of these ships afloat? It isn't easy, but it is possible.

First of all, all women are not domestic any more than all men are carpenters around the house in their spare time. A man who is not handy with tools, however, has it all over the women. He just turns to the Yellow Pages. Women are stuck. Like it or not, they must keep their houses running (maybe not smoothly, but running). Still, there is a distinction. You can be a good homemaker even though you may not be a perfect housekeeper. Here are some suggestions.

1. You get rid of self-pity. No matter how much the housework piles up, you must not feel sorry for your lot. Instead of brooding about the dishes, beds, dusting, scrubbing, washing, and ironing that have to be done *after* working hours, you should spend that energy developing a better system. Working out a time-and-motion study for the household duties usually results in reduced time and a better-kept house.

2. Avoid all time-wasting activities that you do not enjoy. One could spend hours each week telephoning friends, visiting the neighbors, creating culinary masterpieces, indulging in shopping sprees or in gossip parties. But a working wife must write them off as luxuries she cannot afford.

3. You might work out an organization chart to be tacked to a bulletin board. On this chart show the duties (rotated frequently) of each member of the family. When there are only two members of the family, the prob-lem may not be particularly pressing; but the working wife with growing children *must* make a definite assignment of duties. One of the important segments of this assignment is delegating to others those duties ordinarily performed by the stay-at-home mother. For example, each high school member of the family is responsible for the following duties:

    a. Picks up his or her own clothes.
    b. Makes his or her own bed — not very well, perhaps, but he or she sleeps in it, so it is his or her problem.
    c. Washes his or her own fragile clothes.

d. Does his or her own pressing.
e. Buys his or her own small articles from the drugstore.
f. Takes his or her own clothes to the cleaners or arranges for them to be picked up by the cleaner.
g. Makes his or her own dental and doctor appointments.

Other household tasks, such as cleaning, ironing, dishes, and so on, are assigned on a weekly basis. One of the children can be made a temporary "supervisor" to back the work of the others.

4. Make a flexible working plan for each day. At the top of the list (as in your organization of office duties) goes the really important task that must be done no matter what crisis occurs. Each item on the agenda is assigned a place on the list, in order of importance. After the first item, our "merely human" working wife does the best she can. Also, being human, she won't reach some of the items at all; and, toward these unaccomplished tasks she must develop an easy-going attitude. Some of the tasks may never get finished, since they are always at the bottom of the list; but you must be able to say, "So what?" and let it go.

Financial Icebergs

What will you do with the money you earn? This question appears to be a simple one, but its answer has caused tears, accusations, and divorces. It is such an important question, in fact, that you should decide with your husband just what these financial arrangements are to be before you take your first job. If it is too late for that solution, memorize this statement: His and her paychecks can be dangerous. A plan that has worked for many couples is as follows:

1. Both paychecks go into the same bank account.
2. Both get experience in the job of paying the bills.
3. A certain percent goes into savings.
4. A certain amount is given to each partner for general spending.

This is one good way of learning about the consequences of foolish vs. wise spending.

More Do's and Don'ts

There are a number of possible disadvantages to the suggestions given in this chapter, but perhaps a caution or two will change them to advantages. For one thing, you'll have to grow up. You can't be childish and keep all of your ships afloat. Also, you must take care of your health. Plenty of rest, good food, exercise, vitamins if needed, regular visits to your doctor and dentist, enjoyable vacations, and enjoyable days off for both you and your husband are absolutely essential. You may have to give up some of your pet hobbies, but squeeze one in if you possibly can.

One final advantage of a "double" life is for neurotics only. All well-adjusted women get out of bed every morning and tackle the jobs that need to be done. What is more, they do the jobs without batting an eye. But if, like so many of us, you tend to shrink from unpleasant tasks, the definite routine of a job is a life and sanity saver.

Now that you have settled everything, take a minute in your busy life and, perhaps, throw some of your roles *out* of the cast. Those walk-on roles are not too rewarding, you know. If you get rid of a few, your life will be less complicated. But just one more thought: Be sure to save part of your life for being an audience. About half the time turn the spotlight on the other members of your cast. *Listen* to your husband, your children, your employer, your co-workers. Let them play the starring roles they need and want.

FOLLOW-UP ACTIVITIES

1. For one day, list the irritating things done in business or at school by one member of the opposite sex.
2. For one day, list the irritating things done in business or at school by a member of the same sex.
3. Compare the two lists. Which sex tends to irritate you the most? Do you think you may be doing something to bring out the worst in some people? What are some of the things you do that might irritate women? that might irritate men?
4. For one day, casually express appreciation for everything that is done for you. If anyone opens a door, helps you carry anything, passes you the sugar, or is of assistance in any other way, say, "Thank you," and smile. Report to the class whether it made your day any more pleasant.
5. Have you ever lost your temper or in any other way lost control of your emotions in a working situation? If so, what was the result? Do you see any other way you could have handled the situation? Explain.
6. If you are working, make up a budget for one month. Include all your expenses of any kind. (If you are not employed, find out what beginning salaries are in your area and use this figure.) Take the amount you have listed for entertainment and divide it by 4. Spend exactly this amount for entertainment this weekend. Are you living within your entertainment budget at present?
7. This week, every time a person says anything to you of a complimentary nature, say, "Thank you." Force yourself to do this.
8. This week, casually compliment five of your co-workers or classmates. Keep your words and tone casual — but not sarcastic.

9. Write a short "thank you" note for some favor that has been done you in the past year. Keep the note short, sincere, and conversational. (If you are unable to think of any favors done you, write a "thank you" note to a member of your family.) *And mail the note.*

10. For one week, keep a record of your moods. Each night before you retire, write down which of the following phrases best described your prevailing mood that day:

Very happy   Somewhat depressed
Moderately happy   Very depressed
Neither happy nor depressed

At the end of the week, see if you need to work on your emotional habit patterns.

CASE PROBLEMS

1. Is Behavior Caused?

Natalie Groschalk, a young-looking and attractive woman, has recently been widowed. In order to prepare to support her family, a boy of 16 and a girl of 12, Natalie is attending a private business college. She worked before her marriage but has not worked since. Natalie is having grave problems with her son, Karl. Karl has always been difficult, but her husband had taken care of all disciplinary matters. Now, Natalie does not know where to turn. Her son refuses to study, his school grades are low, and he goes out on school nights and refuses to tell Natalie where he has been. He will not do anything around the apartment to help Natalie. Every morning is the scene of a verbal battle between Karl and his mother.

1. What past or present experiences of Karl's do you think may be contributing to the problem?
2. If you were Natalie, what would you do?
3. Write the solution you favor, using the five-step method.

2. Is a Whistle a Compliment?

Lester MacDonald has a secretary, Valerie, who is a striking beauty. She wears extreme clothes that attract attention. The men in the office seldom think of her only as part of the office machinery. Responding to their interests, her manner is a little too warm and her smile a little too intimate. His colleagues tease Lester about his secretary. At first he tried to be a good sport. Now the ridicule is becoming embarrassing. After all, he wants to work in his office, he loves his wife, and he is tired of his colleagues' jokes. He asks an older woman in the office to speak to his secretary.

1. If you were given this task, how would you begin?
2. What would you suggest in the way of appearance?

3. What would you suggest in the way of behavior?
4. How could you soften the blow so the secretary would really want to follow your suggestions?

3. Private Lives

Maria Perri has recently been granted a divorce from her husband on the grounds of mental cruelty. Maria was married only two years, and she feels that she is a complete failure. She has returned to work at her old job as a clerk-typist for Specialty Foods, Inc. Maria is a good worker, but she is not adjusting well from her divorce. She spends a good deal of time talking with the other girls about her unhappy marriage; she cries if reprimanded, and she talks to her mother on the telephone for about twenty minutes every day during business hours. Mr. Rugerri has tried to be patient with Maria, knowing her capabilities and realizing the difficulties of her personal life. Now, however, he decides to tell Maria that she must be more businesslike in the office.

1. If you were Mr. Rugerri, what would you say to Maria first?
2. Would you give Maria a warning?
3. Do you think Maria should be discharged?
4. What other action could Mr. Rugerri take?

4. His and Her Paychecks

Mary Jackson, a pretty black girl, has had an unfortunate marriage and was divorced four years ago. A year and a half ago she married again, this time to a young policeman, very ambitious and proud of his wife. Mary loves her job, but recently Sam, her husband, has been asking her to give it up and stay at home. Since they have no children and Sam's salary is not high, Mary refuses to give up her job. Mary comes to you and asks you what she should do. After some questioning, Mary says Sam's parents are interfering. She then says Sam doesn't like her cooking. Finally, she admits that she buys clothes and things for the house with her money and that Sam pays all of their living expenses from his salary.

1. Should you give Mary direct advice? Why or why not?
2. If you think you could get Mary to see her own problem, write your part of your conversation with Mary.

5. "Who's Afraid . . . ?"

Mr. Kane left the office a little early in the afternoon. He told Jane Starr, his secretary, that he would not be back during the day. Soon after he had left, Mr. Dodson, an important customer, came in.
"Is Mr. Kane in?"

"I'm sorry, but he has gone for the day. May I make an appointment for you for tomorrow morning? Or how about my calling you as soon as he comes in?"

"No, I shall be in town for only a few hours. See if you can find him for me."

Jane knew that Mr. Kane liked to forget the office as soon as he left it and would be irritated if called at his home. She hesitated for a moment before answering, then said, "I'll see if I can reach him for you." Risking Mr. Kane's anger, Jane dialed the number of his home.

1. What would you have done in Jane's place?
2. If you decide you would not call Mr. Kane, what would you say to Mr. Dodson?
3. If you did as Jane did, what would you say when you get Mr. Kane on the telephone?
4. In case Mr. Kane is angry with you the next day, what would you say?

part
five

getting the job you want

chapter 13

applying for the job you want

Today we hear the word "relevance" applied to education and to education for business in particular. Students of all ages want their schooling to lead to some worthwhile purpose. While young people may do well to listen to the answer when they ask the questions, "What good is this subject going to be to me?" or "How is studying this course going to help me be a better, happier person?" they still may prefer to think the answer through for themselves. One part of your education, however, is relevant — the part that is devoted to preparing you to earn your own living. Of course, you may have earned your own paycheck before now. You may have worked during vacations and part time while attending school, or you may have recently returned to school after an absence of several years, some of which were spent in the world of work. In any case, you know that financial independence is a real goal, one to which much of your education has been geared. Earning a good-sized paycheck is an important goal. Exciting as this prospect may be, however, there is another side to the picture.

When you work in business, you spend around eight hours a day, five days a week, and about eleven and a half months a year in a certain kind of work. This is a lot of time, particularly when you multiply it by the thirty to fifty years that you may be a member of the labor force. Naturally, you want to make this vast amount of time as enjoyable as you can. If you do enjoy your work, you will be a much more pleasant person; and your chances of living a happy life are increased. If you dislike your work, on the other hand, you can see the hours of misery that will be added one upon the other.

Finding enjoyable work is not a simple matter. Many young people have no particular inclination toward one certain job at first. They discover their liking or disliking for their jobs only after they have been working for months or even years. Any formula that will help you to choose wisely, therefore, is a valuable tool. Some of the parts of such a formula are your schooling, your skills, your hobbies, your personality traits, your energy, and your health. The list is actually endless. You can see, though, that you must understand yourself before you can find the job for which you are best suited.

YOUR JOB CAMPAIGN

If you want to find the right job, you should allow about eight weeks of continuous effort for the project. This may seem a great deal of time, but you will find that half-hearted attempts rarely result in success. If you must obtain work immediately upon graduation from school, you will need to begin your job-finding campaign while you are finishing your final term. A better solution, however, is to devote your full time to the job-finding project. Take your time; work hard at each step in the process. You will then be much more likely to find a job that gives you personal satisfaction. Since you are actually marketing your skills, knowledge, ability, and personal qualities, you must learn all you can about them or, in effect, about yourself.

Making Your Inventory List

The first step in learning about yourself involves making a personal inventory of everything you can think of that would have a bearing on your success. One good way of doing this is first to jot down items as they come to you. For example, you might make a list beginning with the following:

Born August 22, 1953
Enjoy sports: tennis and swimming
Participate in drama and dance
Father's occupation, owner-manager of printing business
Father's education, technical college
Mother's occupation, office manager
Mother's education, business college
Physical handicaps, none
Height, 5' 7"
High school attended, West High
Courses taken, college preparatory and business electives
College, Westfield Junior College
Courses taken, liberal arts and secretarial
Best grades in English, shorthand, and typewriting
High school activities:
    Senior class president
    Member, dance club

      School plays and dance concerts
      Editor, yearbook
   College activities:
      Student body vice-president
      Member, dance club
      Activity editor, yearbook

This is not a complete list, of course, and these items seemingly have no relationship to each other. Organizing your information comes with the second step. Now you do nothing but write down items about yourself. Just to be certain you omit nothing important, keep in mind the following additional areas: (1) your skills (typewriting, shorthand, machines, musical instruments, foreign languages), (2) subjects you have studied in school, (3) your hobbies, (4) your liking for people. Some jobs require the ability to meet the public, to mix well with others; in other jobs you may work entirely by yourself. It is important to rate yourself in this area and also to see how any prospective job can be evaluated with respect to this quality.

There is one other part of your inventory demanding some attention. You may be a person with many talents, one who changes his career choice with every new class he takes. If this description fits you, there are two ways of getting down to your fundamental interests. The first one has to do with routine work. All jobs have some dull, routine sides to them. If you dream of becoming a great ballet dancer and have never studied this art, you may know nothing about the six hours a day of endless exercises that must go on for years and years before a young dancer is permitted to do any actual performing. Make a list of all the routine activities you can think of that you rather like to do. Perhaps you don't mind tinkering with cars (and this would be drudgery to some people); maybe you find proofreading something of a challenge; or you may enjoy checking figures. After you have made your list, choose the routine activity you would dislike the least. This may be a real indication of your fundamental interests.

The second way to cut through too many interests in order to find the real one is to go back to your early interests. What activity did you enjoy the most when you were in the elementary grades? If you can remember back to the first three grades, you will find your interests before they were changed by favorite teachers, pressures from parents, and so on. If you were always elected president of your class — even in the elementary grades — you may safely say you get along well with others, or at least you have that basic ability. Or you may have been the one who was chairman of committees when you were ten or eleven. If so, you may naturally lean toward a job involving some leadership. Were you the class poet in the second grade? This may mean you have abilities in writing. With the increasing importance of communication in business, such a talent is vitally needed.

Organizing Your Inventory List

When you have written down every item you can think of (and you should have at least thirty items), you must organize the items into separate classifications. Some of the headings you might consider are the following:

Schooling
Early interests and routine enjoyed
Work experience
Abilities or talents
Skills
Machines
Physical details
Liking for people
Organization memberships
Appearance

Now take a large sheet of paper and turn it the long way. Enter your headings across the top of the sheet. Below the headings, list the items from your inventory that belong in each category.

When each item has been placed in its proper place, see if you can rank the categories in the order of their importance to you. Which classification has the most important items? Mark this classification "I" and the next most important "II" and so on. After you have arranged your headings in this manner, write down the first three. Assume that your first three were the following:

I. Skills (high-speed typewriting and calculating machines)
II. Interests (have always liked detail)
III. High grades in math and accounting

You can see that these three items suggest work in an accounting firm, either as a junior accountant or a combination statistical typist and clerk. Whatever your three highest classifications may be, they will give you a similar lead into the type of work you will likely do best and find most satisfying. Keep this classification at hand; you will use it next in preparing your data sheet and application letter.

Sources of Possible Jobs

After you have analyzed the product (yourself), you must analyze the market (the jobs available). Look over your own qualifications again. What other possible lines of work do they suggest? After you have settled on two or three alternative lines of work, the next step is to look around for one or more specific jobs. There are a number of sources where you might inquire: school placement service, newspaper want ads, state and federal merit tests, public employment bureaus, private employment agencies, and dealer agencies.

School placement services. Larger schools now have formal offices concerned with placing their students. The placement officer will ask you to fill out an application blank or data sheet; he will interview; and he will consult the references you give him. This is an excellent source for you to consider. The school may know more about your abilities than any of the other sources named could possibly know. Businessmen who have had good results with such offices are glad to use their services again. In this way, a knowledge of the available openings is assured. One caution should be given in connection with the use of references. Always ask the former teacher or former employer if you may use his name as a reference. This is a courtesy to your reference, but it is also good insurance for you. Teachers, particularly, have so many students in one year that they may be grateful for the opportunity to renew your acquaintance. This, in turn, will make it possible for them to give you a more detailed recommendation.

Small schools usually do not have placement services. This does not mean, however, that you should not keep in touch with your former school in such cases. Placing of graduates in small schools may be handled by the business teacher, the teacher in charge of the work experience program, the school counselor, or by the principal. Ask your former business teacher whom you should consult; then go to this person and leave your name and your qualifications and references.

Your responsibility does not end (in either the formal or informal placement situation) with the interview. You should cooperate with the placement officer by following his leads *at once*. If the placement officer receives word that a job is available at 9 a.m., it may be taken by 2 p.m. A second need for promptness lies in reporting the results of your job interview with the placement officer. If you are given the job, he should send no other applicants for it; if you were late in applying and the job was taken, you should give the placement officer this information. If you did not get the job and it is still open, the placement officer will want to send other applicants. In the latter case, too, he may be able to refer you to other positions.

Newspaper want ads. You should always take advantage of the help wanted ads in your daily newspapers. These are not only a source of openings; they also show a trend as to the type of openings most prevalent. If you are undecided between two possible areas of work, for example, a study of the available jobs listed in the help wanted section should tip the scales in favor of the one providing the best opportunities. A further help can be found in the want ads, namely, the level of competence desired. In the secretarial field, for example, the majority of the ads may specify 60 words a minute in typewriting and 100 words a minute in shorthand dictation. A clerical job may ask for skill on the calculating and adding machines. A receptionist ad may ask for experience on the switchboard.

There are certain dangers to be avoided when responding to a want ad. Some of them are disguised attempts to sell merchandise. Be wary, then, of those asking for a cash deposit, or those asking that you buy samples. If the job requires that you take a course for which you pay tuition, this, again, may merely be a device for attracting students rather than a *bona fide* job opportunity.

Assuming, however, that the ad is for an actual job, there are two ways of replying to it. If an address is given in the want ad, you must go in person for an interview. This topic is discussed in Chapter 14. If a box number is given, you must reply with a data sheet and an application letter. These topics are discussed on the following pages.

State and federal civil service tests. Two excellent sources of jobs are the federal civil service and state civil service. If you are interested in either of these opportunities, you should inquire at the respective office building in each case. Federal civil service tests are given frequently throughout the year. The dates and places of these tests can be secured at your federal building or post office, either in person or by letter. State examinations are customarily given in the spring, and information concerning these tests can be obtained at your state capitol.

Public employment bureaus. The United States Employment Service conducts tests, arranges interviews, and provides job leads without charge. This service was established in 1933. Agencies are located in the larger cities of all the states. The USES is an excellent employment agency and one that merits your acquaintance. Businesses using the USES turn the screening of applicants over to the agency. Two or three applicants considered best suited for a certain position are then sent to the firm requesting help. Beginners in business, especially, will do well to visit their public employment bureau to learn about the services offered.

Private employment agencies. In addition to the public employment services, there are many private agencies operating in most cities. These agencies do charge a fee for placement. In some cases the applicant is expected to pay this fee (which involves a certain percentage of the salary received in the first months of employment); but in many cases the new

employer pays the fee. The advantage of the private agency may rest
on the fact that these agencies often specialize in certain types of jobs.
One may specialize in placing executives, others may place clerical workers, and so on. With such specialization, of course, the agency should have
a deeper knowledge of the field covered and may have the exact job for
a certain applicant. Before registering at a private agency, it is a good
idea for a beginner to inquire of his former teachers or employers as to
the particular agency's suitability for him.

Dealer agencies. There is still another source available to beginning
office workers. Some companies dealing in office machines and appli-
ances are able to help young people who are skilled operators of their
equipment to find openings. If you are a fast and accurate typist on a certain electric typewriter, for example, you could get in touch with the
local sales office of the manufacturer of this typewriter and ask about
any leads they might have. Because it is to their advantage to place skilled
workers on their machines, they are usually glad to help you. If you should
get a job through a dealer, be sure to call the person who helped you and
thank him.

Preparation for Placement

The law of supply and demand has a great influence on both securing
and keeping a job. If the supply of workers with a particular skill is large,
the employer can be selective in employing and retaining personnel. If
the supply of workers with specialized training is smaller than the demand,
then the worker can be selective in choosing a position. The present market is, and has been for some time, an excellent one for office workers, and
an increase in these opportunities is expected to continue through the next
decade. Such factors as tax laws, social security regulations, and the increase of service industries all combine to create more and more office
positions.

There is one change, however, that has already begun to operate.
This change is in the opportunities available to the unskilled office worker.
There was a time when a beginner with no training could start as an office
boy and learn the business on the job. This picture has changed completely.
There is no place in business now for the person without education or
skills. The higher both of these qualifications are, the better the opportunity in business. As the job classifications go up, the number of jobs
available also increases. There is no place in business for the high school
dropout. Conversely, the more skill, knowledge, efficiency, and desirable
personal traits you possess, the better you can compete for the job you

want. This means that you will do well to obtain the best training you can afford. This training may be obtained in schools plus experience or in schools alone.

The wise businessman and woman will realize, too, that times of great opportunity will not always exist. If you are wise, therefore, you will get all the training you can. If possible, such training should precede employment; but if this cannot be arranged, additional training after you are hired should not be overlooked. In cities many private and public schools and colleges offer night courses or Saturday classes. If arrangements cannot be made to take these classes, you might consider home study courses. These courses have one distinct advantage for the working student: They may be completed at the rate you set for yourself. Information regarding home study courses may be obtained from the National Home Study Council, 1601 18th St., N. W., Washington, D.C. 20009. The Council publishes the *National Home Study Council Bluebook*, which lists thousands of excellent home study courses.

YOUR DATA SHEET

Perhaps the most important single job-finding aid is your data sheet. Whether you apply for a job on your own, without invitation, or whether you are asked by an executive of a firm to come in for an interview, your cause will be aided if you have a neatly typed data sheet to submit. One reason for the popularity of the data sheet is the ease with which it can be scanned by the interviewer. Whatever he may wish to look over, he can find in a moment. It is also helpful for the firm hiring you if they keep the data sheet in your personnel file. When opportunities for advancement arise, your data sheet will provide, in concise form, the information that will help them make a choice.

To be effective, your data sheet must "put your best foot forward." Go back, now, to your personal inventory list. See if you have checked off every item as you added it to your classified inventory. Then look over your classified inventory for "best feet" or plus factors. Your data sheet consists of an outline of these plus factors arranged attractively under centered headings. The headings covered in your data sheet should include the following:

Personal Information

Education

Work Experience
  (or Experience with People if you have never worked)

References

PERSONAL DATA SHEET

Ann Wilcox
3729 Bullard Avenue
Minneapolis, Minnesota 55401

Personal Information

Age:	23	Weight:	120 lb.
Telephone:	825-6412	Health:	Excellent
Height:	5'3"	Marital Status:	Single

Education

College: Four years' study at Cutler College (1969-1973);
   B. S. degree; major in office management and secretarial
   Science; A-minus average
High School: West Hills High School, Rochester, Minnesota

Related Courses

Data Processing   Human Relations
Office Management   Office Procedures
Report and Letter Writing   Economic Theory
Survey of Office Machines   Accounting
Advanced Typewriting (80 wam) Advanced Shorthand (120 wam)

Work Experience

1972-73 Secretary for Mr. Thomas A. Jennings, Manager,
   General Electronics, Inc., Minneapolis, Minnesota;
   part-time while attending college
1970-72 Typist for Mr. H. M. Wells, Project Engineer, Wells
   Construction Company, Springfield, Illinois; worked
   summers for three years

Organization Memberships

Phi Chi Theta (business/professional)
Delta Zeta (social)
University Methodist Church

References (by permission)

Mr. Thomas A. Jennings, Manager, General Electronics, Inc.,
   1067 Main Street, Minneapolis, Minnesota 55402
Mr. H. M. Wells, Project Engineer, Wells Construction Company,
   1549 Somerset Road, Springfield, Illinois 62707
Dr. Morton L. Smith, Professor of Economics, Cutler College,
   Minneapolis, Minnesota 55402

Data Sheet

Personal Information

Some data sheets begin with personal details or vital statistics, such as age, height, weight, health, hobbies, marital status, and military status. You may list a minimum of organization memberships in this section. The heading, *Personal Information*, should be underscored; and other titles should be followed by a colon, as follows:

Personal Information

Age:	23	Weight:	120 lb.
Telephone:	825-6412	Health:	Excellent
Height:	5'3"	Marital Status:	Single

Education

When you list your education, you should list first the last school you attended, with your major field of study and the date of your graduation. For example, if you finished four years of college work, leading to a degree, you make a statement such as the following:

Four years' study at the Cutler College (1969-1973); B. S. degree; major in office management and secretarial science; A-minus average.

If you graduated from a junior college, this fact is shown as follows:

Two years' study at Monterey Peninsula Junior College (1970-1972); Associate in Business degree; major in Secretarial Science; A-minus average.

If your education beyond high school did not lead to a degree, you should make a statement similar to the following:

One and one-half years' study at Clarke College (1971-1972); will complete work for certificate by correspondence; major in Distributive Education; B-plus average.

If your final schooling was high school, this fact is shown as follows:

Four years at West Hills High School, graduating in 1972; major sequence in Business; B-plus average.

Some of you may prefer to list your class standing rather than your average grades. In that case, you might end your statement on education with the following: graduated in upper third of class. Since some schools use 3.0 for an A, while others use 4.0, do not use a grade point average unless you show the method by which the average was calculated, as follows: grade point average, 3.2, with 4.0 equal to a grade of A.

Following the statement of schools attended, degree or diploma received, and so on, you may wish to list the courses you have taken that are related to the job for which you are applying. The title of this section may be *Related Courses*, or you may use a longer title, as follows:

Courses Related to Work as Supervisor
of Machine Section

Accounting, elementary	Human Relations
and intermediate	Economic Theory
Data Processing	Statistics
Office Management	Survey of Office Machines

Work Experience

In listing your experience, it is best to be quite specific. Such statements as, "Worked in grocery store," do not give enough information. Dates, names of companies and employers, plus a description of the work, are needed. Another important point is to list the jobs you have held in reverse order (the last job first). Following is an example, assuming you have worked in two different jobs:

1972-73   Secretary for Mr. Thomas A. Jennings, Manager,
General Electronics, Inc., Minneapolis, Minnesota;
part-time while attending college.

1970-72   Typist for Mr. H. M. Wells, Project Engineer,
Wells Construction Company, Springfield, Illinois;
worked summers for three years.

If you have held more than five different jobs, it is best to choose only the latest ones or the most important ones. The experience section of your data sheet is to show concisely that you are capable of doing satisfactory work, that you know what it means to do a day's work for a day's pay. The listing of additional positions adds nothing new and takes up valuable space that can be better used in other ways.

Experience with People

If you have never had a job, full time or part time, the work experience section of your data sheet is headed *Experience with People*. Here you should list organizations you belong to, dormitory offices, church offices, and school activities. Of particular interest to employers are leadership activities in debating, campus newspapers and literary organizations, athletics, and class offices. It is believed that such activities denote a person who can communicate well and who has learned to work as a part of a team. These qualities are vitally needed in the business world.

References

The last section of your data sheet should contain the names, titles, and addresses of three or four individuals who can recommend your work, your scholarship, and/or your character. These should be arranged attractively:

References

Mr. Thomas A. Jennings	Mr. H. M. Wells
Manager	Project Engineer
General Electronics, Inc.	Wells Construction Company
1067 Main Street	1549 Somerset Road
Minneapolis, Minnesota 55402	Springfield, Illinois 62707
Dr. Morton L. Smith	Mrs. Harriet Sholund
Professor of Economics	Business Department
Cutler College	Cutler College
Minneapolis, Minnesota 55402	Minneapolis, Minnesota 55402

Photograph

One small investment you can make when applying for a job is to have a number of photographs (2″ x 2 1/2″) made in conservative business dress. This can be done quite inexpensively, and a photograph makes your data sheet much more personal and alive. When you are ready to start your job-finding campaign, you should arrange to have at least twelve of these pictures made. Then attach a photograph to each copy of your data sheet that you send out. No employer can require that you enclose a photograph with a data sheet, nor can an employer require one for an application or as a condition of hiring. The completed data sheet could be arranged as shown on page 183.

As shown in the illustration, your data sheet will look better and command more attention if it is arranged with plenty of space around each section. Do not crowd a data sheet in order to save paper. You should be willing to invest in your future to the extent of buying good quality bond paper for your data sheet.

YOUR APPLICATION LETTER

While a data sheet is often used in both personal applications and those carried on by mail, the application letter will not always be necessary. Ordinarily, you will send a letter in answer to a newspaper want ad or as an unsolicited application. You may write a fairly long letter and include the necessary details if you wish. The most effective method, however, is to write a short letter introducing yourself and to enclose a data sheet with picture.

The beginning of an application letter is the hardest part. What you should remember, though, are your selling techniques. Your application

Mr. Robert L. White, Manager
Apex Enterprises, Inc.
5932 Wilson Avenue
San Bernardino, CA 92405

Dear Mr. White

Have you ever wished you had an assistant who could turn out
your correspondence, contracts, and specifications quickly--
with that important touch of accuracy? I might be the one.

On June 16 I shall be graduated with honors from Cutler College
with the degree of Bachelor of Science in Business Administra-
tion. This course of study has covered two years of general
education, one year of business and economics courses, and one
year of intensive training in office procedures and management.
My favorite course in college was business writing; I like
writing both letters and reports.

Since last September I have been working part time for General
Electronics, Inc. On this job I have gained the experience of
working under pressure. When my family decided to move to San
Bernardino, my counselor suggested that I write your firm for
an interview. Mr. Thomas A. Jennings, my present employer,
will be glad to write you about my qualifications. His address
is given on the enclosed data sheet.

I plan to be in California with my family the last week in
June. May I call you for an interview for July 1?

Sincerely yours

Ann Wilcox

Miss Ann Wilcox

enclosure

Application Letter

letter must interest your prospective employer in you. The first thing you must do, then, is get his attention. If you know someone who is a friend of your prospective employer, you might (with permission) begin your letter with this fact. The second good beginning is to show what *you can do* for your reader.

For example, a young graduate of a four-year college wished to get a secretarial job with the State Department in a foreign country. She was an honor student, and she had had unusual experience in college activities. Yet a government official suggested that she begin her letter with an accomplishment that was sure to be in demand: her ability to type 100 words a minute. Look over your personal inventory. See what ability you have that would be of help to the reader of your letter.

The second paragraph should show that you know something about the work and the company and should give some information about your training. This may require that you do some research on each company before you send your letter. In this paragraph, as in the first, you will stress the reader's interest rather than your own.

In the third paragraph you should put in a personal touch, something that makes your letter different from all others that may be received. This touch will give your reader an idea about your personality. For example, one girl mentioned in her letter that she had spent the preceding summer making telephone appointments for an appliance sales firm and had learned the importance of a low, friendly voice and clear enunciation in telephone conversations. Her letter stood out from the others.

Your final paragraph is short. All it does is make it easy for your reader to get in touch with you. Just one sentence is enough: "Will you call me at 322-2410 and suggest a time when I may come in to talk with you?" This short sentence suggests action; it gives the reader your telephone number again; and it also shows courtesy. All of these factors will help you persuade your reader to give favorable attention to your application.

You can see that such a letter will follow the principles of successful selling. You will get attention, then create interest, next add a personal touch, and finally make it easy for the reader to act — by getting in touch with you. One final warning: Don't copy application letters verbatim from textbooks. In the first place, they will not represent you; in the second place, your reader may already have received dozens of that same letter. Just talk, conversationally and respectfully, to your reader as you follow the foregoing four steps. An illustration of a letter of application is given on page 187.

Now that you have composed your letter, to whom should you send it? Your first task now will be to find as many prospects as you can. This involves another principle of selling. Your campaign should be planned to cover several weeks and to involve from twenty to thirty companies.

The beginner in business who tries for one or two jobs and then takes one that is not right for him may never find the right job. Before you send any letters, you should make a list of prospective jobs. This list should cover all available sources: want ads, leads given you by friends, leads given you by placement bureaus and employment agencies, and some companies to which you have not been referred but for whom you would like to work.

When your list is ready, you should decide on which companies you will make a personal call and to which you will send an application letter. For the latter group, you must type an original letter. You may decide to use the same letter for each company, with minor changes, but you *must* send each firm an original copy. Nothing will get your campaign off to a worse start than sending out mimeographed letters. *Never* send a carbon copy of an application letter. You should also enclose a data sheet (an original), complete with photograph.

Another important point is to address your letter to an officer of the company. This makes your letter more personal and may have a direct bearing on its reception. If the firm is in your city, all you need to do is call the company and ask the person who answers if he will please give you the name of the person you want. This might be a department head or a personnel manager. If the company is out of your city, you should inquire of your public or school library for an index giving this information.

When you have sent out your letters, take your time about making a decision, and don't get panicky when your favorite firm fails to answer. One or two answers for each ten letters is average; you should send out enough letters to assure yourself of three or four answers. The more letters you send out, naturally, the more responses you are likely to receive. Your letter will have a better chance, though, if it is mechanically perfect, if it is typed with clean type and a medium dark ribbon, if there are no erasures (or the erasures are invisible), and if it is attractively arranged on the page. Make certain of these details. If you are asked to come to one firm for an interview, you should consider your mail campaign to be a success. In Chapter 14, you will find a discussion of the interview.

HELPFUL QUALITIES IN YOUR JOB-FINDING CAMPAIGN

When you embark on a job-finding campaign, qualities particularly helpful to you are foresight, thoroughness, and self-judgment.

Foresight

Perhaps the most important trait you can develop to help you succeed in your job-finding campaign is foresight. Foresight has been defined as the act of looking forward, of planning for the future. This trait is one that separates the leaders from the followers — in business as well as in other walks of life. Foresight consists, too, in anticipating life's difficulties before they arise. It means you will notice that supplies are getting low as well as prepare for the job ahead of you on the office ladder. If you have foresight, you will be able to think of many opportunities for exhibiting this trait. The following list should be helpful.

English — both spoken and written — is needed in every business job; and the higher you go, the more important it will become to you. You will show foresight, then, if you constantly strive to improve your English through general reading and specific study.

You will be using foresight if you learn as much as you can about the latest trends in business and economics. Regular reading of the magazines and newspapers of business is one excellent way of keeping abreast of the rapid changes that are constantly taking place. You should also learn all you can about your specific industry or service.

When you are employed, you soon discover that certain questions, comments, and complaints tend to be repeated by customers or clients of your firm. You will show foresight if you prepare in advance an answer for the most commonly asked questions and if you know in advance to whom you should refer the names of the products or services provided by your firm.

When you apply for a job, you will show foresight if you look ahead to the years to come. Is there a possibility of advancement in your job? If there is such a possibility, accepting a lower starting salary might be wise. If you are employed and see no advancement in your present job, you should plan for another one.

An important aspect of foresight is intelligent listening. Through listening and asking intelligent questions you can learn much that is now unfamiliar to you. Be careful, however, that you review what has been told you so that you need not ask a question more than once.

Thoroughness

The second trait of great value to you both in getting and in keeping a job is thoroughness. If you are thorough, you finish what you start, you persevere, and you display exactness. It is difficult to impress most beginners with the importance of thoroughness. Good intentions are not enough. Every task entrusted to you in business must be performed completely and accurately. Following through is as necessary in business as it is in tennis or golf.

One habit you should develop is that of thoroughly checking your work. You must be able to evaluate critically the work you do. You must

learn to check off details as they are completed. Particularly at the close of
the working day, you must check to see that all details have been taken care
of before you leave the office. The rewards in business are reserved for
those who do all that is required of them and a little bit more.

If you are selling, you must make out all sales slips completely,
accurately, and legibly. If you do bookkeeping work, you must see that
each entry in your books is carefully and correctly made. You must be
sure that the statements you send out are correct. You must be thorough
in making out all reports. You must check the correctness of all data in
the correspondence you transcribe and make sure that all questions have
been answered. If you have *any* doubts about the meaning or spelling
of a word, look it up in the dictionary. Proofread every word of every
page you type, and check the enclosures that accompany the correspondence.

One habit of thoroughness that pays big dividends is learning the
names and faces of important customers. If you can remember a customer's name and business after having heard it only once and use his name
when speaking to him, that customer will consider you a brilliant addition
to the firm.

Self-Judgment

The third trait that is needed when applying for a job is self-judgment,
which means self-analysis. You must have the ability to evaluate your
own skills, knowledge, training, and personal traits if you are to succeed.
And you must make this evaluation objectively. This means you cannot
let yourself be sensitive, that you must not become emotional in your
analysis. One good way is to think, "So what?" as you note your various
good and bad points.

Believe it or not, you will make more improvement as a result of
your self-analysis if you keep your emotions out of the picture. When
your emotions become involved with your feelings about yourself, it is
almost impossible to accept any kind of help from others. No matter what
the criticism, you immediately rush to your own defense. A friend may
tell you, with the kindest of intentions, that you have a tendency to complain a great deal. This is actually an easy habit to break. Yet, if you are
emotional about criticism, you will only be hurt and angry at the person
for criticizing you and make no effort to stop complaining. Saying "So
what?" to yourself is a graphic way of expressing emotional detachment,
and saying it will help you build detachment.

Too much introspection, or thinking about ourselves, is not good for
us; so taking stock of our good and bad qualities should be done rarely. One
time should be just before or after you get your first job. This is true be-

cause you may have had no need to do this before and thus have an unclear picture of yourself. The next time you will need to take stock is when you first become dissatisfied with your work. Small disappointments come to all workers, of course; these do not call for self-analysis. If you should have an extended period of disliking your work, however, you should take stock. Your feeling of dissatisfaction may be caused by a job that is actually unsatisfactory, or it may be caused by personal factors that are frequently unrecognized.

The best way to find out exactly how others are affected by your personality is to have some other person tell you. This is easier said than done, however. No one wants to make an enemy; you may take offense even if you ask another person to point out your faults. And this is true regardless of how much you assure the other person you will not be offended. If you have a good friend with whom you might trade suggestions, and if both of you are tactful, both parties should benefit.

Being tactful is extremely important. If your friend asks you to tell him frankly if you can understand why he was not promoted when he had expected to be, you must not say, "Because your work is always late." This may lose you your friend, and he may fail to profit by your suggestion in his anxiety to explain to you just why he was late. A better way is to start with his good points. You might mention his accuracy, his good judgment, his care in checking all details. Then you might say, "Perhaps that's it. You may be too conscientious. Your boss may prefer to have you submit some of your projects immediately, rather than take longer to check and recheck." If you can get your friend to make this suggestion himself . . . but, then, you could be a counselor instead of a friend!

If you would rather not undertake a combined improvement campaign, you can follow this same suggestion yourself. Write down all of your good points on a sheet of paper; underline the ones you consider outstanding. Take the most outstanding virtue you have and look at its opposite. For example, the other side of generosity is selfishness. And every virtue, if carried to extremes, can become a vice. See, then, if you could possibly be going too far in that particular direction. Are you thrifty? Look at yourself again. Compare yourself with one of your more popular classmates or co-workers with respect to this trait. Just how thrifty are you? If you are much more thrifty than John, the man who was promoted instead of you, then it may be possible that you have gone too far with this virtue and become stingy!

Try the following plan with at least three of your predominant traits; the results may surprise you! When you have compared yourself with a successful friend and found that you need some improvement, it is really a simple matter to improve. Any negative trait can be eliminated. First, you attack one trait at a time. Second, you must plan in advance. If you are going to make yourself be more generous, for example, you must make a plan and carry it out. It is not enough to be more "giving" when the opportunity comes up. You must make your own opportunities. Ask one of your friends to have lunch with you, and get the check first. Keep working on one trait until your overdoing in that direction has been eliminated. Then go on to the next one.

FOLLOW-UP ACTIVITIES

1. Interview an experienced worker in a job that you would like to have. Ask this worker to tell you something about the qualities needed for the job, the personality traits that are aids to success, and something about the standards of work.
2. Interview an executive. Telephone for an appointment and ask if you may question him about the type of employee he seeks. Take notes on all that is told you.
3. One of the hurdles you must conquer in getting a job is talking with an interviewer. How do you rate when you talk with strangers? If you feel insecure in this respect, do some practicing. Talk with someone whom you do not know about employment matters. Possible sources are librarians, teachers in your school whom you do not know, the placement director in your school. Try to get over your fear before you go to an actual interview.
4. Practice interviewing a friend for a position you would like. Ask this friend such questions as the following:
   Why do you want to work for this company?
   How long do you plan to stay in one job?
   What machines can you operate? Do you consider yourself a competent worker on these machines?
   What make of typewriter do you prefer? Why?
   Are you married? engaged? What are your plans?
   These questions may be asked you in an interview. What attitude should you have toward semipersonal questions of this sort?
5. Office work is competitive. How will you compare with other applicants for the job you want? Rate yourself on the following qualities as follows: plus — very good; check — average; and minus — poor.

Reliability	Manners	Leadership
Good nature	Poise	Intelligence
Honesty	Concentration	Accuracy

Now rate three of your friends who are also ready to look for their first jobs. Be honest — and do not refer to your own scores — and then compare yourself with your friends. If you score higher, you are probably ready for employment. If you score lower, you have more work to do.

CASE PROBLEMS

1. Experience or Change?

Ben Mendoza has just graduated from high school. He has two job opportunities for the summer. One is a general office job in a large manufacturing company. The other, which pays more, is driving a truck. Ben likes to drive and enjoys out-of-doors. He is planning to go to a nearby community college in the fall to study computer science. If you were Ben, which job would you take?

1. What advantages would each job offer? What disadvantages?
2. How should Ben rate the following three factors in choosing a summer job: salary, change of activity from school, and experience allied to his chosen career?
3. Should Ben's national origin background influence his decision?

2. What About English Mechanics?

Barbara Chamberlain, a black 20-year-old stenographer, has a job in the office of a construction company. In the letters her employer dictates, he is very careless about his English usage. Such matters as grammar and old-fashioned phrasing seem of no importance to him. Barbara has always done well in English courses in school and has also done well in a course in business communication.

1. What should Barbara do about the situation?
2. It has been said that policies and facts are the responsibility of the dictator, but that spelling, punctuation, and grammar are the responsibility of the stenographer. If this is true, should Barbara say anything about the matter to her employer? Why or why not?
3. If Barbara decides to correct the mistakes in grammar, how far should she go in changing her employer's style or characteristic way of expressing his meaning?

3. Who Is Responsible?

Claire Baker usually proofreads all letters after she transcribes them. Her employer dictated several letters at 4:15 p.m., and because Claire was in a hurry to leave, she mailed these letters without proofreading them. In one letter that asked for the payment of a past-due account of $50, she typed the amount as $40. A prompt reply was received with a check for $40 in full payment of the account. Claire's employer insisted that she make good the difference. Claire agreed, but she thought his demand was very unfair.

1. Who is responsible for errors of this type, the business or the employees who make them?
2. What is the rule when cashiers make mistakes in giving change?
3. Why does business insist on accurate records where money is involved?
4. What opinion might the customer who paid $40 likely have of the firm?

4. Be Specific

A wholesaler of carpenters' tools has a vacancy in the sales department. Mr. Peterson, Director of Sales Personnel, calls the local college and asks that interested young men submit letters of application and data sheets. When the letters arrive, he narrows them down to two, one from Charles Pittman and one from Joe Anderson.   The letter from Charles Pittman contains the following as part of his third paragraph: "I am confident that I can sell tools because I am prepared to sell. I get along well with people. I believe that I can sell the tools because I have always been interested in selling. As I am going to be married soon, I am interested in a permanent job."

In the third paragraph of Joe Anderson's letter are these statements: "I like to make bookcases and do odd jobs around our house. When you have a hobby like carpentering, you appreciate the value of Camp's forged steel tools. Although I have not sold tools, I have been a clerk in a drugstore, where I learned the techniques of selling."

1. Which person do you think Mr. Peterson will employ? Why?
2. Why is it better to speak of specific facts than to make general statements when applying for a job?
3. What specific statement could Charles Pittman have written as evidence that he gets along well with people?
4. Is approaching matrimony a good selling point? Why or why not?

5. Constructive Criticism

Dan O'Riley has the common habit of saying "You know" three or four times in every conversation.   In fact, he sometimes repeats this meaningless phrase twice in one sentence. Peter Neerings, who works at the next desk with Dan in the credit department of a large firm, has noticed how Dan's repetition of the phrase annoys their supervisor. Peter decides to mention the matter to Dan. He tells Dan, however, that the mannerism annoys him — rather than mentioning the supervisor.   Dan is hurt by the criticism but asks Peter what he can do to break the habit, since he is not aware that he repeats the phrase at all.

1. Assuming you are Peter, can you make any suggestions to Dan to help him break this habit?
2. What do you think of Peter's assuming sole responsibility instead of bringing in the supervisor's name?
3. Can you think of a tactful way of bringing up this matter to avoid hurting Dan's feelings?

chapter 14

interviewing for the job you want

You may have heard that the interview is the place where you put your best foot forward. In a way, this old saying is true; but only in a way. If you try too hard to make a good impression, the impression you make will be one of effort, of strain. Of course, your first interview may be rather frightening. Any first experience has its hazards. One sure way to make it more frightening than it need be, however, is to worry about what may happen. Don't even think about the success or lack of success in your first interview. Instead, consider your interview to be a pleasant conversation in which you will do your best to answer all questions promptly and correctly. Also, be ready to ask questions of your own when the opportunity arises and try to appear at ease.

Why is it important to refrain from looking ahead to the probable results of your interview? The answer is contained in one word, tenseness. If you are concerned with the results of what you are saying, of the success or failure of the impression you are making, you will become tense. Tenseness causes all kinds of unfortunate reactions. Your memory fails you; you hesitate in answering the simplest questions, thus appearing to be unsure of your answers; your expression, your voice, your posture, all advertise that you are frightened. All of this can be eliminated if you concentrate on the *now* rather than on the future. Chalk this interview up to experience. Resolve to do your best, but possibly just for practice. Decide before you begin that the first two or three interviews will be for the sole purpose of learning how to be your own real self in a new situation.

If you can eliminate tenseness by being relaxed, you will be able to show the real you to your interviewer — something you will not be able to do if you are tense. After all, your interviewer will appreciate your relaxed attitude. It is not pleasant to inspire fear in people you talk with,

and your interviewer does not enjoy this any more than you do. Your
interview will be much more successful if you are relaxed and if you are
prepared. Successful preparation involves your appearance, proof of what
you can do, and perseverance.

DRESSING THE PART

If you were cast in a school or community play as a successful young
worker in the firm of your choice, how would you dress? This is the
question you must answer when you get ready for your first interview.
First impressions are often lasting ones, and just as often they are made
on the basis of your appearance. Your friends may judge you or excuse
you on the basis of your kind heart or your past actions, but none of this
information is available to your interviewer. He can judge you only on
what he sees. He may actually make decisions about your personality
and capability on the basis of that first impression. You can make that
first impression work for you if you dress the part.

To make sure you are dressing the part, visit the leading business
firm in your city or town and see for yourself how the young, successful
workers dress. You may discover that sport clothes and campus outfits
are not worn in leading business firms. While the old advice to wear only
dark colors to the interview is no longer followed, it is still best to avoid
extremes but to follow fashion with simple lines and good quality.

Extreme styles should be avoided, though some of the workers in
the firm you visit may be wearing them. Remember, you are the newcomer. Until you can be sure of your acceptance, it is better to dress in
fashion — but not in the most extreme fashion that is being worn. Makeup
for girls and women should be applied with an artistic and not too lavish
hand. Men should take note of the hair length that is followed by the young
men employed in the responsible positions of the firm. Extremes beyond
these norms may handicap them in getting the job they want.

Grooming for the interview should be perfect. Never skip any detail
of grooming when dressing for an interview. Clothing should be clean
and fresh. Be sure to use an effective deodorant and a mouthwash. Carry
a clean handkerchief. Wear new hose or socks to reduce the possibility
of snags, runs, or holes. Avoid too much jewelry. While tastes of executives
differ in this regard, you will never be criticized for wearing too little
jewelry.

WHAT YOU CAN DO

Next to your appearance, your interviewer will want evidence of your
abilities. The reason your abilities come second is that your appearance is

infinitely easier for your interviewer to evaluate. Also, he will read into the neatness of your dress certain estimates of the way you will work. These estimates will be supplemented with questions and, possibly, tests. When questions are asked, general statements of what you like to do, of your interest in people, and so on are of little help. A company wants to hire workers who have proved themselves. You may feel that you have no proof; and, when you seek your first job, you may feel completely inadequate. What you may not realize, though, is that experienced executives understand this feeling; they consider it natural. What they will not understand is any attempt on your part to "gild the lily." If you have had absolutely no previous experience, you must state this frankly when asked. You must not pretend to be something you are not.

An executive is interested, however, in any kind of work you may have done. Although you are applying for office work, the executive will be glad to know about newspaper routes, care of young children, playground directing, leadership in summer camps, manual labor, and many other forms of honest work you may have performed. Vacations spent in worthwhile work tell your interviewer that you have formed desirable work habits.

What You Can Do For a Specific Company

Before you go to any company for an interview, learn all you can about it. Find out what products are manufactured or sold, what services are performed, the location of branch offices in other cities. Ask your librarian for indexes containing this information. You may be surprised to know how much information is available to you. Whether you have an opportunity to display this knowledge is not too important. What is important is the confidence you will gain when you succeed in becoming acquainted with the company.

When you know something about the company, you will be better prepared to display what you can do. First, gather together samples of your work. If you are young and inexperienced, you may not have many exhibits to present. What you do put into your portfolio, however, should be of the highest quality. Depending on the kind of job for which you are applying, you should gather exhibits that will show you are familiar with the type of work done in the company. Actual evidence is much more effective than any unsupported statement you could make.

If you are applying for a stenographic position, you might include in your portfolio the following materials:

1. To show skill:
   2 letters perfectly typed and artistically arranged
   2 form letters with fill-ins

2 examples of statistical typing
An example of forms filled in with a typewriter
A stencil you have cut
Certificates of proficiency in shorthand and typewriting
2. To show personality traits:
Clippings from the school newspaper showing activities in which you participated
Copies of minutes of meetings (you were the secretary)
Data sheet

If you are applying for a position in the bookkeeping department, you might include in your portfolio:

1. To show skill:
The journal record of a completed set
Several invoices, statements, and receipts attractively written
A copy of your balance sheet that had been selected for class display
2. To show personality traits:
Financial statement that you, as treasurer of the student body, issued at a recent meeting
A letterhead that you designed for school use in a typewriting class
An issue of the school paper containing art sketches you made
Data sheet

You can see that almost any evidence of worthwhile activities in school, clubs, or community projects is of interest to the prospective employer. Although such activities may not be directly related to the assignments you will receive on the job, they do show personal qualities that may interest the employer. Samples of your work should be kept from your school classes whenever they appear to be valuable evidence to show when you apply for a job.

There are other bits of information you should have at your finger tips. First, you must know your social security number if you have one. If you don't have one, you should get one before you go for an interview. Second, keep in mind the dates of important events in your life, the names of your former employers, and the kind of work you did in each case.

If you are applying for specialized work, you will need the tools and materials required in case you take tests. For instance, if you are applying for a stenographic position, you should take a shorthand notebook, a pen, a pencil, a type eraser, and a small pocket dictionary in case you are asked to take dictation and transcribe. For all kinds of jobs you should take a pen, a pencil, and a pocket dictionary. You may be filling out forms even if you are not required to take any of the tests required by industry.

Take a Deep Breath

No matter how well prepared you may be, the effect will be ruined if you appear for your interview looking as though you just barely made it. Take plenty of time. Allow yourself twice as much time to get to your destination as you would normally require. If you drive, you may have car trouble; if you take a bus or a train, you may have to wait longer than you expected. And, regardless of your means of transportation, always go to your interview alone. Any young person who needs the support of a friend is not mature enough to take a job.

When you go into the reception room of the company, you will give your name and the time of your appointment (and the name of the interviewer if you know it). The receptionist will probably ask you to be seated and wait. Don't be alarmed if there are other people waiting, too. Be friendly, reply to all questions courteously, but do not bother the receptionist or other employees with questions.

Even if you wait for some time, try to relax; think of a pleasant subject. Above all, don't anticipate difficulties when your turn comes to go in to talk with the interviewer. Even with the best of intentions, you may find yourself suffering from stage fright as you walk into a strange office. It may help you to know that stage fright often acts as an aid to the sufferer. "Butterflies" may mean that you are keyed up to a high level of alertness, and your first words to the interviewer will banish your nervousness. In any case, the following suggestions may help you.

Stand tall. The first impression you make is certain to be a better one if you stand tall. This does not mean a stiff, military posture. Raise your chest, keep your ears lifted, and your posture will be as it should be. One hazard may happen to you: the employer may be busy when you go into his office. If this should happen, do nothing except stand quietly until he looks up. Don't do anything with your hands as you stand. Putting them in your pockets, moving your handbag from one hand to another, crossing your arms, all advertise that you are ill at ease. Just let your hands hang at your sides. Regardless of how this feels to you, it looks more relaxed than any other attitude you could assume.

Think about something pleasant. Have you ever had someone ask you to look pleasant as he snapped your picture? And, as you looked pleasant, how did the snapshot turn out? Was the smile you forced a natural one? Probably not, yet this is usually the way any attempt to look pleasant turns out. A better way to achieve the appearance of being comfortable in your surroundings is to think of something pleasant. If you do this, your "look" will follow suit, and it will also appear more natural. Perhaps the best thing to think about is some good point you have noticed about the company. If you are interested, you will look interested — and this is a pleasant sight for the interviewer to see. It can set the tone of the entire interview and contribute to your getting the job.

What should you say first? Suppose you have been standing in front of the interviewer's desk for several moments and he finally looks up at you. What should you say? Remember, the employer does not know you; so the first thing you say is your name. In your most natural manner, tell the employer who you are — and use the employer's name. Say, "Mr. Eccles, I am John Cardwell. You asked me to come in this morning." It is pretentious to give yourself any title whatever, so don't say you are Mr. Cardwell or Miss Ellsworth. And don't supply your middle name unless you go by both names. It sounds all right to say, "I am Mary Jo Smith, Mr. Eccles," but to say, "Mr. Eccles, I am John Kennleworth Cardwell," is too much. After you give your name, the interviewer will ask you to be seated and take the interview from there.

What do you do with your belongings? In cold weather, it is best to leave your outer coat, boots, or other paraphernalia in the reception room, hanging them up if there is some arrangement such as hooks, hat racks, or closets available. It is decidedly awkward to carry excess clothing into the employer's office. You girls will carry your handbag and perhaps gloves. If your bag is large, put your gloves inside it and place the bag upright at your feet. If it is small, hold it in your lap. You men should hold your hats in the same way if you wear one, and place your briefcase on the floor beside your chair. If you are asked to write something, do so at your chair. Do not touch the employer's desk. Don't put anything on it, and don't look at anything on it (letters, contracts, and the like). If you can keep your hands quiet, you will add to the good impression you make. Any kind of activity of the hands, turning a ring, smoothing your hair, touching your face, will show that you are nervous.

What Do You Say?

The employer will lead the interview, but there are a number of directions he may take. Some interviewers ask many questions. When this happens, be sure to answer with enough detail. For example, if an employer should say, "You say your name is John Cardwell," you might answer, "Yes, sir." A more detailed answer is better, however. If you continue, "Mr. Kent from the Central College placement office asked me to see you," this places you more exactly than merely answering in the affirmative could do. This answer, too, will naturally lead into a discussion of your school work, the subjects you liked best, your grades in your major field, school activities, and so on.

It is important that you answer all questions without hesitation. You may be asked why you want to work for this particular company. Such a question is frequently asked, so it is wise to be ready with an answer.

If you have a friend who is employed in the company, this is a valid reason. Or you may answer that you are interested in this business (banking, manufacturing, the oil business, or whatever it may be). Another reason may be that you have been a customer of the company and have admired the way they deal with the public. Whatever your reason may be, give it promptly and sincerely.

Controversial questions. Some interviewers make a practice of asking a question or two that is controversial. Such a question might have to do with politics, religion, racial matters, or economics. If this kind of question is asked you, give a mild but straightforward answer. It is important that you refrain from anything that may sound argumentative no matter what your interviewer may say. It is possible that such questions are asked to see if the applicant can remain calm under pressure. No matter what the motive, however, it will be to your advantage if you *do* remain calm. A good mental attitude is recognition of the universality of different opinions.

Your previous employer. You must avoid saying anything negative about a former employer or teacher. Your interviewer will assume that you will be just as likely to knock him and his company to someone else. The reputation for loyalty is built up by saying positive things about former associates of all kinds. An employer who asks about your low grades in some school subject will appreciate your taking the blame. If you say you didn't work as hard as you should, or that you spent too much time on extracurricular activities, you will make a better impression than if you blame your low grades on a poor teacher. Because he dislikes hiring a troublemaker, an employer will avoid hiring a person who whines or knocks. Saying negative things about former associates is one symptom of the troublemaking habit. Be careful that you keep away from any possibility of having the tag of troublemaker applied to you.

What about salary? Should the beginning applicant say anything about salary? In general, it is best not to bring up the matter too soon. Don't ask the interviewer how much the job is worth at the beginning of the interview. On the other hand, you should be prepared with some statement about salary if the question is asked you. What should you say if the interviewer asks, "What salary do you expect?" If you are currently employed or if you have worked recently, you might mention the salary you made or are making, with the qualification that you would expect an advance if you are working. The beginner, however, does not have this advantage. What should you say if you are seeking your first job? In this case, you need not mention a specific amount. You might say you are interested in advancement, but that the interviewer would have more of an idea what the particular job is worth. This statement would open the matter for discussion.

Before you go to your first interview, you should find out what beginning office jobs are paying in your community. Possible sources of information about salaries are your school placement service, the United States Employment Service, and the business teachers in your school. If you should reach the end of your interview and find that nothing has been said about salary, you will have to bring up the subject. You might say, "Could you give me some idea of the salary?" Stated this way, the question sounds reasonable rather than grasping. It should merit a factual reply.

When discussing salary, you should be perfectly frank. Do not say you have been offered some amount if it is not the case. The quickest way to be blacklisted among businessmen is to misrepresent facts when applying for a job. If you should be seriously considered for employment, your would-be employer will certainly check on the information you have given him. On the other hand, you should not understate your desires. If you are willing to work for the salary suggested, that is one thing; it is another if you agree to the suggested salary in order to get the job and then regret your decision.

Remember that a business is not a charitable organization. You should not explain why you need a job or why you need a certain salary. The employer is interested in what you can do for the company. It is much better, then, for you to emphasize your abilities and skills, your knowledge of the work to be done, and your interest in the field.

What Do You Do?

In a way, an interview can be a miniature working situation. You may be given a test that simulates the work for which you are applying. If you are asked to take dictation, for example, try to be calm. It is better to go slowly and accurately because hurrying will cause mistakes which, in turn, will make you more nervous. You have been instructed to have a pen, notebook, small dictionary, and type eraser with you when applying for a secretarial position. This is because asking to borrow some needed item during the test session will look anything but efficient to the person conducting the test.

You fill out an application blank. One activity is customary when you go to a firm for an interview; this is filling out an application blank. Again, do not hurry. Take enough time to read each item carefully. Notice if your name is to be written or printed and whether your last or first name is to appear first. Unless you are asked to typewrite the information, the blank should be filled out in ink. Careful reading of each statement will eliminate erasures and strikeouts. You should answer all questions, leaving no blank spaces. If the question does not apply to you, draw a horizontal line in the space provided. This indicates that you have read the question but that it does not apply to you. If you leave a blank space, this could mean that you failed to see the question or that you did not wish to answer it for some reason.

Be as neat as you can, both in writing and in keeping the blank free from smudges, wrinkles, and fingerprints. Be extra careful to carry out all directions that are printed on the blank. Some firms consider the ability to follow directions one of the best indications of the applicant's suitability for employment.

You leave promptly. When you have finished taking any tests that are required and filled in the required forms, and when the employer has asked everything he wishes to know, he may indicate that the interview is over. This indication may be a statement, a question, or merely a long pause. You must be perceptive enough to catch your cue, whatever it is, and to act upon it at once. Long, drawn-out leave takings are inappropriate and will do you harm. You should pick up your belongings (such as a briefcase or a handbag), rise, thank the employer for considering you, say good-bye pleasantly, and then go. There is one thing you might make sure of, however. The employer may tell you he will call you in a few days, after he has consulted your references. If he says nothing, you may ask if it will be all right if you call in a week or so to see if a decision has been reached. In any case, whether you mention the matter or not, following up on a job you want is good strategy, for it will indicate to the prospective employer that you have a sincere interest in getting the job. Ways of following up are discussed below.

You follow up. It is courteous to write a short letter of appreciation for the interview. Then, after several days, you may call the employer and ask if he has filled the position for which you applied. If the job is still open, the telephone call may bring your application to his attention; if it is filled, knowing about it at once is preferable to waiting. Some excellent jobs have been won because of persistent follow-up on the part of the applicant.

Keeping yourself in the picture is usually to your advantage; but whatever happens, you must not give up. You will learn a great deal from going on several interviews. If you consider each interview as a stepping-stone to the job you want, you will be less likely to try too hard to impress any one employer. Just be yourself; it is the most impressive *you* that you can present.

APPLICATION FOR EMPLOYMENT

Full Name (Print)
Mr.
Miss
Mrs. _____
                        FIRST   MIDDLE   LAST

Present Address _____Telephone No. _____
                        STREET AND NUMBER

_____
            CITY OR TOWN   STATE   ZIP

How long have you resided there? _____

Permanent or Home Address _____
                                    STREET AND NUMBER

_____
            CITY OR TOWN   STATE   ZIP

How long did you reside there? _____

Date of Birth _____Age _____
                    MONTH   DAY   YEAR

Are you single? _____married? _____widowed? _____

separated? _____divorced? _____

Have you any relatives in the employ of this company? _____

If so, give name, relationship, and position. _____

APPLICANTS SHOULD NOT WRITE BELOW THIS LINE

Interviewed by:	Date of interview	Date applicant available for work
Applicant's Areas of Special Strength and Interest		

Date Employed	Clock Number	Enrolled in Bonus Plan	Classification
Enrolled in Group Insurance	Enrolled in Pension Plan	Blue Cross-Blue Shield Coverage ☐Ind. ☐Fam. ☐Surg.	
Date Employment Terminated	Reason	Consider for Reemployment	

Application blank

EDUCATIONAL RECORD

School	Name and Location	No. of Yrs.	Date of Graduation	Specialized Subjects
High School				
College				
Others (Specify)				

Are you now attending school? _____

If so, give particulars. _____

_____

What office machines do you operate? (typewriter, keypunch, etc.) _____

_____

Are you a skilled operator in the use of these machines? _____

Give experience. _____

_____

What experience have you had as a stenographer? _____

_____

What foreign languages do you speak? _____

What foreign languages do you read and write? _____

_____

_____

Application blank (continued)

EMPLOYMENT RECORD

From		To		Name and Address of Employer	Nature of Work	Salary (Monthly)	Why did you leave?
Yr.	Mo.	Yr.	Mo.				

If you are employed at present, why do you wish to leave? _____

_____

_____

May we write to your present employer concerning you? _____

Have you ever been dismissed or requested to resign from any position? _____

If so, when, where, and for what reason? _____

_____

_____

_____

PERSONAL DESCRIPTION

Height _____

Weight _____

Color of Eyes _____

Color of Hair _____

Have you any physical defects or deformities that might affect your work?

_____

Explain fully.

Is your sight or hearing impaired in any way?

_____

_____

Have you ever been accused of or convicted of any crime? _____

Give particulars. _____

_____

Have you ever had a surety bond canceled or an application declined by a bonding company? _____If so, state particulars. _____

_____

_____

Application blank (continued)

PERSONAL REFERENCES

List the names of three persons, other than relatives, to whom we may refer concerning you.

NAME AND ADDRESS	OCCUPATION	YEARS OF ACQUAINTANCE

DEPENDENTS

NAME	AGE	RELATIONSHIP

THE SPACE BELOW IS FOR THE USE OF THE INTERVIEWER:

_____

_____

_____

_____

_____

_____

_____

_____

_____

_____

Application blank (concluded)

Which Job Should You Accept?

If you are well qualified, you may have your choice of several positions. You may be hesitant to accept a position that is available because you may think you can find a better position elsewhere. This attitude may or may not be realistic. If you cannot perform your best work with maximum satisfaction in a particular job, you are wise to discover the fact before you begin work. If you are reluctant to accept an available job because your salary or prestige demands are too great, then you may have to adjust your demands. However, as you want to build a satisfying career for yourself, you should not sell yourself short just to obtain immediate employment. Your goal is to market your services for the best possible measure of job stimulation and challenge, security, appreciation, and other rewards.

In deciding whether or not you will accept a position, the following questions should be considered:

How stable is the firm? Is it just getting started? What are the indications that it will succeed or grow?

What opportunities are there for advancement?

What promotional policies has the firm established?

Will I need more education if I remain with the firm? Have I formulated plans for such education?

When a vacancy occurs in a better position, is someone likely to be brought into the firm to fill the vacancy?

What is the reputation of this firm? Within the company itself? Among the personnel? Among customers or clients? Among other people?

What security does the position offer? In times of depression what layoff policy will be followed? Can the employers usually be depended upon to be just and fair? Will the employers keep their word? If sickness takes an employee from his work temporarily, will his job be filled by someone else?

What social security does the position offer for retirement? For unemployment? For sickness and hospitalization? For injury?

Will the work be challenging enough during a period of years?

Do you like the employers and your immediate superiors?

Do you have the aptitudes, interests, and abilities required by this job?

Are there any negative characteristics? Some people want to avoid night work, travel, and so forth.

In answering these questions, you will have to find sources of information about labor trends, industrial expansion, technological changes, and other factors. Many books and magazines discuss opportunities for employment and advancement in great detail.

If You Like the Job

If you like your new position, do all you can to express your appreciation by doing your best work. You may find that you can achieve greater satisfaction by growing in the present position than by competing for advancement. If you make a decision to grow in the present capacity, you must constantly try to improve your efficiency. If you have no ambition to advance or to improve in your present assignment, you will grow stale and become both bored and boring.

Length of service in a single capacity offers opportunity that is rewarding. By familiarity with the position, you can obtain more knowledge and skill. You will become more expert in your duties and will assume more responsibility. This thoroughness and familiarity may make you more secure in times of staff reduction. If the human relationships afforded in the present capacity are pleasant, you may find that continued work with the personnel will be more rewarding than adjusting to new co-workers.

Some people cannot perform their best work in a competitive situation. By growth in a job instead of ambition to advance, the stress of competition can frequently be avoided, and yet a feeling of success can be attained.

THE EXTRA MILE

What does "going the extra mile" mean to you? About fifty years ago, the word "character" was in common use. Character meant the ability to remain steadfast under difficulties; and, in that bygone day, strength of character was the most important attribute that an individual could possess. Now, however, we don't hear much about character; the word seems actually to have gone out of fashion. In its place, let's substitute "going the extra mile."

How do you know if you can go the extra mile? One clue is this: Can you keep going when the going gets rough? Another clue is whether you can stand on your own two feet. People who lean on others, who always ask for help, who are filled with self-pity are not the kind who go the extra mile. They are the ones who give up. Everyone has problems; but he who can go the extra mile masters his problems.

It takes courage to go the extra mile. It also takes courage to admit your mistakes. Once having admitted them, however, you will find your path much smoother. If, on the other hand, you cover up your mistakes, you will spend far too much time making excuses, blaming your troubles on others, depending on the alibi. If you admit an error in judgment, you may feel chagrin — or you may even be punished — but eventually you will be respected for your honest admission.

You demonstrate your ability to go the extra mile by taking responsibility for your errors, by facing irritations without reacting to them, by defending the policies of the firm, by ignoring pettiness and gossip that may involve you, by standing up to be counted for that which you know is right. You go the extra mile when you cheerfully perform the difficult, tedious, or unpleasant task when it falls to you. You go the extra mile when you perform your work with poise, dignity, and patience although conditions at work or in your private life may be distressing. You go the extra mile when you do not take unnecessary advantage of illness, physical handicaps, or interruptions to avoid work.

The strong person is rarely rewarded early in his career. You should prepare yourself for the fact that, like the reward for many other positive qualities, the reward for going the extra mile may be delayed. Still, if you are really the person who goes the extra mile, your own self-knowledge will be reward enough. You will know that you can cope with whatever you need to do. Eventually, others will know that in a crisis, great or small, they can depend on you.

In Chapter 2, the three selves each of us has inside us were discussed. The Adult self is the self that is strengthened when you go the extra mile. The Adult self is then able to take control. When you have a strong Adult self, you will refuse to become ruffled, no matter what the provocation. Anyone in business who can remain calm under pressure becomes a valuable asset to the firm. You see, emotions are contagious; both hysteria and tranquility are catching. Modern business is filled with emergencies, crises, pressures. Someone who can remain calm will act as a human tranquilizer to those about him. To paraphrase Kipling, if you can keep your head when those about you are losing theirs — you will be a real addition to the staff of the firm.

An Adult self in control has another side, as well. Not only will it help you control negative emotions, but it will act as a self-starter to make yourself do the things you should do. Actually, your success in business will depend to a great extent upon your ability to control your work habits. Innate intelligence is highly overrated by many people as a factor in success. A brilliant mind helps, of course, but it will not insure success. Interest in your work, enthusiasm, work habits, carefulness in checking details — all these play an important part.

You may have observed someone with great talent who was at the top of his profession. What you did not see was the long period of hard work that had gone into this person's career. The axiom that genius is 90 percent perspiration and 10 percent inspiration is true. Even gifted men and women must work hard if their talent and intelligence are to benefit themselves and others; work always requires self-control. In long-range planning, all of us want to work; but doing the job in front of us requires much personal discipline. If a supervisor oversees the work, this outside force helps you to settle down to work. If you have a job you must do without prodding from others, you must have adult self-control to work efficiently.

Some of the common ways to put off applying adult self-control are used by all of us. We get a drink of water; we adjust the ventilation; we become distracted at the slightest interruption and find it hard to pick up the thread again. All of these preparations for work must be forgotten. The best way to start working is to sit down and begin. Get started with a stubby pencil. Save that drink of water for a reward at the end of your first completed page. Adjust the ventilation as a reward for the completion of your second. If you use adult self-control the first few times, you will form the habit of concentrated effort. With this habit, you will find yourself becoming a much more productive worker.

There is no simple formula for controlling efforts and emotions. By trial and error you will discover ways that work for you. Just remember that practice in adult self-control builds strength. The following list will provide you with opportunities for building a strong Adult self. If you find habits in this list that you would like to acquire, begin now to make such habits a part of your own personality.

Ability to work at a task that evidently does not offer immediate interest or pleasure

Ability to work on a fixed schedule, even when you are your own taskmaster

Ability to work instead of participating in pleasant sports or entertainment when the work cannot be postponed

Not waiting until the last minute before beginning a necessary task

Attending to the most demanding duties first, rather than doing the most interesting work first

Conquering evidences of anger, impulses to "tell off" other people, and smouldering resentment

Ability to control giggling, idleness, tears, and visiting

Ability to spend some time alone in quiet work or recreation

Ability to work in the presence of distracting influences — physical discomfort, noise, emotional stress, heat, etc.

Ability to work when weary, even late at night if the occasion demands "burning the midnight oil"

Expecting oneself to perform assignments, not just satisfactorily, but well

Ability to take justified correction or criticism without malice, anger, or tears

Ability to tolerate differences of opinion, injustices, and impositions without a display of emotion

Ability to be objective and impartial when working with others, regardless of friendly or unfriendly feelings toward co-workers

Ability not to spend money for something that will give immediate pleasure when the money can be set aside so that it can provide greater satisfaction in the future

Ability to save some money for emergencies

Ability not to indulge in pleasures that cause injury to the body, mind, or emotions

Ability not to boast, even though there may be cause

Ability to keep confidential information secret

Patience when other people make work difficult

GOING THE EXTRA MILE IN GETTING A JOB

If you have developed a strong Adult self, your job-finding campaign will be a much more rewarding experience. You may be lucky and find the job you want with your first interview. There *is* an element of luck involved in getting the right job for you: being in the right place at the right time. It is more likely that you will just miss that golden opportunity —and more than once. Just keep telling yourself that the Parent self in you feels resentment and talks about discrimination and unfair practices when you don't get the job. The Child self in you gives up, causes you to take the job you don't want, or turns to an easy way out that is rarely the right way. The only self who can help you find the job you want is your Adult self. Learn to go that extra mile; strengthen your Adult self in every way you can.

FOLLOW-UP ACTIVITIES

1. It has been said that if you work for two weeks, eight hours a day, as hard as you would on the job, you will get the job. Outline two weeks of activities on a job-finding campaign that would bring this kind of success.
2. How many businesses can you count in your town where you might apply for a job you would like?
3. Survey 10 business firms in your town regarding the future openings for some kind of work that you can do. Present your findings to the class orally.
4. If you had your choice, in what area of business would you like to work? How many such businesses are there in your town? Prepare a summary if requested by your instructor.
5. Suppose you were being interviewed today. In the space provided, write the adjective that would best describe the way an interviewer would probably rate you in the following:

Appearance _____   Attitude _____
Approach _____   Temperament _____
Dress _____   Knowledge _____
Hands and face _____   General
Speech _____   Reaction _____

6. Which of the following descriptions would you use to describe the way you meet people during an interview? What can you do to improve your rating?

| Lacks ease | Slightly nervous | Averted eyes |
| Nervous | At ease | Great poise |

CASE PROBLEMS

1. If at First You Don't Succeed . . .

Carla Mendoza is about to graduate from the junior college in her town and has begun her job-getting campaign. On Tuesday morning she mails ten application letters with data sheets enclosed to the leading firms in the area. On Thursday there is one reply. The office manager of Stewart Electronics, Inc. asks her to call for an appointment for an interview. Carla calls and is told to come the following Monday. When Carla arrives, she is told that Mr. McKay has been called out of town for a week. Carla asks if there is someone else she can see, but the receptionist answers that no one else in the firm can hire office workers. Greatly discouraged, Carla goes back to her typewriter and sends out ten more application letters.

1. If you were Carla, what would you have done in this situation?
2. Which would you consider the most effective follow-up in this case, a letter, a telephone call, or a personal call at the office the following week? Why?
3. Why might Carla take the initiative, even though she did not break the appointment?
4. What attitude should Carla take when she sees Mr. McKay? Why?
5. Why is it inappropriate for Carla to show any resentment because of the broken appointment?

2. It Works Both Ways

Dick Bennett is badly in need of a job, as his father has recently had a heart attack and is temporarily unable to work. Dick hears of a job in a box factory and applies at once. He is interviewed by one of the company officers and is given a series of tests. The following day Mr. Daynes, the man who interviewed Dick, calls him and says that he has not been given the job because his test scores were too high. Dick insists that he would be happy to take the job, no matter what the test scores say. Mr. Daynes insists, however, that it is company policy to give routine, repetitive jobs only to applicants of average ability. Dick feels that he has been treated unfairly.

1. Why would such a policy be made? What is its purpose?
2. Do you agree that Dick might not enjoy working at repetitive, monotonous work?
3. What should Dick do now? Is there any place he can go for further advice?
4. What other policies can you suggest for dealing with this problem of repetitive jobs?

3. Make Your Own Opportunities

Dale Evans and Joe Packard are good friends. Both have finished school and are ready to look for work. Both are good typists and both have studied accounting for two years. Joe feels that opportunities are limited in his town and is thinking of moving to a large city if he doesn't hear of an opening soon. Dale has no money to keep himself in a larger city and decides he will have to find something on his own. Consequently, he maps out a campaign. At the office of the local Chamber of Commerce he gets a list of all of the business firms in his town that employ more than two hundred office workers. Dividing the list into geographical areas, he visits ten firms a day. At each firm he either speaks to the office manager or makes an appointment to do so later. At the end of a week, Dale has had five offers of employment.

1. In what ways are getting a job and selling a product from door to door similar?
2. A rule of selling is to see as many people as you can. How does this apply to finding a job?
3. It is not easy to be given a refusal. What attitude can a job applicant take toward a refusal that will help lessen its sting?
4. Are there other job sources Dale did not cover?

4. Salaries and Advancement

Gloria Mong has applied for several jobs and has gone out on three interviews. In the first interview she found her training was not adequate; in the second, a small office, the salary was excellent; but there seemed to be no chance for advancement. The last interview is most interesting to Gloria. The job is secretary for three doctors. The beginning salary is low, but Dr. Meade (who interviews Gloria) informs her that by the end of the year the office manager, Mrs. Smott, will be retiring and, if Gloria seems capable of filling the job, she might be considered. Gloria is undecided. She dislikes refusing a good salary on what is actually just a chance that she will be offered the office manager's job six months later. She asks for a day to think the offer over.

1. Assuming that you are Gloria's friend and that she asks your advice, what would you suggest?
2. Besides salary and opportunity for advancement, is there a third consideration of even greater importance?
3. Is there a possibility that Gloria could be advanced too rapidly? Explain.
4. It is said that slow, steady progress is more likely when the ultimate job is a good one. Do you agree?

5. Are You a Team Worker?

Max Loeb has been a brilliant student in high school and college, but he has never shown an interest in athletics or school activities. There are two jobs open in the Peerless Bonding Company. One requires that the individual be able to work with others and prefer this type of work to that done alone. When the head of the firm, Mr. Kenny, interviews Max, he suggests that the actuarial job, requiring no group work, might be the better choice for Max. This suggestion is agreeable to Max, but he wonders how Mr. Kenny was aware of his preference.

1. Do you agree with Mr. Kenny that participation in school activities indicates a liking for people?
2. What jobs can you list that require team effort?
3. Which ones can you list that need no ability to work with others?
4. Which of your lists is the longer? What does this fact indicate?

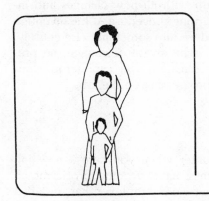

chapter 15

growing on the job you like

Why is it important for you to find a job that you like, that you enjoy, that adds to the best you? The answer to this question is complex, but one part of the answer lies in the number of hours you work in a day. Even with a shorter workweek, you spend more time on your job than you do in any other one activity. Those hours should add, not subtract, from your best self. If you are happy in those seven-eight hours a day, your overall mental and emotional health are enriched. If you are bored, unhappy, or filled with anxiety during those hours, the negative feelings you experience are sure to affect the way you live your life the rest of the day. Furthermore, your after-work hours may be filled with escape mechanisms in which you try to dull the unhappiness you have been experiencing. Such escape mechanisms include overuse of alcohol, drugs, and other self-destructive devices. On the other hand, if you are happy in your work, you will find that happiness spilling into your after-work hours.

Your first goal, then, is to find a job that fits you. Such a fit does not mean that you are equal to your first job; it means that you have the potential for growth, that you will become equal to the demands of the job. One important area of fitting into the demands of the job is that of working alone or with people. If you like to work with people and your work demands that you work alone, with a machine, all day, you may find yourself becoming irritable and greatly fatigued. For it has been found that much of the fatigue we experience comes from work that does not fit — rather than from too much work.

Guidelines for a job that fits can be applied only loosely, however. A new job is rarely tailor-made to your abilities and training. This is partly a result of the vast multiplicity of business operations in themselves. Still another factor is the swiftness of technological change. The most modern, up-to-date school cannot possibly keep up with all new changes and inventions in business. While students are learning procedure A, the invention of machine B may be changing the procedure into something else entirely. All you can do under the circumstances is be aware of change, be prepared for it, get the best training and education you can before your employment, and continue learning and progressing on the job.

KEEPING AHEAD OF OBSOLESCENCE

The first inadequacy you may encounter when you take a new job is in your technical preparation. You may have become proficient on a certain machine, only to discover that your employer has installed another. You may find that the methods, systems, and routines of the new firm are entirely different from those you learned. What should you do?

First of all, keep a learning attitude. No matter how "sold" you may be on the equipment and procedures used in your training or your previous employment, try to adjust to those found in your present job. It will be helpful, also, if you refrain from mentioning how you solved the problem at your former school or on your other job. Like the customer, your boss is always right — at least until you have given the new situation a fair chance.

A learning attitude means that you will be alert for any departure from your present knowledge or training. Suppose your supervisor suggests that you do a certain task in a new way. Pay attention, and ask questions if you have any doubts. Write down and number each step of the new method. Ask that it be demonstrated and see if you can follow the demonstration by trying it yourself. Most supervisors would rather spend extra time with a new employee than have errors appear in his work. Be appreciative of the extra help you receive, too. A considerate employee will find that his supervisors will usually respond with equal consideration and will be glad to help him when he needs it.

On-the-Job Training

Large firms may recognize the importance of the need for special training for new workers by organizing specific training courses. These may be training at the time of employment, called induction training; on-the-job training when new procedures must be learned or difficulties are encountered; and promotional training.

Induction training is usually required of all new employees, and you should be eager to learn all you can when you have such an opportunity.

One vital part of such training is becoming acquainted with the overall business of the firm. Learn all you can about the product your firm manufactures or the service your firm performs. Find out about the extent of its operations and the location of its branch offices. Learning these things will result in an increased interest in your job. You will no longer be an unimportant cog in a huge machine if you realize just how your job fits into the whole.

The second type of on-the-job training may be offered to certain employees who have been transferred from other departments, those employees who lack certain needed skills, and those who are expected to work on new equipment or with new procedures. If such training is given you, welcome the opportunity to learn something new. This alone will set you apart from the other employees, as resistance to change is a common trait. Even if the training involves longer hours, be glad for the opportunity. Learning something new is a guaranteed way of improving your vigor and effectiveness. Take advantage of each opportunity that comes your way.

If, after you have been working in a firm for several years, you should be considered for advancement, you may be asked to take some sort of promotional training. Special training is usually needed before a worker is promoted to a supervisory post. If such an honor should come to you, be aware of the benefits such training will bring you. For example, you may be given help in developing your leadership qualities, in planning your work and the work of others, in developing desirable attitudes, and in evaluating your work and the work of others. This type of training is sure to be helpful to you through all your working life.

Serious Reading

Reading has been an educational tool for thousands of self-made business leaders. Regular reading for short periods of time and on one subject is the secret. Decide to become knowledgeable in some area of interest to you. Get a book or two on the subject from the public library. Start reading. That's all there is to it. It will help if you set aside a special time for general reading of this type. Just before retiring is a good time. Fifteen minutes each night (before you turn to your brand of escape reading) spent on a serious subject should greatly improve your education. Good reading has a further advantage, too. Teachers of writing tell us that the best way to increase your vocabulary is through reading and that the best way to learn spelling and punctuation is through reading. Such a rewarding activity should not be overlooked.

In case you have no particular interest that you care to pursue, a good start may be made by subscribing to a weekly or monthly magazine devoted to articles of general interest. Another possibility is a subscription to a business periodical. If you are interested in faraway places and cultures different from your own, you may wish to subscribe to the *National Geographic* magazine. The thing to do is get started. Serious reading is an addictive habit that is good for you! It has been said, by the way, that a mind expanded never returns to its original boundaries. Just as true is the statement that a mind never expanded tends to shrink to even less than its original boundaries.

College Courses

In some types of businesses, for example, banking and insurance, special courses are offered in local colleges and universities. These courses are for the benefit of employees of such businesses and are supported by banking or insurance associations. College credit may be earned if it is desired. These courses provide a splendid opportunity to the ambitious worker, whether he is a beginner or veteran employee.

In addition to prescribed courses, you will find night classes offered at universities and colleges. These classes become more popular each year. In fact, many colleges have an "extended day" enrollment equal to that of their regular programs. As business continues to emphasize automation, communications, accounting, and economics, the college degree becomes more and more essential. If you have not yet graduated from college, extended day courses leading to a college degree will be worthwhile.

Still another kind of self-improvement study can be pursued through correspondence or home-study courses. These have been discussed in describing job preparation, but they are just as helpful as part of your improvement-on-the-job program. As was stated before, the major drawback in working by correspondence is that you must motivate yourself. Developing such self-discipline, however, is in itself a valuable accomplishment.

LEARNING TO BE A WINNER ON THE JOB

Do you feel like you are a winner or a loser? If you want to grow on the job, you must learn to feel like a winner. Part of growing on the job involves getting promoted to the next rung of the ladder. Losers seldom get promoted; therefore, you should do everything you can to show your supervisor, your co-worker, and particularly yourself that you feel like a winner. A winner has a "can do" attitude; he keeps working on a task until it is completed. He has a positive attitude toward life, toward other people, and toward himself. It isn't enough to feel like a winner, though. You must work at being a winner. Such work involves preparing for the next higher job, brushing up on your human relations skills, and learning how and when to speak up.

Prepare for the Next Higher Job

The best time to plan for advancement is before you take a job. One of the considerations you should weigh is the job's promotion possibilities. A well-established firm may offer more security than advancement. A new firm, on the other hand, may provide rapid advancement to those employees who are promotable material and yet be less stable than an older firm.

If you are serious about advancement, you should study the possible jobs to which you might be promoted. What other skills, abilities, and traits in addition to those you now possess are needed in the new job? Be willing to prepare yourself in these areas before asking for advancement.

Planning for advancement also means that you will develop more dependability. Be the sort of worker who completes the assigned task, no matter how dull or unchallenging it may be. If you have responsibilities (such as locking files or doors, or closing windows), never neglect them. Follow the rules and regulations established by the company, such as directions for smoking, taking coffee breaks, turning off lights. Last, and most important, do not blame others for any of your errors. A leader faces up to his own mistakes; he does not make excuses.

Brush Up Your Human Relations Skills

The way you get along with your co-workers will have much to do with your promotional chances. One important factor is your ability to be friendly with everyone without becoming involved in office feuds. It is wise to remain somewhat impersonal and detached at first, as you may not be able to detect factions and dissensions until you become more familiar with the firm. You will be slow to confide with others. Be a listener instead of a confider. Keep the confidences of others, and keep your own confidences to yourself.

Be willing to help others on occasion, but do not permit yourself to be exploited. In every office there are workers who try to find someone to do their work for them. Becoming a party to this sort of thing merely encourages irresponsibility in others. This type of worker is of no use to the firm, and if you should become a supervisor, he would continue to expect favors. A better way to handle this situation is to encourage the "leaner" to do his own work, to stand on his own feet.

A part of your human relations skill must go to keeping yourself in a good frame of mind. When you take a new job, you will probably go through periods of discouragement and dissatisfaction. You may receive reprimands, or you may be impatient with your mastery of the new position. When such times of disappointment come, try especially hard to do your job well. Self-discipline means you will not let your productivity respond to the variation in your own feelings. Knowing that there will always be difficult times in any job may help you.

There are cases where employees become indifferent to the demands of their jobs or where they are poorly prepared for the jobs they hold. If this should happen to you and someone in authority should point it out to you, your reaction should be one of gratitude. You would attempt to find and correct the source of the trouble. In other instances, however, even well-prepared employees with good work habits and good attitudes feel tense and ill at ease in new positions.

Psychologists say that many people are too sensitive. If you are sensitive to the point that you feel other people are often sniping at you, criticizing you, or cheating you, you should examine your own feelings. Suspicious people cannot be happy or work easily with others. Self-understanding and self-discipline can frequently relieve this excessive sensitivity and give you a trust in others, enriching all your relationships. Sometimes all you need to do is recognize excessive sensitivity for what it is: self-consciousness or thinking too much about yourself.

Psychologists say that many employees are anxious. Of course, if you are not performing your best work, you may have reason to be anxious. In such a situation *action*, not anxiety, is required. Whatever is bothering you should be studied and remedied. Work habits and attitudes can be changed by a determination to do so; lack of technical training can be remedied through further education and experience.

When the anxious feeling does not seem to be caused by any actual failure, discovery of the reason may be impossible. There are steps you can take, however. You can do the very best work of which you are capable, *not* because you want to appear efficient in your employer's eyes, but because you want to do well. Second, you can make yourself think of something else every time you begin to worry about yourself. Make it a point to say something cheerful and pleasant to someone else when you feel anxiety coming on.

One of the best bits of therapy for excessive anxiety is talking it out with a counselor. Large firms may employ a company psychologist, or they may assign this task to the personnel director. If you can discuss your fears with such a professional, you may be better able to understand your weaknesses and how to overcome them.

Anxiety may manifest itself by worry or by excessive fatigue. Of course, fatigue may be actually merited. You may be getting insufficient sleep; you may be overworking; you may be involved in too many out-side activities. If there seems to be no actual physical reason for your fatigue, however, anxiety is probably the cause, and monotony the symp-tom. If you do find your work monotonous, you might suggest to your supervisor that you rotate with other workers on repetitive jobs. Another suggestion is to change the way you do your work. One successful device is to time yourself on repetitive tasks, trying to cut down on the time taken while you continue to maintain high accuracy. If you can increase the interest and attention you give your work, you may be able to increase your enthusiasm for it.

Another change of pace that helps fatigue is a complete change of activity outside office hours. If you sit at a desk all day, you will benefit from physical activity after work. Bowling, tennis, golf, swimming, and other sports all contribute to zest for your work and increased efficiency.

Learn How and When to Speak Up

So much depends on speaking — when to speak, when not to speak, what to say, and what not to say — when working for advancement. It is true that sometimes silence is golden. A beginning worker, for example, should be slow to suggest changes in working procedures. Before you make such suggestions, you should study the reasons for the present processes. You might learn from such study why your changes would not be practical at the moment. Suggesting changes just to prove you are alert and up to date is a practice that can only be detrimental to you.

Another time when silence is golden is when you are tempted to criti-cize another worker or an employer. Idle criticism will only earn you a reputation for being a troublemaker. Oftentimes, too, when you know the reasons for a person's actions, you will recognize that your intended criti-cism is undeserved. When you do decide to say something critical, it should be said *to* the person involved and not about him.

Think before you speak. There may be times when you have con-structive suggestions to make. The first rule is to learn when and where you should express your views regarding the firm, your office, a particular job, process, or decision. Until you can learn the appropriate timing for such expressions, you should say nothing. Even when you know the right time and place for stating your views, you should do so concisely. Come directly to the point. If explanations are essential, organize them in logical form. It may be that your employers will welcome your suggestions. If, however, you find that your superiors have different ideas on the subject, you must abide by their decision. You must never argue or refuse to cooperate. Your superiors are older, wiser, and more experienced.

Asking for a raise. The ideal situation exists when true merit is recognized and need never be called to the employer's attention. If your situation is not ideal, what can you do? Obviously, there is only one answer: You must bring the matter up; you must ask for a raise. All that has been said about timing your speaking applies here with extra force. Before you speak at all, however, you must precede it with considerable thought and study.

First, see if you are justified in asking for a promotion or a raise. If it appears that you are, make out a good case for yourself *in writing* — but be objective. What about your production? Is there a standard for your work in your office? If so, how does your production compare with this standard? How many mailable letters do you transcribe in an hour? How many papers do you file in an hour? How many customers or callers have you handled without a complaint? What additional preparation have you made since you were hired? Have you attended extension courses? If you were to take an employment test at this point, would it be significantly higher than the one you took when you applied for your job?

Second, check your attitudes and work habits. Are you always prompt in arriving for work? Do you work overtime without complaint when it is necessary? How many days of work have you missed because of illness? Are you considered cooperative by your supervisor and your co-workers? When you finish the work assigned, do you find something else to do?

Third, ask your employer for an appointment. Of course, you will not tell him the object of your request. Merely ask if you may speak to him one of the following days. Mondays and Fridays are busy days, so it is better to ask (on Tuesday) for an appointment on Wednesday or Thursday. It is good persuasion psychology to give an employer a choice of days. Notice his mood, however, and wait for another week if he seems busy or worried.

Fourth, if your request for an appointment is granted, bring your notes with you to your interview. You might begin your remarks with something like the following: "Mr. Blank, I have enjoyed my work here very much. As I was hired two years ago, you may be interested in the progress I have made since then." And then tell him how much progress you *have* made. If you are confident of your worth, you will be able to respond pleasantly to any gruffness or lack of enthusiasm on your employer's part. If he challenges your statements, see that you neither back down nor get on the defensive. Simply and calmly bring up the case that you have prepared. After all, it is merely another employment interview, and you passed the first one!

Fifth, as in other interviews, when you have stated your case, you should thank your employer for the interview and for his time and leave.

Go back to your work and be patient. Even if your employer has seemed impressed with your facts, you must not expect your raise to be forthcoming at once. He may intend to grant your request after conferring with other members of the firm. Don't ruin a good case by becoming a nuisance. If you hear nothing about your request after two weeks, you might ask your employer if any decision has been made. Both when asking for a raise and following up, keep your tone friendly but impersonal. Too much emotion has on many an occasion ruined more than one otherwise good cause.

GETTING YOURSELF TOGETHER

One of the difficulties encountered in growing on the job is that of becoming a whole person — in other words, getting yourself together. In fact, no big step should ever be taken when you feel torn, splintered, not all together. The ideal state of affairs, of course, would be to go through adolescence "in one piece." This ideal seldom comes about, however, and the newcomer to the job market may feel pulled apart. Well-meaning teachers, friends, relatives, future bosses, all give conflicting advice. Before you can begin to grow, therefore, you must get yourself together, find out who you are, know what you think and feel. In short, you must become a real person — not just somebody's daughter, son, wife, husband, employee, and so on. Becoming a real person takes time, however; in the meantime, you may be helped by standing firm in relation to some of your co-workers.

Like the old stock companies of your grandfather's day, the office has its stock characters. These may be recognizable at once, or they may be hiding behind a facade that is entirely different from the real person. This fact is one reason why you should take your time in joining one of the many groups you will encounter. The secret of a successful entrance into a new office is to be pleasant to everyone. Say "Good morning" to the janitor and to the president. Be sure to avoid becoming part of a clique until you have become better acquainted.

Don't React to Office Characters

One of the stock characters you will meet is the office grouch. A beginner may become upset over the office grouch, but remember he is not mad at you. There may be several reasons for his crankiness: his home life; finances; or his responsibilities in the office. If you are pleasant and sympathetic, if you refuse to take his complaining personally, you may make him less of a grouch.

What about the bossy "nonboss"? There is usually one around every modern office. This person criticizes everything you do (and everything others do, too). Remember that this bossy person is mainly dissatisfied with himself. Calling attention to the faults of others is just his way of easing up on this self-dissatisfaction. Pay no attention to the bossy person if he is your co-worker. If he *is* your boss, however, you will help him by paying careful attention to detail and by following his directions as accurately as you can.

The office complainer is more dangerous than these other office characters because complaining is highly contagious. The best thing you can do is politely avoid the complainer. Trying to counter complaints with cheerful, positive statements is useless because the complainer is interested only in gloom. Whatever you do, don't let the complainer influence your thinking so that you become a complainer, too.

Another dangerous character is the tattletale. You can recognize him by the stories he tells you about other employees. No matter what the provocation, even if he repeats what one of the employees said about you, don't retaliate. A tattletale will go back to this person and repeat what you have told him. Gossip is unwise at anytime, but gossip with a tattletale is positively dangerous. When such a person starts telling you some tale about another person, be polite but firm. Suddenly remember a pressing engagement. There are plenty of your co-workers who will listen to him, unfortunately. The tattletale will leave you alone if you refuse to listen.

The best insurance against office characters is a busy social life outside the office. With the assurance friends of your own give you, you will not be upset by the office tease. You will be able to smile and agree with him good-naturedly, no matter how it really gets under your skin. The office wolf will be less of a menace, too. Remember, in any situation with an office wolf, it is best to be casual. Whistles and the like will be discontinued if you fail to react. The best way to handle the office wolf is to be pleasant but firm, pretend not to hear him, and have a sense of humor that puts him in his proper place; he will soon move on to greener pastures.

Don't Become an Office Character

There is one office character that you may become — the favorite employee. Try to keep such a situation from developing if you can. If, in spite of your efforts, the boss seems to favor you, do everything you can to stay on good terms with the other workers. You must never try to capitalize on such favoritism. Even though your employer may call you Jack, or Mary, or Bill, you must not call your boss by his first name. You will have everything to gain and nothing to lose if you treat all superiors with "distance" — that slight formality that indicates respect.

Another character you must not assume is that of the arguer. It is possible to avoid unnecessary arguments; it takes only two ingredients, relaxation and patience. If someone makes a controversial statement, relax. Feel your muscles go limp. Then wait and listen until you have heard the whole story. Many arguments are merely the result of not letting the other fellow finish his story. Decide to say nothing until your "opponent" has talked for at least three minutes. By that time, particularly if you are relaxed, you will find yourself much less likely to say something rash, something that might hurt the other person's feelings.

Have an Emotional Outlet

An important part of keeping your emotional balance in the business world is having an emotional outlet outside of office hours. Sports provide this outlet for many young people, but everyone does not enjoy sports. To be effective, your hobby must be one that *you* enjoy. There is no definition of a good hobby. Anything you can lose yourself in is good for you. If you have a talent, expressing that talent is the best hobby for you. There can be tremendous emotional release in little theatre productions, amateur orchestras and quartets, painting, photography, or writing.

If you have no talent but have goodwill, you can find just as effective an outlet. Helping the helpless brings greater emotional satisfaction than any other activity. Call your hospitals. Ask if they need someone to read to crippled children. Call your blind centers and ask if readers are needed. In most universities there is a great need for readers for those students who have poor vision. Local rest homes offer unlimited opportunities for bringing happiness to those who feel unwanted.

No matter what your business life may offer, you need an outlet that *you* consider rewarding. And don't let someone else tell you that the hobby you have chosen is without value. People's emotions are the most individual phenomena imaginable, and only you can make your choice.

Take Your Emotional Temperature

No matter how you have felt about your personality in the past, the important point is how you are doing right now. You see, the trouble with many improvement campaigns is that they go the wrong way. We measure the mistakes we have made, how we have failed. A much more fruitful exercise is to measure how we have succeeded. Furthermore, your personality growth is an individual matter. It won't help you if you pattern your personal qualities after those of someone else. What you need instead is some kind of standard, some indication of your own personal growth.

Following are fourteen points taken from A. H. Maslow.[1] These fourteen points might be considered your emotional thermometer against which you can measure how you are doing from time to time. Remember, though, that there is no end to personal growth. We will never be totally free from personal faults. No one ever reaches the state of being cured. Still, it will help if we can see measurable improvement over the years. Maslow's fourteen points make up a description of a person who is all together, who is OK, and who feels that he is OK. Measure yourself against these standards today; then go through the fourteen points again in six months. See if you have made any progress.

1. You will be able to detect the fake, the phony, the dishonest, and to judge people correctly and efficiently. You will be able to perceive reality and be comfortable with reality. You will not be frightened by the unknown.

2. You will be able to accept. You will be able to accept yourself, accept others, accept nature without thinking about it much one way or another. You will enjoy your physical side without guilt. You will be able to be yourself and you will dislike artificiality in others. What you will feel guilty about are shortcomings that could be improved: laziness, hurting others, prejudice.

3. You will be spontaneous, simple, and natural. Your codes of behavior may be strict, but they will be your own. You will be ethical, yet your ethics may not be the same as those of the people around you.

4. You will be problem centered; you won't fight the problem to defend your own ego. You won't spend time worrying about yourself but will do what needs to be done. You will be concerned with the good of mankind in general, with all of the members of their families in general. You will seem to be above the small things of life, and this will make life easier not only for you but for all who associate with you.

5. You will need detachment and privacy. You will like to be alone more than the average person does. You will be able to take personal misfortunes without reacting violently, as the ordinary person does. You may even concentrate so much on the main problem that you earn the "absent-minded professor" title.

6. You will become independent of your environment; you will be interested in growth rather than in attaining some goal. Less healthy individuals must have people around them; but the self-actualizing person, the person who is concerned with personal growth, may be hampered by the clinging demands of others.

7. You will have the capacity to appreciate freshly, again and again, the basic goods in life. Any sunset is as beautiful as your first sunset; any flower is of breathtaking loveliness even after you have seen a million

---

[1]A. H. Maslow, *Motivation and Personality* (New York: Harper & Row, 1954), pp. 203-234.

flowers. You will be as thrilled with your luck in finding a good wife or a good husband as you were in the first moment of falling in love. But you will derive ecstasy, inspiration and strength from the basic experiences of life — not from going to a nightclub, or getting a lot of money, or having a good time at a party.

8. The mystic experience will be fairly common to you. The feeling of being simultaneously more powerful and more helpless than you ever were before, of great wonder and awe, of the loss of place in time and space will happen to you again and again.

9. You will have a deep sympathy and affection for human beings in general. But self-actualizing people are very different from other people, and you will sometimes feel like an alien in a strange land. Very few will really understand you, yet you will have a feeling of older-brotherliness toward other people.

10. You will have a few very close friends. The ones you love profoundly will be few in number. In fact, you may spend a good bit of your time trying to escape gracefully from getting involved with a host of admirers.

11. You will have an unhostile sense of humor. The kind of jokes Lincoln told — mainly on himself — will be the type you like.

12. You will be creative, original, inventive. This does not mean the special creativeness of Mozart, but rather you will be a creative clerk, a creative shoemaker, finding joy in a new approach to your task.

13. You may not be well adjusted. You will get along with the culture in various ways, but while you will not be rebellious in the adolescent sense, you will resist conformity.

14. You will make mistakes. Because you are strong, you may marry out of pity; get too closely involved with neurotics, bores, and unhappy people. You will not be free from guilt, sadness, and conflict — because these conditions are normal in our lives today. But you will be able to accept your own blame and pick up the pieces and go on.

WANT TO GROW AND TO SHARE

If you have ever tried to reform another person, you have probably discovered what an impossible task it is. The reason for the difficulty lies in a simple fact: Change and growth come to a person because *he* wants to change and to grow — not because someone else desires the change. In order to grow, then, you must have a deep desire to grow.

Desire for Improvement

The desire for improvement is a wish to enhance oneself in value or quality. Everyone has vague desires for improvement. With success, however, you become aware of what is involved in achieving greater success and are able to set more realistic goals. For example, the untried schoolboy may dream of handling scores of workers with a word, of swaying great audiences with his eloquence. A businessman who knows what is involved in leading others, and who knows the difficulties he is likely to encounter, will set his goals within the realm of possibility. For this very reason, a realistic desire for improvement is usually stronger after the worker has had some success in his work.

A number of studies have been made of successful young people. One such study asked many questions of young people who had succeeded. In their answers, successful beginning workers said they did not expect success to come to them without effort. They stated that nothing comes to those who only wait for it. They believed that successful people must work hard, adjust to life's problems, want to improve, and make a determined effort to become more capable.

You probably know someone who is bitter because success did not come to him. That person may explain that he did all that he was told to do. Unfortunately, however, doing only what you are told to do or meeting the minimum expectations of a job is not enough to bring success.

The successful businessman must go beyond the call of duty. He must do what is expected of him — plus. In adding this plus quality that is needed for success, he must not be aggressive or obtrusive. Instead, he should, in a quiet, confident way, give more thought and work to the assignment. This plus quality has two parts. One part is a desire for improvement; the other is doing something about the wish to improve.

The desire for improvement may be expressed in being proud of the growth of your firm, in watching and helping that growth. If you have this pride, you will also be proud of the amount of work you can do in a certain time. One of the joys of any kind of work is pride in good work.

Even after the day's work is finished, you can express pride in your work. Read the newspapers and newsmagazines for items that may affect your firm. Keep in touch with current and local affairs.

A desire for improvement is shown in your attitude toward your work. You will welcome and encourage suggestions from your superiors for doing your work more efficiently. You will be alert to suggestions for improving your work when they come from fellow employees. If someone tells you about an unconscious mannerism you have that is making you conspicuous, you make a determined attempt to eliminate it.

Desire to Share

To be unselfish means that you are willing to share, to pay attention to the interests of others, and to be generous with your time and talents.

The selfishness of business has been the object of humor since business began. All human traits are found in business because businesses are composed of human beings. Yet, while selfishness can be found in business, unselfishness and many other positive qualities can also be found. As an employee, you must be aware of your interests but also aware of the interests of others.

The ability to share is sure to be appreciated by the companies for which you will want to work. All businesses are working hard to create goodwill with their customers and their potential customers. If this same quality is evident among the employees of a firm, it will help them create a good feeling with the public. Sometimes you may see cases where it appears that selfishness is rewarded and unselfishness unnoticed. Such instances do occur, of course, both in business and in all other areas of living. The results of an unselfish attitude toward others will be evident in your personality, however, if you continue this trait. Appreciation of unselfishness may be slow, but it will be sure.

If you have the opportunity, talk with experienced businessmen and women about selfishness and unselfishness in business. You will discover that most people have a basic respect for fair play and unselfishness. Your co-workers will dislike you if you violate these basic values. To be accused of unfairness or selfishness would cost you more than any reward you could attain through pursuing these qualities.

You may express unselfishness by lending or sharing your materials and equipment with other employees when there is a need. You will give information, time, or services when your department is working under pressure. You will work overtime when this is necessary to complete the job on time. When there are unpleasant duties to be done, you will do your share willingly. All of these suggestions are familiar to you. Most of you have grown up with such maxims. All that is necessary is to make them habitual actions.

There is another side of unselfishness, however, that is not stressed; yet it is even more important to the smooth working of the business team. This side is the ability to accept gracefully the praise that is given your superior when you were largely responsible for the work, the idea, or the plan. Developing this kind of unselfishness is not easy. In our fiercely competitive society most of us try to shine individually; we dislike sharing honors rightfully belonging to us with others. Yet an old saying is true: You can get anything done so long as you don't care who gets the credit.

There are steps in developing this cooperative kind of unselfishness. First, you refrain from talking about your high skills, high grades, successes in general. Rather, you help another person to accomplish something and then praise the one you helped. This is the way to begin. After a while you will receive a greater feeling of pleasure from the success of the one you helped than you ever would from your own successes.

From this beginning it is a short step to a glow of pride when others in your department or your company achieve honors in which you had no share. Envy and jealousy — two most unattractive traits — can be eliminated from your nature with this sort of practice. All it takes is practice each day. If you can become the kind of person who is pleased when he hears words of praise for someone else, you will have taken a giant step toward emotional health. Nothing is so destructive to the personality as resentment.

Desire for Civic Sharing

As you grow in your ability to share with your fellow workers, you will need to expand your horizons to the community in which you live and work. You will then have civic or social consciousness, having a desire to further existing institutions if they are working for the public good. If you see a need for change in the local government bodies, you will be willing to do your share to bring such change about. Working for public betterment is one of the hallmarks of an adult person. You know, of course, that business depends on society and that society regulates business. You know, too, that the services of all legitimate institutions have value. You also serve society in your capacity of employee, no matter how humble your position.

When you are called upon to contribute to your Community Fund, the Red Cross, and the various other drives, you are glad to do so. The request usually comes through the business that employs you, and that business is judged by the social consciousness of its employees. If you are asked to work for some civic organization for the general good of the community, you are glad to be of help. When requests for information come to you, you answer them promptly and courteously. You obey the laws of your community; you set a good example to others in your conduct and in your speech.

As you mature in business, you in turn become a leading citizen of the community — one to whom your fellow citizens will turn for leadership. This day will come more quickly if you get the feeling of civic responsibility early — responsibility for those less fortunate than you, responsibility for helping to maintain and carry on the worthwhile institutions of today. Your service to society is a debt you owe in payment for the privileges that are yours.

FOLLOW-UP ACTIVITIES

1. After you have been working for one year, ask a friend to rate you on the following scale. You might suggest that you rate each other.

You must both be absolutely objective in your ratings, however. Flattery will get you nowhere! If you can get an honest appraisal, and if you can work on improvement where it is needed, you will be surprised at your progress. The results of this rating should be kept and the same appraisal made a year later. A comparison of the results will show you "how you are doing."

Check each item from 1 to 4 according to the following rating: 1 — Good, 2 — Average, 3 — Fair, and 4 — Needs Improvement.

Rating

a. Good Grooming _____
b. Cleanliness _____
c. Appropriate Dress _____
d. Dress Suits Your Personality _____
e. Color Combinations _____
f. Posture and Carriage _____
g. Correct English _____
h. Voice and Diction _____
i. Facial Expression _____
j. Poise _____
k. Health _____
l. Vitality and Enthusiasm _____
m. Self-confidence _____
n. Cheerfulness and Sense of Humor _____
o. Friendliness _____
p. Sincerity _____
q. Willingness to Cooperate _____
r. Consideration for Others _____

2. *Helps Toward Growth.* On a form like that below, keep an up-to-date list of suggestions you encounter in your work and in your reading that you think might help you to grow. Check each suggestion that you try out. If you find the suggestion helpful, put an asterisk (*) beside the check mark.

Suggestion	√	°

3. Everyone has a mental picture of himself. Sometimes it is a good likeness, and sometimes it is not. In Column 1, check the statements that correspond to what you think you are like. In Column 2, check the statements you believe other people think you are like. In Column 3, check the statements that you would most like to be someday.

a. *How I Feel About Myself*

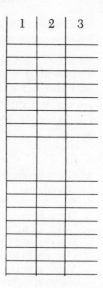

Inferior to most of my associates
Superior to most of my associates
Self-confident
Lacking self-confidence
Conceited about my achievements
Conceited about my appearance
Modest about my achievements
Ashamed of my appearance

b. *How I Feel Toward Others*

Tolerant
Intolerant
Friendly
Unfriendly
Like to be with others
Dislike to be with others
Like most people
Dislike most people

	1	2	3

4. Psychologists say that we become what we think. As part of your improvement campaign, try keeping an improved mental picture of yourself in mind. Write down the statements from No. 3 that you checked that indicate what you would like to be someday. Visualize yourself as being this way for the next three months. At the end of that time, try this rating again. The results may be a pleasant surprise to you.

5. Following is a form to help you take your emotional temperature, as suggested on pages 227 through 229, using Maslow's fourteen points. In the left-hand column are listed words standing for each of the fourteen points. Across the top are listed the five steps in Maslow's Needs Hierarchy. Place a check mark in the proper rectangle, indicating where you are in regard to each of the fourteen points. If you are not even started with that particular point (because of physical deprivation), place your check mark under Need Level 1. If you are trying, but feel insecure about yourself and are not making much headway, place your check mark under Need Level 2. If you are doing fairly well with the particular point but are more concerned with what your friends are doing and approving, place your check mark under Need Level 3. If you are doing very well with that particular point but still need to have recognition for doing well, place your check mark under Need Level 4. Only if you feel the description of a particular point fits you well, and only if you have no need for the approval of others in that regard, should you place your check mark under Need Level 5.

Fourteen Points	Level 1 Physical Needs	Level 2 Security Needs	Level 3 Belonging Needs	Level 4 Recognition Needs	Level 5 Self-Actualization
1. Being Real					
2. Acceptance					
3. Spontaneous					
4. Problem-Centered					
5. Detachment					
6. Growth-Oriented					
7. Simplicity					
8. Mystic Experience					
9. Humanitarian					
10. Few Close Friends					
11. Unhostile Humor					
12. Creative					
13. Resist Conformity					
14. Admit Your Mistakes					

CASE PROBLEMS

1. Criticism Trap

Sarah Dornbush is a student in the local community college. Only a few of Sarah's former high school friends are attending the college. One of these is Sarah's best friend, Miriam, a pretty and popular girl with the men students but who seems to take delight in putting Sarah down. Whenever Sarah meets a new friend and starts dating him, Miriam makes some critical remark about the fellow to Sarah. Even though Sarah realizes that she should not let Miriam's criticism affect her, Sarah usually breaks off with the new friend. Sarah also notices that she is becoming critical of the other students, especially of their clothes, hair length, and general actions. Sarah seems to be "catching" Miriam's negative attitude toward strangers.

Following the five-step problem-solving plan described in Chapter 3, suggest a solution to the case from Sarah's point of view.

2. Future Dividends

Ted Tyler was employed as one of two bookkeepers in a small manufacturing concern. Mr. Christopher was the manager of the accounting department. Ted found that he could work much faster and more accurately than his fellow employee. He thus had time to spend in doing extra work or in helping the other bookkeeper. Things seemed to go just as well, however, if he took more time with his own tasks. He worked more slowly, therefore, so he would not have to do anything extra.

At the end of the year some special reports and records had to be prepared. A new man, Henry Mack, was employed as an extra bookkeeper for one month. Although his work was temporary, Henry was interested in the job and worked as hard as he could, doing exceptionally well. At the end of the month, when Henry was scheduled to leave, Mr. Christopher became ill and had to resign. Mr. Christopher recommended that Henry be given his vacated post as department manager, and this was done.

1. Do you feel Mr. Christopher was justified in overlooking Ted's seniority in the firm?
2. Do you think Ted had any claim on the position as department manager?
3. In working slowly, what impression did Ted give Mr. Christopher as to his ability?
4. If Ted had worked more efficiently and then spent the extra time in helping the other bookkeeper, would this have gone unnoticed?

3. Competition or Cooperation?

Tina Castro and Melinda Duval are secretaries in a large company. Both have done well and both are being considered for the position of office manager. Tina has been given the job of making a survey of equipment needs in the various offices. She comes to Melinda for data in her office. Melinda gives Tina the data she needs; but, as she looks over the work Tina has already done on the study, she discovers a serious error in Tina's calculations. Melinda realizes that if Tina makes a success of the survey, she will probably get the promotion instead of Melinda. She hesitates about calling the error to Tina's attention in any case because she does not want to hurt Tina's feelings by criticizing her. After much thought, Melinda decides to say nothing about the error.

1. In thinking about not hurting Tina's feelings, do you think Melinda was "rationalizing" or finding a good reason for doing something she wants to do?
2. What, if any, bad effects may come to Melinda if she lets the error go by?
3. If Melinda had pointed out the error to Tina in a tactful manner and Tina had received the promotion, would Melinda have been hurt in the long run as far as her career is concerned?
4. Was Melinda thinking of the good of the company when she made her decision?

4. Reducing Resistance to Change

One of your duties as the newly appointed assistant purchasing agent is the supervision of the stock room. In charge of the stock room is Mr. Black, who has been with the company for thirty years. It is he who devised and installed the system of records used in the stock room. This system is now out of date, clumsy, and too elaborate.

A major item of concern is how to get Mr. Black's cooperation in making the change from the old system of records to one that is more efficient.

1. How will you win the confidence of Mr. Black?
2. Write down the opening statement you will make when you bring up the matter of installing a new record system for the first time.
3. Assuming that you win Mr. Black's cooperation, what will you say when Mr. Black makes a suggestion that you feel is not a good one? Give your conversation in detail.
4. The new system is now ready to be installed. What will you say to Mr. Black to help get the system off to a good start?

5. Giving One's Talents

Mildred Taylor, a talented pianist-singer working as a secretary for the Acme Company, has been asked to perform at a benefit show to be given by the company to raise money for the Red Cross. All of the employees of the company are participating in the show, performing, helping backstage, providing refreshments to be served after the show, or selling tickets. Mildred feels that she has been imposed upon, as she is asked to play for something nearly every week. She tells the chairman of the show that she would rather give $5 to the fund and be excused from playing.

1. Is it true that talented people are sometimes imposed upon?
2. If Mildred were justified in refusing some of the requests to perform that she receives, where should she draw the line?
3. In considering such requests, should Mildred weigh the purpose for which the performance is to be given?

appendixes

SUPPLEMENTARY READINGS

Axline, Virginia M. *Dibs: In Search of Self*. New York: Ballantine Books, Inc., 1967. (Paperback)

Berne, Eric. *Games People Play*. New York: Grove Press, Inc., 1967. (Paperback)

Buber, Martin. *I and Thou*, 2d ed. New York: Charles Scribner's Sons, 1958. (Paperback)

Bugental, James F. T. (ed.) *Challenges of Humanistic Psychology*. New York: McGraw-Hill Book Company, 1967. (Paperback)

Fromm, Erich. *The Art of Loving*. New York: Harper & Row, Publishers, 1956.

_____. *The Revolution of Hope: Toward a Humanized Technology*. New York: McGraw-Hill Book Company, 1967. (Paperback)

Goffman, Irving. *Stigma: Notes on the Management of Spoiled Identity*. Englewood Cliffs: Prentice-Hall, Inc., 1963. (Paperback)

Gordon, Thomas. *Parent Effectiveness Training*. New York: Peter H. Wyden, Inc., 1970.

Green, Hannah. *I Never Promised You A Rose Garden*. New York: Signet Books, 1964. (Paperback)

Hall, Edward T. *The Silent Language*. Greenwich, Connecticut: Fawcett Publications, Inc., 1961. (Paperback)

Harris, Thomas A. *I'm OK — You're OK*. New York: Harper & Row, Publishers, 1969.

Hayakawa, S. I. *The Use and Misuse of Language*. Greenwich, Connecticut: Fawcett Publications, 1962. (Paperback)

Huxley, Laura Archer. *You Are Not the Target*. New York: Farrar, Straus & Giroux, Inc., 1965. (Paperback)

James, Muriel and Dorothy Jongeward. *Born to Win*. Reading, Massachusetts: Addison-Wesley Publishing Co., Inc., 1971.

Jourard, Sidney M. *Disclosing Man to Himself*. New York: Van Nostrand Reinhold Company, 1968.

_____. *The Transparent Self*. New York: Van Nostrand Reinhold Company, 1964. (Paperback)

Katz, Robert L. *Empathy*. New York: The Free Press, 1963.

Lair, Jess. *I Ain't Much, Baby — But I'm All I've Got*. New York: Doubleday & Company, Inc., 1972. (Paperback)

Maslow, Abraham H. *Eupsychian Management*. Homewood, Illinois: Richard D. Irwin, Inc. and Dorsey Press, 1965.

——————. *Motivation and Personality*, 2d ed. New York: Harper & Row, Publishers, 1970.

——————. *Towards a Psychology of Being*. New York: Van Nostrand Reinhold Company, 1962. (Paperback)

McNeil, Elton B. *The Quiet Furies: Man and Disorder*. Englewood Cliffs: Prentice-Hall, Inc., 1970. (Paperback)

Menninger, Karl. *Love Against Hate*. New York: Alfred A. Knopf, Inc., 1959. (Paperback)

Otto, Herbert. *Group Methods Designed to Actualize Human Potential*, 2d ed. Chicago: Stone-Brandel Center, 1967.

Rogers, Carl R. *Freedom to Learn*. Columbus, Ohio: Charles E. Merrill Publishing Company, 1969.

Schutz, William C. *Joy: Expanding Human Awareness*. New York: Grove Press, Inc., 1967. (Paperback)

Shostrom, Everett L. *Man, the Manipulator*. Nashville, Tennessee: Abingdon Press, 1967.

Skinner, B. F. *Walden Two*. New York: The Macmillan Company, 1962. (Paperback)

Sohl, Jerry. *The Lemon Eaters*. New York: Simon & Schuster, Inc., 1967. (Paperback)

index